Frommer's®

The Balearics

with your family

The best of Mallorca, Menorca, Ibiza and Formentera

Alex Leith, Georgina Bromwich &
Donald Strachan

Wiley Publishing, Inc.

Published by:
Wiley Publishing, Inc.
111 River St.
Hoboken, NJ 07030-5774

ISBN: 978-0-470-05529-8

UK Publisher: Sally Smith
Executive Project Editor: Martin Tribe (Frommer's UK)
Commissioning Editor: Mark Henshall (Frommer's UK)
Development Editor: Donald Strachan
Content Editor: Hannah Clement (Frommer's UK)
Cartographer: Tim Lohnes
Photo Research: Jill Emeny (Frommer's UK)
Wiley Bicentennial logo: Richard J. Pacifico
Production by Wiley Indianapolis Composition Services

For information on our other products and services or to obtain technical support, please
contact our Customer Care Department within the U.S. at 800/762-2974, outside the U.S.
at 317/572-3993 or fax 317/572-4002. Within the UK Tel. 01243 779777; Fax. 01243
775878.

Wiley also publishes its books in a variety of electronic formats. Some content that appears in
print may not be available in electronic formats. Printed and bound by Printer Trento in Italy.

5 4 3 2 1

Contents

About the Authors

Alex Leith is a freelance writer, who has contributed regularly in recent years to the *Independent* and *Independent on Sunday* travel sections, as well as numerous other national newspapers. He is the author of football/travel book *El Becks – A Season in the Sun*. Having lived for two long spells in Barcelona, Spain, he currently resides in his home town of Lewes, East Sussex, where among other things, he edits cutting-edge magazine *www.vivalewes.com*.

Georgina Bromwich is a geography graduate from Jesus College, Cambridge University. Georgina Bromwich has travelled extensively for work, study and pleasure. Having spent much time in Latin America, on mainland Spain and island hopping between the Balearics, she worked in publishing in the UK before finally moving abroad. She currently lives in Menorca with her husband and baby son, where she contributes to several travel and lifestyle magazines and writes for the local press.

Donald Strachan is a London-based writer, editor and copywriter. He has written about travel to European destinations for the *Sunday Telegraph*, the *Independent on Sunday*, the *Sydney Morning Herald* and *Zest* magazine. He lives in Hackney with his partner and two young daughters.

Acknowledgements

Thanks to IBATUR, particularly David Sastre Camps, Ben and John of Astbury, Formentera and Francisco of Formentera Tourism Board as well as many other inhabitants of this enchanted island he finds it hard to keep away from. (AL)

Thanks to Maria and the staff at the Tourist Information Office; Nicki for her ideas; Caroline for being practical; and Amalio and Samuel for rediscovering Menorca with me. (GB)

Thanks to Becs for my first assignment, J. D. for the belief, Mark for the commission, Stephen and Justin for the inspiration, and most of all Lucia, Lili and Ruby, without whom this would be a different book altogether. (DS)

An Additional Note

Please be advised that travel information is subject to change at any time and this is especially true of prices. We therefore suggest that you write or call ahead for confirmation when making your travel plans. The authors, editors and publisher cannot be held responsible for experiences of readers while travelling. Your safety is important to us, however, so we encourage you to stay alert and be aware of your surroundings.

Star Ratings, Icons & Abbreviations

Hotels, restaurants and attraction listings in this guide have been ranked for quality, value, service, amenities and special features using a star-rating system. Hotels, restaurants, attractions, shopping and nightlife are rated on a scale of zero stars (recommended) to three (exceptional). In addition to the star rating system, we also use 4 feature icons that point you to the great deals, in-the-know advice and unique experiences. Throughout the book, look for:

FIND	Special finds – those places only insiders know about
MOMENT	Special moments – those experiences that memories are made of
VALUE	Great value – where to get the best deals
OVERRATED	Places or experiences not worth your time or money

The following **abbreviations** are used for credit cards:

AE	American Express
MC	MasterCard
V	Visa

A Note on Prices

Frommer's provides exact prices in each destination's local currency. As this book went to press, the rate of exchange was 1€ = £0.67. Rates of exchange are constantly in flux; for up-to-the-minute information, consult a currency-conversion website such as www.oanda.com/convert/classic. In the Family-Friendly Accommodation section of this book we have used a price category system.

An Invitation to the Reader

In researching this book, we discovered many wonderful places –
hotels, restaurants, shops and more. We're sure you'll find others.
Please tell us about them, so we can share the information with your
fellow travellers in upcoming editions. If you were disappointed with
a recommendation, we'd love to know that too. Please write to;

Frommer's The Balearics with Your Family, 1st edition
John Wiley & Sons, Ltd
The Atrium
Southern Gate
Chichester
West Sussex, PO19 8SQ

Cover Credits

Front cover: Large Image: © Stuart Abraham / Alamy.
Small Images (from left to right on cover):
© Ian Dagnall / Alamy
© Andreas von Einsiedel / Alamy
© Ian Dagnall / Alamy
© Ian Dagnall / Alamy
Back cover: © Peter Adams Photography / Alamy

Front Matter

p. i: © Stuart Abraham / Alamy; p. ii: © Ian Dagnall / Alamy; p. ii:
© Andreas von Einsiedel / Alamy; p. ii: © Ian Dagnall / Alamy;
p. ii: © Ian Dagnall / Alamy; p. iii: © Ian Dagnall / Alamy; p. iii:
© Andreas von Einsiedel / Alamy; p. iii: © Ian Dagnall / Alamy;
p. iii: © Ian Dagnall / Alamy.

Inside Credits

© **Alex Leith**: p. 5 bottom; p. 241; p. 245; p. 247; p. 252; p. 256.

© **Cathy Limb**: p. 4; p. 9; p. 151; p. 165; p. 168; p. 175; p. 186;
p. 194; p. 197.

1 Family Highlights of the Balearics

Even though you're only reading the first line of this book, you probably already know plenty about the Balearic Islands. So does your neighbour. And your boss, your brother and your postman. There's the high-rise hotels, the sunkissed strips of sandy beach. The child-friendly villas, the English cuisine and the charter flights. The banana boats, the glass-bottomed cruises and the tourist buses. And you're all right, partly. You'll certainly find each and every one of those on a family trip here, if you know where to look. But if you think that's all you'll find, think again. Or even better, read on.

The Balearics pretty much invented the package holiday – it still thrives at key resorts, and has much to offer family travellers. But independent travel to the islands has become much easier, too. During the summer months, Mallorca, Ibiza and Menorca are well served by low-cost airlines. Formentera's just a short onward hop by ferry. It's all just far enough away to guarantee sun from May to October; just close enough to make the flight bearable with toddlers. Know where to search and you can find your own accommodation quicker than ever. There's no need to stay in high-rise hotels if you don't want to: self-catering options are unending, apartments, villas, farmhouses, whatever you like. Sort out some transport for your stay, and you're off.

While the sun and sand may be what attracts you in the first place, a closer look while you're here reveals much more. Don't be put off by a handful of infamous resorts on Mallorca and Ibiza. These are just one tiny side of these multi-faceted islands, easily avoided once you know where they are, and when not to visit. Take a walk in Mallorca's mountains, or through the cobbled streets of Sóller, or in towns where you'll hardly hear Spanish spoken, never mind English, and you couldn't feel further from Magaluf. On Ibiza, tiny whitewashed villages littering the island's interior mark a sharp contrast with its fame as a clubbers' haven. Menorca's prehistoric and military heritage is a constant reminder that tourism is still a relatively new development here, and in fact has barely stained Menorca at all. And Formentera is little more than one giant sand dune: hire some bikes and you'll find all sorts of fun within a few miles of its tiny port.

For all the compromises these islands have made to tourism (not all of them bad), it's still refreshing to travel inland and see that much remains unaffected, whether it's the almond harvest in Mallorca, Ibiza's hippy markets or dairy farming in Menorca. Throw in some cobble-stoned hill towns, the odd rural frustration, a great place for you and the kids to stay in, and, yes, a spin on those banana boats, and you have the makings of a great family holiday. Enjoy!

Bilingual Balearics: Chatting in Catalan

Alongside Spanish, Catalan is the second official language of the Balearic Islands. Its use is widespread – particularly in government offices, in schools and on road signs. In smaller towns and villages, it thrives. Spanish tends to dominate in cities and resorts, however, as many Spaniards travel to the Balearics from the mainland to work during the summer season.

There are few islanders who will actually describe their local language as Catalan, though – for fear of Barcelona claiming the islands as part of their vision of a Catalan Country. So expect to hear it described as *mallorquin*, *menorquin* and *eivissenc*. Those who have studied French may find many Catalan words familiar, and with a good knowledge of both French and Spanish, you can often piece together a conversation.

Each island has developed its own dialect, and many unique words. Menorca is a special case. As the British dominated the island for the best part of the 18th century, several local words reflect that influence, like *xoc* (chalk), *mèrvils* (marbles) and, most famously, *gin*.

An attempt to speak in Catalan will be highly appreciated, even if it is just a brief greeting in a shop or bar. Here are a few words you may come across:

Bon dia – good morning
Benvinguts – welcome
Gràcies – thank you
Si us plau – please
De res – you're welcome
Adéu – goodbye
Platja – beach
Ajuntament – town hall

Gelat – ice cream
Formatge – cheese
Peix – fish
Carn – meat
Vi – wine
Aigua – water
Llet – milk
A poc a poc – little by little

BALEARIC FAMILY HIGHLIGHTS

The Best Beaches You're hardly short of choice on Formentera, but a trip to the island isn't complete without walking the A-list strip of sugary sand at Platja de Ses Illetes. It's the place you'd take a Martian who wanted to know what a perfect beach should look like. See p. 248.

Mallorca's best beach requires a boat ride from Port de Sóller: Sa Calobra. It's the stuff of movies, with towering granite cliffs, sparkling turquoise water and bottle-green umbrella pines providing pockets of shade for those who get here early. If all your kids want to do is mess about on the water, this is a treasure island. See p. 76.

Son Bou is Menorca's longest beach, and even on the hottest

At the Beach, Menorca

summer day, if you walk westwards away from the bars and activities, you're still guaranteed a patch of sand all to yourselves. See p. 166.

The Best Markets There may not be many hippies left, but the hippy markets around Santa Eulària des Riu on Ibiza are still going strong 30 years on. The incense and the kaftans you probably expect; the fine crafts and kiddie crèches might come as a surprise. See p. 217.

You can't leave Formentera in the summer without stopping at La Fira de la Mola, the tiny island's unique market. Your kids will love the place, particularly the central plaza where a 60-something hippy sits on a high-stool playing the slide guitar. See p. 247.

For hand-made toys, jewellery, pottery and trinkets on Menorca, Maó's artesan market on Fridays during July and August may be small, but it is well worth strolling through. See p. 163.

Sineu's Wednesday market is one of the oldest on Mallorca, with a long tradition as a meeting point for the *campesinos* of Es Pla. It's also become something of an attraction, with gifts and souvenirs, from hand-made pottery and herb-infused olives, to artesan cheeses and colourful strings of peppers. See p. 142.

The Best Nature Reserves There is nowhere quite like Ibiza's Ses Salines Nature Reserve. The bleached salt hills and pink pools make for an unreal landscape. Migrating flamingos and herons rest here from July to October, and February to May, so pack the binoculars and rent some bikes. See p. 213.

When Menorca was declared a Biosphere Reserve in 1993, the 2000 hectares of marsh, dunes and headland at S'Albufera d'Es Grau was designated its core. Over 100 bird species can be sighted, or just follow the nature trails to hunt for animal footprints. There are even pushchair-friendly walkways. See p. 167.

The Best Animal Attractions Top billing goes to the brand new Palma Aquarium. An iconic building, it draws visitors across shimmering pools, through tropical rock gardens and beneath waterfalls as a backdrop to its incredible diversity of aquatic life, including giant sunfish and white-tipped sharks. It's perhaps the finest animal kingdom in all of Spain. See p. 55.

Not quite in the same league, but you can't leave Menorca

Palma Cathedral

The Best Cities The Balearic Islands' capital, and their only real city – **Palma** – is an unlikely but great spot for a fun-filled family weekend. From chi-chi shopping to stunning architecture, and getting pleasantly lost in the twisting cobbled streets, there's plenty to keep everyone happy. See p. 43.

Don't miss the views from Ibiza's old town, the **Vila Dalt**. Declared a UNESCO World Heritage site in 1999, it's a living testament to battles, defeats and conquests of the island's 1000-year history. See p. 43.

without taking the kids to meet the red cows at **Lloc de Menorca**. See p. 167.

If you prefer your nature a bit wilder, **Cabrera National Park** is a Galapagos in the Med. If you're really lucky, you might even spot Audouin's gull and Eleanor's falcon. The children will love the boat trip to get there, too. See p. 124.

The Best Adventures on Water If you want your children to learn to windsurf, kayak or sail, the **Escuela Municipal de Vela** on Formentera is one of the very best places in Spain. Run with passion by a former Olympic windsurfing instructor, the school has produced a number of Spanish and international

Platja de ses Illetes

Wooden Train to Sóller

champions – but prices remain reasonable. See p. 243.

In Menorca, renting a **canoe** from **Es Grau beach** is a cheaper, slightly more genteel, way to get out and about on the water. The shallows of Es Grau's enclosed bay means that even little ones are safe in their life jackets. See p. 166.

While for many parents waterparks can be a trial, **Aqualand,** near Magaluf in Mallorca, is a cut above the rest, continually renewing itself with ever wilder and more wonderful rides to keep little ones quiet. Even teens will return in awe of the Tornado and the Boomerang. See p. 62.

The Best Train Ride Okay, it's pretty much the only train ride on the islands, but the little wooden train that bores through the Tramuntana, from **Palma to Sóller,** is a real family highlight. See p. 74.

The Best Sunsets The 14th century **Castell de Bellver** holds

a lofty spot above the bay of Palma, flanked on either side by pine woods and framed to the west by the hazy outline of the Tramuntana. It's a magnificent sight, and has the most spectacular view of the city below. See p. 54.

For a bird's eye view of Menorca at the end of the day, drive up to **Monte Toro** to watch the sun go down. It's a privilege

Castell de Bellver

to see the fields, towns and water in Fornells' bay gradually change colour as the giant orb melts into the water. See p. 179.

The Best Active Fun The flat terrain around Ciutadella, makes for perfect cycling, even with little children in tow. From the town centre, it's an easy ride through fields bordered by dry-stone walls down to isolated beaches. Several of Menorca's prehistoric sites are also within reach. See p. 159.

There's no shortage of fantastic dive schools on the islands, but Ibiza's Punta Dive is perhaps the best. It offers dive sites for all levels, and 'Bubblemakers' courses to get young kids interested. The adjacent beach is a winter kite-surfing mecca, too. See p. 220.

The Best Museums A museum with exhibits indoors and out, Menorca's Ecomuseu de Cap de Cavalleria brings its interior alive by linking it to the surrounding countryside. Children will be especially intrigued by the Roman city of Sanisera that was swallowed up by the sea. See p. 183.

This long-overdue Robert Graves Museum, a tribute to the poet who put Deià on the map, was finally opened in July 2006. It's an absolute must for anyone who wants to understand Mallorca's artistic appeal. See p. 79.

You can't miss the fake castle on the Palma–Manacor road: Vidrierias Gordiola, a glassmaking factory that's been in the

Off the Beaten Track

same family since the 18th century. Watching craftsmen blow bubbles from molten glass is a jaw-dropping experience for little ones, especially when you tell them that the fires are as hot as volcanoes. See p. 141.

The Best Buildings Built to protect Menorca from an attack that never happened, the old military fortress on La Mola at the mouth of Maó's port impresses with its rock-solid construction above and below ground level. The guided tour will keep family members of all ages entertained, with stops at tunnels, gloomy prisons and immense British cannons. See p. 168.

Valldemossa's magnificent sandstone Carthusian monastery, the Real Cartuja de Jesús de Nazaret, dates back to the 17th century, and still presides regally over this sleepy hill town. These days, it provides children with a wonderland for exploration. See p. 77.

No trip to Mallorca is complete without taking in the **Catedral de Palma.** This magnificent pile, converted from a mosque in 1229, is one of the most extravagant Gothic cathedrals in the world. See p. 52.

The Best Family Walks The **Parc Natural de Mondragó,** near Santanyí, is one of Mallorca's best-kept secrets. Finding your perfect patch of sand means a walk through pine trees and sand dunes, dodging basking lizards and chirruping birds, and drinking in stunning views along the way. Take picnic fodder, sunscreen and some shade, and find a secluded spot in the dunes for a long, lazy day out. See p. 108.

Menorca's perimeter path, the **Camí de Cavalls,** is gradually being opened up to the public. The walk along low-level cliffs between Punta Prima and S'Algar takes you past a restored defence tower perched on a key lookout point. See p. 173.

With older children who don't mind a 4–5-hour hike, a lovely way to take in southern Mallorca's wild places is on foot from the **lighthouse at Cap de Ses Salines** to **Còlonia de Sant Jordi.** There are a couple of virgin beaches, and plenty of scrambling over rocks. See p. 126.

The Best Fiestas Alcúdia's **Fiesta de Les Llanternes** on 24th August is designed with tots in mind. The town's littlest children parade through the streets at night carrying lanterns made from melons, singing traditional folk songs. It's one of the cutest sights in Spain. See p. 91.

To close Menorca's summer-long party season, **Maó** holds a three-day fiesta in early September. It ends with a bang: two nights of fabulous underwater fireworks. See p. 161.

The annual **Regata Internacional 'Bahia de Cala Millor'** takes place during the last five days of October. It attracts hot-air balloon aficionados from all over Europe, the US and Africa, filling the sky above Mallorca's east coast with colour. See p. 107.

The Best Caves The **Cuevas del Drach** is hands-down one of Mallorca's top sights. It's a mysterious underground labyrinth of stalactites and stalagmites, dripping from the ceiling and rising from the floor like great wax sculptures. Your kids will spot a Buddha, fairies, witches and warlocks, all in the rocks around them. As mesmerising as anything Disney imagined. See p. 109.

Though it morphs into a nightclub after dark, Menorca's **Cova d'en Xoroi** is not to be missed during the day. Or even better, find a perch on its terraces to watch the sunset. See p. 167.

One of Ibiza's must-sees, the old smugglers' **Cova de Can Marçà** is over 100,000 years old. Your children will sense the magic right away. See p. 225.

The Best Art Stop For budding painters in the family, no course of study is complete without a peek into the world of Pablo

Old Wooden Door

Dimoni in Sa Pobla is one of Mallorca's underrated attractions. See p. 96.

The Best Shops Menorca is internationally renowned for designer footware, and leading labels **Jaime Mascaró** and **Pons Quintana** both have factory shops on the island. Grab yourself a bargain. See p. 186 and 187.

Joyas Forteza in Palma may just be the place to buy your little darling her first string of pearls. Specialists in typical Mallorquín jewellery, they stock a wide range of Mallorcan grey pearls, as well as diamonds and other precious stones. See p. 60.

THE BEST ACCOMMODATION

The Best Hotels for Families
In Menorca, **Punta Prima's Insotel Hotel and Apartments** are a haven for family holidays. With pools, tennis courts, bikes for hire and the beach just a couple of minutes away, you could easily spend your break without leaving the resort. The rooms are spacious, with satellite TVs, and there are babysitters on hand if Mum and Dad need a night out on their own. See p. 188.

Just outside the pretty village of Porreras in Mallorca's quiet interior, **Can Feliu** is an old farmhouse with tasteful rooms, as well as a working organic farm. You can pick fruit straight from the tree for your breakfast, and enjoy the other farm produce during your stay – you can

Picasso. At Palma's **Es Baluard,** you can enjoy his works alongside that of his friend and contemporary, Joan Miró, who lived on Mallorca until his death in 1983. The architecture of the place is a highlight in itself. See p. 56.

The Best Attractions for Free
Swap flip-flops for trainers, and explore the pine gorge between Es Migjorn Gran and Binigaus beach, Menorca to discover the **Cova des Coloms**. The cave itself is an incredible 24 metres high, so it's no surprise that locals nickname it 'the cathedral'. See p. 181.

On a smaller scale, in **Sóller,** you can enjoy works bequeathed to the town by Joan Miró and Pablo Picasso for free at the train station above Plaça Constitució. See p. 75.

Kids love nothing more than a spook or a ghoul, and the collection of benign 'demons' at the **Museu de Sant Antoni I el** even roll up your sleeves and muck in. There are bikes for hire and a secret Wendy house hidden in the trees. See p. 143.

The Best Family Boutique Hotels

In fact, few of the islands' stylish hotels are suited to children, but Ibiza's clifftop Hacienda Na Xamena is a bit different. The interiors are eclectically fitted with Indian and Asian artifacts, and the terrace has some of the best views in the Med. Best of all, it's a bargain for what you get. See p. 226.

You've got to love a town where even the trendiest boutique accommodation welcomes the kiddies with open arms: Palma's Hotel San Lorenzo certainly fits the bill in the style department. A converted 17th century town house in the old quarter, its best features include a Parisian Art-Deco bar, and an oasis-like swimming pool surrounded by lush plant life. It doesn't come cheap, of course. See p. 63.

The Best Self-catering Accommodation

Menorca's Son Bou Gardens have well-equipped apartments in a perfect setting for children. They can play in ample gardens while you keep a watchful eye from your terrace. There are pools and restaurants nearby, as well as water slides, a giant maze and tennis courts, all within the complex. See p. 192.

Astbury Formentera have been in business for 25 years renting islanders' bungalows, villas and apartments from the beginning of April to the end of October. Having your own place eases the stress of *hostal*-dictated life and enables you to move at your own island pace, in a place which soon feels like home. See p. 251.

The Best Setting

The spectacular, windswept Sa Duaia feels like the edge of the world, a remote and untouched corner of Mallorca surrounded by umber mountains and rippling wild grasses. It has a decent-sized swimming pool, with wild and romantic terraces that could have been plucked from the Arizona desert. Book early: it's small and great value. See p. 99.

The Best Country Retreat

Located in a 17th century mill-house, the renovation at Son Mas, close to Mallorca's east coast, is sympathetic and tasteful, opening up the building to let in natural light while preserving original features. It's a home-from-home for anyone looking for something a little special – and your kids are very welcome. See p. 114.

THE BEST EATING OPTIONS

The Most Child-friendly Restaurants

In Menorca, you'd be hard pushed to find a better family eatery than Cala en Porter's La Salamandra. With a great-value set menu, a nearby playground and tortoises living in the flowerbeds, your children will love it. See p. 197.

Practically an Ibiza institution, don't miss a trip to **Daffers** in Cala Sant Vincent. With its cavernous interior strung with Moroccan lanterns and intimate nooks, it's a cut above the local plastic places – and it makes a change to go somewhere where the children's choice is as wide as the adults'. See p. 222.

The Best Seafood

It's certainly not cheap, but it's hard to find a better lobster stew on Menorca than **Es Cranc's**, in Fornells. The owners have their own fishing boat, so it's as fresh as it gets. See p. 195.

There's no special tourist treatment at Port de Sóller's **Ca's Mariner**, just superb home cooking and the island's best catch. Try the *bandeja de marisco* (a selection of seafood including clams, mussels, three different kinds of shrimp and razor clams) or *parrillada de pescado* (a mixed fish grill). See p. 85.

The Best Outdoor Dining

Handily placed in Ciutat Jardi, just a short hop from Palma, **El Bungalow** is an essential water's-edge dining experience. This charming fisherman's

Ca's Mariner

cottage on the beach is everything seaside eating should be: boat-fresh fish and seafood, clams and mussels; whole sea bass baked in salt; and some of the island's best paellas, with crisp, cold white wine to wash it all down. See p. 67.

The Best Fine Dining

Housed in a handsome 16th century olive press, **L'Olivo** in Deià is one of the best dining experiences in Spain. Its soaring rafters and whitewash make it light and airy by day, romantic and intimate by night. If you're with the family, book a spot on the terrace for a long, lazy lunch. See p. 84.

It's only been open a year, but already chef Peter Urbach, who previously had restaurants in Munich, is making waves with his fresh approach to Mallorcan cuisine at **Es Pinaret**. This is a place where kids get to play grown-ups in an enchanted garden, and still get catered for on a menu that features everything from saffron risotto to kiddies' schnitzel. Failing that, the pool should keep them happy. See p. 129.

The Best Ice-creams

No matter where you eat in Sóller, save room for ice-cream at **Sa Fàbrica de Gelats**. People travel from all over the island to taste its 40 excellent home-made ice-creams and sorbets. See p. 86.

The Best Breakfasts

For a Menorcan breakfast (there's no egg and bacon on the menu), visit **Can Pota** in Maó. Stop in for a large plate of tomato-smeared toast, pile it high with ham, sausages and cheese, and finish it off with a strong cup of coffee. See p. 196.

Since opening five years ago in Ibiza, childhood friends Pam and Barbara's **Club Sandwich** in Sant Antoni has become something of an institution. Their famous Potbelly Breakfast is more than just a heaven-sent hangover cure for clubbers – it'll fill hungry teens, too. See p. 231.

The Best Atmospheric Bars

La Fonda Pepe, Formentera's 'Hippy Bar', is the focus of evening action in San Ferran. It's usually warm enough for you to sip drinks outside on the pedestrianised *rambla* and watch the world go by. See p. 246.

Sure, seaside bars are ten-a-penny on Ibiza, but there's only one synonymous with the birth of the Balearic Beat: Sant Antoni's **Café Del Mar**. Grab a beer, get the children a fruit juice, and watch the sun go down. See p. 228.

The Best Picnic Treats

For a tasty DIY-picnic, Balearic style, don't bother making sarnies in advance, just tear open a piece of crusty bread, smear a plum tomato inside and liberally scatter with salt and olive oil – this is the classic **pa amb oli** you'll see in bars and restaurants, occasionally finished off with a wafer-thin slice of Serrano ham.

For sweeter teeth, Mallorca may have claimed **ensaïmades** as its own, but you can find these spiral pastries across the Balearics, in individual portions or filled with angel's hair jam in huge round boxes.

To finish it off, **horchata** may look like a strange milk-shake, but it is in fact made from tiger nuts. It's best drunk poured fresh from one of the glass churns you'll see in bars – not from supermarket plastic bottles.

2 Planning a Family Trip to the Balearics

THE BALEARIC ISLANDS

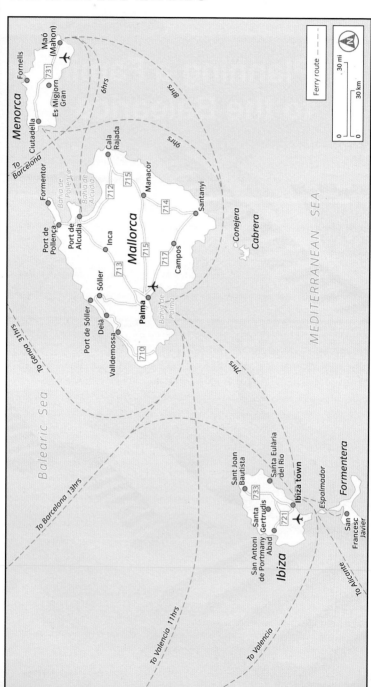

With holiday destinations like the Balearics, the need for planning gets pushed to one side. With a sandy beach just minutes away, and a huge swimming pool in your hotel, what else do you need? While this may suffice for some, each of the islands has **much more to discover.** The Balearics practically invented the package tour, but there are evermore visitors who have decided to do the islands their own way, piecing together transport, accommodation and entertainment options themselves, rather than letting a tour operator make decisions for them. Whichever holiday you choose, you can expect to see very different sides of the islands.

When planning a week or two away, **be adaptable:** what may seem like an ordinary enough beach to you could turn into an adventure for younger children. And make sure you come prepared. Much of the family holiday accommodation on the island is geared towards long days in the sunshine. Many an August thunder storm can scupper these plans, and being stuck between the four walls of a studio apartment is a prison cell for energetic children. If you opt for cheaper accommodation, accept that there will be no TV and little to do if the weather is uncooperative, so have a few rainy-day schedules up your sleeves. If not, at least bring a pack of cards...

WHICH ISLAND?

With four to choose from, finding the right island is crucial: inter-island travel with young children is impractical, especially on a short break. (The exception to this is Ibiza–Formentera). If you plan to visit more than one island during your stay, Mallorca is the best starting point. It has various onward flight and ferry connections to Ibiza and Menorca.

Mallorca As the largest island, Mallorca has more to offer than the others. From water parks to aquariums; golf to mountain walks; secluded coves to shopping: none of the other islands can compete for choice. If you're taking older children, Mallorca is a good option if two weeks on the beach is a boring holiday prospect – rainy-day activities are numerous (especially if you have a car to find them), and there's plenty to keep active children entertained.

Ibiza Ibiza's reputation may go before it, but its popularity with partygoers doesn't mean families should steer clear. On the contrary, Santa Eulària is a family-focussed haven, there are plenty of family beach resorts – and even Sant Antoni is a good place to bring children (just not in July or August). Your teenagers may not be able to get into the nightclubs they'd like, but they can still enjoy a dose of the vibe, over fruit juice cocktails at beach bars.

Menorca For many, this is the Balearic family gold-standard.

There are practically no noisy strips of bars (although there is nightlife if you're prepared to go and search for it), hen and stag weekends steer clear, and instead, peace and quiet prevail. While this makes for a calm backdrop to a family break, it can be frustrating for teenagers. Younger families predominate.

Formentera On an island that's little more than a giant dune, there are limited activities for older children. While Formentera is a safe destination for a family, with clean beaches, little traffic and quiet resorts, older children might get bored unless you opt for an activity holiday: sailing, cycling and diving are all excellent.

Visitor Information

The islands differ considerably in terms of character, so a degree of research before departure will give you a better idea of what's here.

On Spain in general, you can book accommodation and find out about the Balearics from the official tourist board website, *www.spain.info*. The tourist board offices in London (2nd Floor, 79 New Cavendish Street, London W1 6XB; ☎ *0207 468 8077*) also provide information about the islands.

The Balearic Islands' regional government operates *www.illesbalears.es*, which apart from standard information about the islands, including history, gastronomy, towns and local industries, has a list of markets, concerts and fairs.

Another excellent website, *www.infomallorca.net*, covers Mallorca's towns, culture, gastronomy and traditions, as well as links to transport and accommodation. For an unofficial guide, try *www.majorca-mallorca.co.uk* where you can find out about the island by resort, and read comments posted by people who have stayed here. Menorca has its own official site, *www.visitmenorca.org*, with more about individual towns, resorts and services available at beaches. In Mallorca *www.conselldemallorca.net* has weekly and monthly activity calendars on the tourism section of its website; for Menorca cultural events are listed on *www.emenorca.org*; while on Ibiza and Formentera, information is available in English on the Balearic Islands' site, *www.ibatur.es*. The English-language publication *Ibiza Spotlight*, *www.ibiza-spotlight.com*, offers a mixture of island news and information to help your planning. Formentera's town hall has its own website, *www.turismoformentera.com*, with information on the island, or try *www.guiaformentera.com*.

Child-specific Websites

For child-friendly activities, the general island websites are the best sources of information. There are no sites specifically aimed at children. The hotel chain **Sol Melia**

Green Card

After the so-called 'eco-tax' was scrapped, Balearic politicians came up with a new means to generate income for environmental projects, the **Green Card**. Costing €10 (£6.70), this provides discounts at over 900 attractions (including restaurants, museums, parks, travel and sport) across the islands. Valid for 15 days, it also includes 15 minutes in telephone calls to a European landline. The profit made from card sales is channelled into environmental projects. Cards are available from tourist information offices, hotels, car hire companies and participating businesses. See *www.targetaverda.com* or call 📞 *902 929 928*.

(*www.solmelia.com*) has a family section on its website.

General family travel websites *www.babygoes2.com* and *www. takethefamily.com* both have brief sections on the Balearic Islands, recommending accommodation and resorts (although the former omits Ibiza). The Appendix to this book also lists other general family travel resources. See p. 272.

To find your way around, pick up detailed maps from tourist offices once you're there. If you can't wait that long, try *http:// maps.google.com.* You can even zoom in close, right down to the size of your swimming pool.

ENTRY REQUIREMENTS, CUSTOMS & BRINGING PETS

Passports & Visas

Citizens of European Union countries need their national identity card or passport to enter Spain. Non-EU citizens require a passport, and residents of some countries (South Africa is one) require visas. US, Canadian, Australian and New Zealand citizens do not require a visa for stays of up to 90 days that are not for study or work. For up-to-date information on entry requirements to Spain, check the practical advice section on *www.spain.info.*

This site also has links with contact information for Spanish embassies around the world.

Taking Your Pet

EU citizens can bring their dogs and cats into Spain, as long as they have been issued with a passport, fitted with a microchip and vaccinated against rabies. Furry friends are not usually accepted at hotels and self-catering accommodation, so private hire is the best option if you cannot bear to leave Rover at home. In any case, you'll still have to ask the property owner for permission.

See *http://ec.europa.eu/food/ animal/liveanimals/pets/index_en. htm* for information about the movement of animals within the EU.

Coming Home

If visiting Spain from other EU countries, you can bring home any amount of goods for personal use, except new vehicles, mail-order purchases and more than 90 litres of wine, 10 litres of spirits or 110 litres of beer. All visitors leaving with more than €6010.12 (£4026.80) in cash must declare the amount to customs.

MONEY

The Euro

Spain uses the euro (€). A euro is divided into 100 cents, and there are notes for €5–500 and coins for 1¢ to €2. At the time of writing, the euro–sterling exchange rate stood at €1.48 to £1, so conversion from one to another is relatively straightforward: two-thirds of the euro price gives you an approximate figure in pounds. For current rates and a currency converter, see *www.xe.com*.

Credit & Debit Cards

Major shops, restaurants and hotels accept credit and debit cards. While Visa and Mastercard are widely accepted, American Express and Diners Club are usually only taken at expensive eateries and hotels. The local preference is for cash, but do not be put off if a shop

attendant sighs when you attempt to pay by card, even if they ask if you have the amount in cash. High bank charges mean shops usually will not accept cards for payments of under €10.

In smaller shops and restaurants, and isolated resorts, do check whether they accept cards before buying. Some might not.

Payment by card using your PIN number is still in its infancy, although is gradually spreading to more shops and eateries. You will usually be expected to sign the payment slip as well, even if you have already entered your electronic signature.

It is standard practice to show photo ID when paying by card, and some of the larger outlets, mainly supermarkets, may refuse payment unless you can produce your passport or driver's licence.

For lost and stolen cards, see 'Fast Facts: The Balearics', p. 37.

Traveller's Cheques

Traveller's Cheques are now almost a thing of the past, given the abundance of ATMs. If you do decide to cash one, bear in mind that banks have limited opening hours (typically 8am–2pm). Keep a record of the serial numbers in case of loss or theft.

Cashpoints

There are cashpoint machines in all towns, and in most major

What Things Cost in the Balearics	Mallorca	Menorca	Ibiza
1 litre unleaded 95 petrol	€0.92/£0.62	€0.95/£0.64	€0.95/£0.64
Rental of a medium-sized car (per week)	€120/£80.40	€200/£134	€180/£120.60
Bus fare	(Airport to Palma city) €1.85/£1.24	(Airport to Maó) €1.50/£1	(Airport to Ibiza town) €1/£0.67
Admission to zoo (adult)	€8/£5.35	€6/£4	€6/£4
Admission to zoo (child)	free–€4/£2.70	free–€4/£2.70	free–€4/£2.70
Cinema ticket (adult / child)	€5.70/£3.80	€5.50/£3.70	€5.50/£3.70
British newspaper	€1.50/£1	€1.50/£1	€1.50/£1
Local telephone call (per minute)	€0.07/£0.05	€0.07/£0.05	€0.07/£0.05
Menú del día at mid-priced restaurant	€8–15/ £5.35–10.05	€10–15/ £6.70–10.05	€8–15/ £5.35–10.05
Under-12s menu at mid-priced restaurant	€5–9/ £3.35–6.05	€6–9/ £4–6.05	€6–9/ £4–6.05
1 litre milk in supermarket	€0.75/£0.50	€0.79/£0.55	€0.79/£0.55
1.5 litre still water in supermarket	€0.29/£0.20	€0.40/£0.30	€0.35/£0.25
1kg bananas in supermarket	€1.30/£0.90	€1.50/£1	€1.50/£1
Ice-cream in town centre	€1.50/£1	€1.50/£1	€1.50/£1
Packet of 30 nappies in supermarket	€8.50/£5.70	€9/£6.05	€9/£6.05
900g powder infant milk in supermarket	€10.50/£7.05	€11/£7.35	€11/£7.35

resorts. In addition, a growing number of supermarkets have cashpoints. As your bank will charge for each withdrawal made (check charges with them before you leave), it makes sense to take out larger sums of cash. It is advisable to take more than one card with you, in case one gets lost or damaged.

WHEN TO GO & WHAT TO PACK

As the Balearics are still best known for traditional package holidays, July and August are the busiest months, and the most expensive. Once schools break up, the islands fill with families, mostly from the UK, Germany and Italy. Even Spaniards choose

Kids' Kit

The following items can make travelling with babies or young children in the Balearics easier and more relaxing:

Beach tents: When the sun shines, it really does shine, so take care not to get your little ones burnt. While a traditional parasol can be bought cheaply from a resort souvenir shop, a beach tent is more adaptable. If the wind is blowing, your children won't be bothered by sand. You can buy one from most baby shops.

Swimsuits: Protective swimsuits are a good idea for children who won't stay still. Zip them up in a suit with **UV protection,** and they can carry on with their non-stop sandcastle building.

Lightweight pushchairs: The fanciest of pushchairs soon become burdens in town. A walk through the Balearics' historic centres reminds you that they were built long before designer pushchairs had ever hit high streets. To make the ups and downs between the pavement and the road a little easier, bring a lightweight buggy with a narrow wheelbase.

Portable highchairs: As a general rule, few restaurants provide highchairs. Children usually sit on normal chairs or in their pushchairs, so bring one with you. Lightweight options include the supremely compact 'Handbag Highchair' (a loop of fabric that secures your baby to the chair), the foldable Handysitt toddler seat and the Early Years' inflatable booster seat. All are sold at *www.bloomingmarvellous.co.uk*, with prices from £15 to £75.

Nappy bags: Don't waste a precious moment of your holiday searching supermarket shelves for them: there isn't a nappy bag to be had. With domestic rubbish collected on a daily basis, there's no market for them. If you can't live without them, pop a roll into your suitcase.

the islands for their annual holiday – often an entire month on Balearic beaches. The best months of the year to visit are therefore June and September, when the sun shines but crowds are thin.

For when the sun is shining, a few extra towels in your luggage will almost certainly come in handy. Many hotels frown on the use of theirs on the beach.

During low season, you could easily be caught out by storms, so be sure to find space in your suitcase for an anorak. The rainiest months tend to be in the autumn.

Winter is full of surprises. The bitter north wind, or *tramuntana*, that billows down the Pyrenees across the Mediterranean, batters Mallorca and Menorca's north coasts. Legend states that when the *tramuntana* starts, it lasts either three or seven days, so if you're only here for a week, it could be a windy one. But that's

The Balearics Without Breaking the Bank

If you're travelling on a budget, here are a few ideas to make your euros stretch further:

Self-catering Accommodation: Opting for self-catering accommodation, rather than staying in a hotel, is one easy way to keep a tab on spending. Just make sure what kind of a 'kitchen' your apartment has: some are limited to two electric rings and a microwave. When shopping, avoid the supermarkets in resorts, and head to bigger stores in the towns: you'll find a wider selection at much better prices.

Sightseeing: Many of the Balearics' sights are free to the public, and those where you have to pay are usually free on Sundays. If you're planning lots of museums and galleries, invest in a **Green Card;** see p. 17.

Eating out: There's no need to avoid fine dining just because you're travelling on a budget. Instead, visit at lunchtime, for excellent food and wine at a fraction of the price, on a set menu.

On the beach: Renting parasols and sunbeds on a daily basis can be an expensive business: they cost around €5 (£3.35) per day. Instead, buy your own parasol from a souvenir shop – it won't cost more than €10 (£6.70) – and you have it for your entire stay. Even buying a plastic beach chair works out cheaper than renting a sunbed every day. And at lunchtime, take a picnic. Beach bars are ideal for a cool drink or ice cream, but their food is rarely cheap.

Nappies: Nappies are pricey, especially on Ibiza, Formentera and Menorca. If you are only visiting the Balearics for a few days, it makes sense to bring your own. If you're on the islands for 10–14 days, just bring a handful of nappies, and purchase the rest from a supermarket. The small packs on sale in resort supermarkets are expensive, so opt for a bumper-sized bag in town.

Free entertainment: Much of the Balearics' best entertainment is free, especially if you time your holiday right. Ask at the tourist office for information on local fiestas and festivals, and join in the celebrations in island towns without spending a penny. At fiesta time, the streets are filled with activity, including parades, fireworks, open-air concerts and bonfires, all *gratis*.

not to say you're obliged to stay indoors when the wind starts up – with a pair of sturdy walking boots and a warm jacket, you can marvel at the waves. I've also spent many February days walking deserted beaches in short sleeves – it's a real privilege to have a stretch to yourself. Mallorca is particularly suited to winter travel: there are more hotels open all year, and it is well connected to the UK by scheduled flights.

Average Temperature & Rainfall in the Balearics
Palma (Mallorca)

	Jan	Feb	Mar	Apr	May	June	July	Aug	Sept	Oct	Nov	Dec
Temp.(°C)	9.1	9.5	11.0	13.0	16.2	20.9	24.0	24.8	22.0	17.3	13.1	10.8
Rainfall (cm)	3.6	3.2	2.8	3.4	2.7	1.6	0.7	1.6	4.8	6.8	4.8	4.6

Whatever time of year you come, a pair of walking boots, shoes or sandals are essential if you plan to head off the beaten track. Flip-flops aren't practical footwear when you encounter uneven terrain on your way to a secret cove.

The islands, Mallorca aside, have a laid-back feel year-round. In fact, many residents complain they don't have enough opportunities to dress up, so don't feel obliged to pack smart clothes. A shirt is preferred in some exclusive restaurants, especially in Mallorca, however.

Public & School Holidays

The term fiesta applies to holidays of all description, be they national, regional or local celebrations. Should a public holiday fall upon a Tuesday or Thursday, islanders often take the Monday or Friday off as well, to make a *puente* or *pont* (bridge) with the weekend.

In the islands' towns, shops and banks close on such holidays; in resorts, it's business as usual. On Sundays, most supermarkets and souvenir shops close at midday, and during the winter the majority of supermarkets on Ibiza and Menorca do not open at all on a Sunday; only some newsagents and bakeries open until midday.

The main public holidays are: **New Year's Day; Balearic Islands' Day** (1st Mar); **Maundy Thursday** and **Good Friday** (Mar or Apr); **Labour Day** (1st May); **Assumption of the Blessed Virgin** (15th Aug); **National Fiesta** (12th Oct); **All Saints' Day** (1st Nov); **Constitution Day** (6th Dec); **Immaculate Conception Day** (8th Dec); **Christmas Day; Sant Esteve** (26th Dec).

In addition to these holidays, each town also has its own fiesta calendar. Some towns consider Shrove Tuesday a holiday, others take Easter Monday off, and when each town holds its annual celebrations in the name of its patron saint, it normally has at least one additional day's holiday. Don't be surprised to discover small towns closed even in the middle of summer, as many dates – such as **Saint James' Day** (25th July) – are taken as a holiday across the Balearics. The Balearic Government publishes an authoritative list of holiday dates in towns and villages on its website (*www.caib.es*). Use the English drop down menu to access the Ministry of Employment and Training's page, then click on the *calendari laboral*. The list is in Catalan.

Children have school holidays three times a year: two weeks at Christmas and Easter, and ten weeks over the summer, beginning the last week of June. The island is notably busier during these summer holidays. Many offices and factories change their summer working hours, adopting an intensive day, from 8am until 3pm. As a result, beaches are usually more crowded in the afternoon. Many island residents – those who do not work in the tourist industry – take August off, closing up their property in town and moving to a second home on the coast.

Special Events

Each town on the island celebrates at least one fiesta during the course of the year, often in the name of its patron saint. Of the many celebrations held, Palma's festivities in the name of **Sant Sebastià** are one of the highlights in the city's cultural calendar. On and around 20th January, many of the city's squares are transformed with the addition of stages to host concerts. On 23rd June, Mallorcans also celebrate **Sant Joan's** day, with bonfires, music and fireworks. On 24th August, the town of Sóller is filled with fire-breathing demons in the name of **Sant Bartolomeu.** Another highlight is the festivities in the name of **Santa Catalina,** held in late July. Flamboyant floats are accompanied by bands marching through Valldemossa's streets.

In Ibiza Town, the dreary month of February is given a dose of colour and cheer at **Carnival** time, with parades, dancing and live music. In the second week of May, Vila Dalt, Ibiza's old town, celebrates its medieval fiesta with markets, fairground attractions, street entertainers and Arabic dancing. The fair commemorates Vila Dalt being declared Humanity Patrimony by UNESCO in 1999.

On Menorca, between 23rd June and 8th September, every town takes it turn to host days of partying in celebration of its patron saint. Each has its peculiarities, but the essential elements are shared: horses, live music, fireworks and entertainment. The favoured drink at fiesta time is **Menorcan Gin** with lemonade. The fiestas really are a family affair. Away from the main square where the majority of people congregate, don't be afraid to take children up to horses waiting for their turn. Riders will usually let you pat them and admire their decorations close-up.

The major fiestas, some of which can last up to a week, are as follows:

Ciutadella, Sant Joan, 23rd and 24th June; **Es Mercadal,** Sant Martí, second weekend in July; **Fornells,** Sant Antoni, third or fourth weekend in July; **Es Castell,** Sant Jaume, 24th to 26th July; **Es Migjorn Gran,** Sant Cristòfal, last weekend in July; **Llumaçanes,** Sant Gaietà, first weekend in August; **Alaior,**

Sant Llorenç, second weekend in August; **Sant Climent,** third weekend in August; **Ferreries,** Sant Bartolomeu, 23rd to 25th August; **Sant Lluís,** last weekend in August; **Maó,** Verge de Gràcia, 6th to 9th September.

INSURANCE & HEALTH

Travel Insurance

Travellers to Spain from other EU countries now need to carry their **European Health Insurance Card** (EHIC), which replaced the E111 form as proof of entitlement to free/reduced-cost medical treatment abroad. The easiest way to apply for a card is online (*www.ehic.org.uk*). You can also call ☎ *0845 606 2030* or get a form from a Post Office. Be aware that the EHIC only covers *necessary* medical treatment, so is no replacement for travel insurance. When choosing the latter, make sure you read the small print of your home or credit card insurance carefully to check whether it covers you for lost cards, luggage, cancelled tickets or medical expenses. If not, then opting for an annual multi-trip policy is a good bet if you travel abroad at least twice a year. **Moneysupermarket** (*www.moneysupermarket.com*) compares prices and coverage across a bewildering range.

Staying Healthy

Health risks are minimal on the Balearics, and you don't need vaccinations before travelling. To be on the safe side, it's probably best to avoid drinking tap water, especially in resorts. While tap water is safe to drink in the towns and for washing fruit and vegetables, the water is hard. Bottled water is cheap and tastes better.

Another health hazard is **jellyfish.** Depending upon sea-water temperatures and currents, beaches can occasionally be plagued by them. While they are unlikely to bother you with more than an irritating sting, it is advisable to keep an eye on the flag at the Red Cross lifeguard points. If it is red, steer clear of the sea altogether. If jellyfish have invaded coves on one side of the island, it's usually a short drive to clear waters on another stretch of coastline.

INSIDER TIP

Pay attention to the **Red Cross lifeguards** present at all major resorts and on some smaller beaches. There's a simple traffic-light flag system for swimming. **Green** means the water is safe. **Yellow** means swim with caution. **Red** means swimming is prohibited. Even if the water appears calm, a red flag may indicate other hazards, such as jellyfish, so don't ignore the signs. Lifeguards also offer first aid in case of accidents.

If You Fall Ill

Don't forget to bring copies of prescriptions in case any family member loses their medicine or runs out. Note down the generic name, in case local pharmacists are unfamiliar with the brand.

When flying, legislation at the time of writing requires anything other than essential doses for the duration of the journey to be packed in the hold, and liquids cannot be carried as hand luggage in quantities above 100ml; they must also be stored in resealable plastic bags. Check with your airline before travel for an update.

Most resorts have private medical centres with English-speaking staff, to deal with minor injuries or illnesses. In Mallorca, there are several private clinics, including **Policlínica Miramar** (Camino de la Vileta 30, Palma. *971 767000 www.policlinica miramar.com*) and **Hospital d'Alcúdia** (C/Formentera 5, Alcúdia. *971 547373*) in the north. There is also a **British Surgery,** with four clinics in **Magaluf** and one in **Palma Nova** (*971 135022. www.thebritish surgery.com*. The British Surgery operates a 24-hour service, and employs predominantly British staff.

On **Ibiza** and **Menorca**, private healthcare options are limited. On Menorca, there are two private clinics: **Policlínica Virgin de Gracia** (Vives Llull 6, Maó. *971 054507*) and **Clínica Menorca** (Canonge Moll, Ciutadella. *971 480505*). On Ibiza, options include **Policlínica Nuestra Señora del Rosario** (Via Romana, Ibiza. *971 301916*). Private clinics almost

always have translators, but do check that your travel insurance policy will cover treatment.

Under the Spanish public health system, each town has its own health centre to deal with minor problems.

The Balearic Islands' largest and most important hospital is **Son Dureta** in Palma (C/Andrea Doria 55. *971 175 600*). There are full-time interpreters at the hospital, and many doctors also speak English. In addition, if travelling with major tour operators like Thomson, their customer care team can usually help. Elsewhere on Mallorca, public hospitals include **Son Llàtzer** (Crta Palma–Manacor km 4, Son Ferriol. *871 202 000*) and **Manacor Hospital** (Ctra Manacor-Aclúdia, Manacor. *971 84700*).

Formentera's new hospital was scheduled to be opened gradually from early 2007, although given the size of the island, major cases will continue to be treated on Ibiza at **Hospital Can Misses** (C/Barri de Can Misses, Ibiza. *971 397000*). On Menorca, the new **Mateu Orfila Hospital** on Maó's ring road was opened in Spring 2007. Mondays to Saturdays, volunteers from the Red Cross visit English-speaking patients and act as translators. Bear in mind that on the smaller islands, major cases may be flown to Mallorca for specialist treatment.

Should a local doctor prescribe treatment, be aware that green prescriptions receive a discount, red prescriptions are free, and any prescriptions written out by doctors from private clinics are not eligible for any reimbursement. There are always a handful of **pharmacies** on 24-hour call across the islands. Outside normal opening hours, you can find out which is the closest by checking the list posted in pharmacy windows or consulting local press.

TRAVELLING SAFELY WITH CHILDREN IN THE BALEARICS

The Balearics are generally a very safe destination for children, especially away from the crowds. Just walking through any town, you can spot front doors left ajar while owners have popped out to chat to a neighbour. Yet despite this relaxed air, a degree of common sense is required. Make sure you lock cars and apartments. Do not leave valuables in sight: leave them in a safe at your hotel or apartment reception.

Be careful walking in towns and cities. Around popular tourist attractions, such as the streets around Palma's cathedral, **pickpockets** and **bag snatching** are a problem. Similarly, on the coastal road in Mallorca's northwest, be careful when stopping at the numerous view points along the route. Robberies have occurred when tourists leave a car unlocked to take a photo. When walking in towns, do not expect drivers to stop at **pedestrian crossings** – wait until they have seen you and slowed before stepping into the road. Many towns have very **narrow pavements,** so ensure your little ones walk on the inside edge.

In resorts, it is not advisable to leave your belongings in view by a pool or on the beach: don't be an easy target for petty thieves. Obviously, make sure you have adequate **travel insurance** (see above) in case of theft.

Many resorts have play areas or patches of grass for children, but given their usual proximity to swimming pools, don't let them out of sight. On the beach, however shallow the water, do not let small children swim alone. Don't forget to keep an eye on the flags raised by the **Red Cross lifeguards.**

Specialised Resources

For Single Parents

Several websites offer advice for parents travelling alone, and single parents raise no disapproving eyebrows from islanders. The holidays section on *www.single parents.org.uk* provides especially useful contacts and advice.

For Grandparents

The Balearics is a popular location for bringing the grandchildren, although there are no specialist operators. Many who have retired to the island have grandchildren to stay during holidays. Pensioners are entitled to **discounts** on entry to museums and other places of interest: always ask when purchasing tickets and carry photo ID.

For Families with Special Needs

The cobbled streets in historic centres are tough terrain for wheelchair users, but despite this, many access improvements have been made. Most hotels have installed ramps and lifts, but apartment accommodation can be less suitable. Try to reserve a ground-floor unit.

In an attempt to widen access, many **beaches** across the Balearics have been adapted to enable disabled users to swim in the sea. Operated by the Red Cross lifeguards on the beach – just approach their hut to ask for help – users sit in low-lying chairs and are wheeled into the water. Beaches adapted in this way include **Santandria** and **Son Bou** in Menorca; ask at a tourist information office for details of your closest. At **Santa Eulària** in Ibiza, Red Cross volunteers accompany disabled swimmers between 4pm and 6pm during the summer (*℡ 971 390 303*). For Mallorca, the charity **Holiday Care** (*℡ 0845 124 9971. www.holidaycare.org.uk*) publishes a leaflet with travel information for disabled and elderly people. It costs £2.50. A multilingual list of services available at each Mallorcan beach (including information on access) can be downloaded from *www.infomallorca.net/guias/documents/HI-14.pdf.*

Mobile Phones

Switching from a British to a Spanish network is automatic on arrival. Check with your UK provider that your mobile is set up for **international roaming** before you leave. Call charges are higher than within the UK, and you also pay to receive calls.

For regular travellers to Spain, it could be worthwhile purchasing a Spanish pay-as-you-go phone or **SIM card** from a telecoms shop. You can buy a card before setting off from *www.0044.co.uk*. The major operators in Spain are **Telefonica Movistar, Vodafone** and **Amena/Orange.**

Other Phones

Landlines in the Balearics are prefixed **971.** When making calls from payphones, the **minimum charge** is €0.20 (£0.15).

The Internet

As is fitting with the needs of modern travel, **Internet cafés** have sprung up in great numbers. Prices and the speed of service vary considerably: while a café in your resort may be convenient, you are likely to find a faster and cheaper service if you head into town. For recommended Internet cafés on the islands, see 'Fast Facts' on p. 37.

To retrieve your **email,** ask your Internet Service Provider (ISP) if it has a web-based interface tied to your existing account.

If not, then open a free web-based email account with *www.yahoo.com* or *www.hotmail.com*.

The number of hotels with **WiFi** (Wireless Fidelity) is growing, but at the time of writing, Palma, Ibiza and Maó airports did not have WiFi Internet access.

Note that Spanish keyboards include some keys that are absent on British ones.

ESSENTIALS

Getting There

By Plane Just a few years ago, the best option for travel to the Balearics was a package deal, but the boom in low-cost flying has opened up the islands to independent travel, especially in the summer.

To **Mallorca** from the UK, there are countless to choose from, including **Air Berlin** (☎ 0870 738 8880 *www.airberlin.com*) to Stansted; **bmiBaby** (☎ 0871 224 0224 *www.bmibaby.com*) to Cardiff, Birmingham, Manchester and East Midlands; **easyJet** (☎ 0905 821 0905 *www.easyjet.com*) to several destinations; **FlyBe** (☎ 0871 700 0535 *www.flybe.com*) to Exeter and Southampton; and **Jet2** (☎ 0871 226 1737 *www.jet2.com*) to Blackpool, Leeds, Bradford and Newcastle. In addition, **Monarch** (☎ 0870 0405040; *www.flymonarch.com*), **Air Scotland** *www.airscotland.com*) and **BMI** (☎ 0870 607 0555 *www.flybmi.com*) connect to Heathrow to Palma, and

Thomson Fly (☎ 0870 190 0737 *www.thomsonfly.com*) connects Palma with several UK regional airports. There are plenty more, so shop around.

To **Ibiza** and **Menorca,** travel is much easier between May and October when charter flights and low-cost carriers **easyJet** and **Jet2** connect both islands with several UK airports. To Menorca, **British Airways** (☎ 0870 850 9850 *www.ba.com*) and **Iberia** (☎ 902 400 500 *www.iberia.com*) fly direct from London Gatwick, and **Monarch** connects the island with Birmingham, London Luton and Manchester. Monarch also flies between Ibiza and London Luton, Gatwick, Birmingham and Manchester.

During winter, the only company currently offering direct flights between the UK and Menorca is Monarch, connecting Maó with Manchester and London Luton. There are currently no direct flights between Ibiza and the UK in winter. The alternative is to fly via Palma Mallorca or Barcelona, and pick up a connecting flight. Barcelona in particular is an important base for low-cost airlines. Spanish carriers Iberia, Spanair (☎ 902 131 415 *www.spanair.com*) and **Air Europa** (☎ 902 401 501 *www.aireuropa.com*) run regular services between Maó and Ibiza and the mainland, as well as connecting flights from mainland Spain to the UK.

A public service is in operation between Ibiza, Maó and Palma

Mallorca, meaning anyone travelling between the islands is guaranteed a minimum number of flights every day. There are usually at least eight connections with Iberia either way – at a fixed price (currently €167 (£111.90)), so you can make booking changes, subject to availability, without facing penalties. Air Nostrum (part of Iberia) has launched twice weekly direct flights between Mahon and Ibiza.

If searching for flight-only holiday deals, several companies are worth trying: Airflights (📞 0800 083 7007 www.airflights.co.uk); FlightLine (📞 0800 541 541 www.flightline.co.uk); and XL (📞 0870 999 0069 www.xl.com), among several others.

By Ferry There are regular ferry services connecting the Balearic Islands with each other, and with mainland Spain. From Palma, there are ferries to Barcelona (daily in the summer), Valencia and Alicante (weekly), Menorca and Ibiza (daily to both). In the north of Mallorca, Alcúdia's port has connections to Ciutadella in Menorca. From Menorca, you can travel by ferry to Barcelona (daily in high season), Valencia (weekly) and Mallorca (daily); and from Ibiza, to Mallorca (daily), Barcelona (daily in high season), Valencia (weekly) and Dénia (summer only) in Alicante. There are also direct ferries between Formentera and Dénia operated by Balearia (📞 902 160 180 www.balearia.com). Companies operating between the islands and the mainland

include Iscomar (📞 902 119128 www.iscomar.com); Balearia; and Trasmediterranea (📞 902 454 645 www.trasmediterranea.com). Fast ferries connect Ibiza and Menorca with Mallorca in just over two hours. Ibiza is just two hours from Dénia on a fast ferry; Barcelona is an overnight journey.

There are invariably a handful of days a year when bad weather prevents boats departing. If this occurs, companies do not usually offer compensation or accommodation. Children under two travel free on ferries; those aged two to 12 get a 50% discount. Catching a ferry is the only way to get to Formentera. By fast ferry, the journey takes 25 minutes, with several services operating daily. See Fast Facts: Formentera, p. 239, for more details.

PACKAGE DEALS & ACTIVITY HOLIDAYS

Historically the staple diet of Balearic tourism, there's no need to turn your nose up at a package deal to the islands. They often provide better value than attempting to build your holiday independently, especially outside July and August. In fact, if you have children of pre-school age, package deals in June and September are usually excellent value for money, see www.abta.com.

Most package deals include flights, accommodation and transfers. In addition, tour operators usually offer reasonable rates for car hire and excursions.

For the best deals, don't restrict your search to major operators. There are several Balearic specialists.

Majorca Sun Centre (℡ *0870 757 7222 www.majorcasuncentre. co.uk*) recommends resorts for family travel, and you can book online. On the official **Mallorca** site, *www.infomallorca.net*, you book hotels and apartments. Alternatively, book online at the **Mallorca Hotel Guide** (*www. mallorcahotelguide.com*).

Ibiza specialists include the upmarket villa company **Villas in Ibiza** (℡ *971 332 777 www. villasinibiza.com*), while **Ibiza Holidays** (*www.ibizaholidays. com*) has general information about both Ibiza and Formentera, with contact details of hotels and apartments. On **Ibiza Spotlight** (*www.ibiza-spotlight.com*) you can book hotels and apartments.

Both **Tarlenton Travel** (℡ *01604 633633; www.tarlenton travel.com*) and **Celtic Holidays** (℡ *0870 777 9933 www.celtic holidays.ltd.uk*) are **Menorca** specialists.

Getting Around

By Car Although most towns and resorts are well served by public transport, a car is essential if you want to get off the beaten track, to explore the islands' interiors and isolated beaches. The only exception to this rule is Formentera. Here, a bicycle is all you need. See 'Fast Facts:

Formentera', p. 239, for bike hire recommendations.

Driving Rules & Advice

Remember: **drive on the right** in Spain. It's surprisingly easy to forget when you've just stepped off a plane. You are required by law to carry your **driving licence,** as well as a spare pair of **prescription glasses** if you wear them.

You'll find a **fluorescent jacket** inside your hire car. Don't put this in the boot: by law, you are required to have it to hand. In case of a breakdown or accident, you must put it on *before* getting out of the car.

Do not drink and drive. The **legal limit** is much lower than in the UK, at 0.05%. The use of mobile phones is not permitted while driving.

You are obliged to wear **seat-belts,** and children under 1.5m must use a booster seat.

On motorways, the speed limit is **120km/h;** on inter-urban roads this drops to **90km/h.** Within urban areas, speed limits are indicated.

Car Hire

There are numerous car hire companies, from big names such as **Avis** and **Hertz** to local com-panies. If you plan to hire a car, booking in advance is advisable, especially during July and August. If you choose to book through a local company on

Driving Times

At first glance, the islands seem small, but that doesn't mean you can drive anywhere in minutes – distances can deceive. In **Palma,** and to a lesser extent in **Ibiza Town,** the sheer volume of traffic can make crossing the city a lengthy task. Make sure you give yourself plenty of time if you have a town to drive through. Elsewhere in **Mallorca,** the scenic drive along the north-west coast may not look much on paper, but narrow roads and endless twists and turns slow you down. On **Ibiza,** Ibiza Town, Santa Eulària and Sant Antoni are all well connected, around 20 minutes' drive from each other. Once you begin to tackle the interior and sections of coastal road, expect journey times to increase. Finally, **Menorca** has just one central road, so an apparently simple journey between neighbouring resorts, like Son Bou and Sant Tomàs, can take up to 30 minutes: you are forced to drive inland before heading out to the coast again.

Ibiza or Menorca, most will meet you at the airport and take you to the vehicle personally. As Palma is a larger airport, most car hire companies have their own offices. Car hire companies will rent **child seats**, but do order them in advance. Staff at the large majority speak English. Costs for renting a basic model vary considerably, but expect to pay just over €100 (£67) in low season to up to €220 (£147.40) a week in July and August for a small family car. By law, companies cannot rent vehicles to drivers under 21. When collecting your car, you will need your driving licence and additional photo ID, like a passport or national identity card, as well as a credit card. See the relevant chapters for car rental recommendations.

By Bus Although travelling by bus isn't the best way to see the Balearics, public transport has improved in recent years, and connections between major towns are much easier as a result.

In Mallorca, major towns are well connected with nearby beaches and resorts, and there are also regular buses on Ibiza and Formentera. Service information including timetables, bus numbers and maps can be found by contacting the **Balearic Islands' Public Transport** service (TIB) (☎ *971 177 777 http:// tib.caib.es*).

As several private companies operate on Menorca, full information is not available on TIB's website. Instead, consult the back pages of the local press (such as *Diario Menorca*) for details. *Diario Menorca*'s website also lists bus times in Spanish: from the newspaper's homepage (*www.menorca.info*) click on *agenda servicios*, and scroll down to *autobuses*.

On all the islands, frequency of services increases in peak season.

By Train There are no trains on Ibiza, Formentera or Menorca. On Mallorca, services are limited to a tourist route between **Palma** and **Sóller** (see 'The Little Train That Does', p. 74); and a service between **Palma, Inca** and **Manacor**. Service information including timetables, bus numbers and maps, can again be found via the **Balearic Islands' Public Transport** service (☎ 971 177 777 *http://tib.caib.es*).

By Taxi Taxis are a realistic option if you plan to spend the majority of your time in one place. There are taxi ranks at airports and within towns. In **Mallorca,** there are several taxi firms, or in Palma, just hail one on the street. There are several reliable numbers for booking cabs, so don't be surprised to see different numbers advertised. In **Palma,** call ☎ 971 401414 or ☎ 971 201212; in **Calvià** ☎ 971 680970; in **Alcúdia** ☎ 971 546762 and in **Pollença** ☎ 971 866213. On Menorca, Ibiza and Formentera, the numbers for taxis depend on your location. On **Menorca,** call ☎ 971 482 222; in **Ciutadella;** ☎ 971 37348; in **Ferreries** and ☎ 971 367 111 anywhere else. In Ibiza, **airport taxis** can be contacted on ☎ 971 395 481. Elsewhere, call ☎ 971 398 483 in **Ibiza Town;** ☎ 971 343 764 in **Sant Antoni;** and ☎ 971 333 033 in **Santa Eulària.** On Formentera, taxi services can

be booked in **San Francesc** (☎ 971 322 016); **Es Pujols** (☎ 971 328061) and **La Savina** (☎ 971 322 002).

Expect to pay additional charges if you book a taxi through your hotel, if you take a taxi from the airport, if you travel at night, or if you are carrying luggage.

By Bike Cycling is a good way to get to know the Balearics. However, while there are many good short routes, such as around Sóller's port in Mallorca or heading to virgin beaches near Sant Antoni on Ibiza, much of the time cyclists are forced to share the road with traffic, so take great care. Cycle helmets are not obligatory, but are *strongly* advised. **Formentera** is the best adapted to cyclists: flat terrain makes cycling a joy even with small children. There are several bike hire companies; see p. 238 for recommendations.

In Mallorca, **Embat Ciclos** (Bartolomé Riutort 27, Can Pastilla ☎ 971 492 358 *www.embat ciclos.com*) is close to the airport; see p. 172 for more recommendations on the island. Bike specialists in Menorca include **Bike Menorca** (see p. 159).

By Boat Exploring the islands by boat is a unique experience. There are bays and coves aplenty that are only accessible from the sea. However, renting a boat isn't for complete novices. With the exception of very small motorboats, proof of qualifications will be required.

With 41 **marinas** in total, there are several places to hire boats in Mallorca. You can find out about the different maritime companies operating in the Balearics at *www.apeam.com*, where company contact information is also listed. July and August are the best months for sailing, although the weather is usually suitable between May and October.

ACCOMMODATION & EATING OUT

Tourism is the Balearics' most lucrative industry. As you might expect, then, the islands have sufficient accommodation to meet all tastes and budgets. The islands' population booms in the peak months of July and August: expect to pay much more. It's easier to find bargains in May and October, although prices rise slightly for British school half-terms. During winter, accommodation options shrink considerably, especially on Ibiza, Formentera and Menorca. Many hotels and almost all apartment complexes close. If you're visiting the Balearics outside summer, choose your location carefully. While your resort hotel may be open, there's no guarantee that nearby shops and restaurants will.

Note that in many cases, hotels and self-catering are block-booked by package groups.

Hotels

The jury's out as to whether it actually works out cheaper to book your hotel accommodation directly with a hotel, or accept what's on offer in a package. The time of year makes a big difference in terms of availability, and for July and August, unless you book well in advance, you may have trouble finding availability independently. The advantage of booking direct is that you know exactly which hotel you are going to stay in. In May and October, you may find the hotel promised in your package has closed, and you're moved elsewhere. The centralised booking services, *www.mallorcahotelguide.com*, *www.menorcahotelsguide.com* and *www.ibizahotelsguide.com* give a good idea of availability and cost, and provide information about the services each hotel offers. Most are adapted to the needs of young visitors. Expensive hotels often have a **nursery** and **babysitting** services as well, to give you some time out. You'll also find this information in the individual hotel entries throughout this book.

Self-catering

Self-catering is another popular option, with accommodation ranging from simple studios to luxurious villas with pool and garden. Most apartment complexes are set in landscaped gardens so your children will have a degree of autonomy. Apartment complexes also have shared pools, as well as restaurants, supermarkets and souvenir shops to hand, so you can mix meals in with snacks out to suit your budget. One word of warning however: many self-catering apartments have kitchenettes – with just two electric rings and a microwave if you're lucky – so you'll struggle to rustle up gourmet suppers. Another down side of self-catering accommodation is the lack of something for a rainy day. Few apartments have TVs, and in many resorts there is little to do when the weather is poor.

Prices vary considerably depending upon the time of year and type of property. A search on the Internet will give you an idea of seasonal costs. Check with the property agents as to what children's kit there is in the apartment or villa: most have cots, highchairs, and additional beds.

Centralised booking services (see above) also list rental properties. **Owners' Syndicate** (☎ 0871 423 9055 *www.owners syndicate.com*) has a large selection of apartments and villas on the islands. **Owners Direct** (☎ 01372 229330 *www.owners direct.co.uk*) lists several properties for rent in the Balearics, while **Villas Abroad** lists properties on Mallorca and Menorca (☎ 0800 634 1318 *www.villas abroad.com*). In Menorca, try; **Vil·la** (☎ 971 367 852; *www.vil-la. com*) while for up-market properties both **Menorca Private Owners** (☎ 01335 330251

www.villanet.co.uk) and **Owner's Club Menorca** (*www.ownersclub menorca.com*) are worth consulting, as is **Villas in Ibiza** (*www. villasinibiza.com*).

Camping

There are just a handful of campsites to choose from across the Balearics. Not all are within walking distance of the coast, so a car may be an essential additional expense. On **Mallorca,** there is a campsite up in the mountains at **Lluch Monastery** (☎ 971 871 525) and one at Artà, **Club San Pedro** (☎ 971 589031).

There are just three campsites to choose from on Ibiza, **Camping Cala Bassa** (☎ 971 344 599 *www.campingcalabassa.com*), **Camping Cala Nova** (☎ 971 331 774) and **Camping Vacaciones Es Canar** (☎ 971 332 117). On **Menorca,** there are just two campsites: **Camping Son Bou** (see p. 193) is the best bet. Camping is forbidden on **Formentera.**

Eating Out

Fish is inevitably a Balearic staple. Menorca's *caldereta de langosta* (**lobster stew**) is its most famed, and probably most expensive, dish. Ibiza and Formentera have their own **fish stew,** *guisat de peix*. Many of the better restaurants catch their own fish. Meat lovers are generally well catered for: Menorcan specialities include **rabbit** and **partridge.** Menorca also has a thriving dairy industry, and there isn't a menu on the island that doesn't include at least one of three **cheeses:** *tierno* (soft), *semi-curado* (semi-cured) or *curado* (cured). Look for brands that have been awarded the prestigious quality stamp, *D.O* or *denominación de origin.*

The same quality stamp applies to **Mallorcan wine,** with Binissalem and Pla i Llevant both worthy of the classification. Ibiza and Menorca also have their own wines, but are better known for liqueurs: **Herbes** in the case of Ibiza (and also Mallorca), made with a blend of herbs; **gin** in Menorca, a legacy of the British.

In delis, you'll find numerous variations on cold sausages, the most famous being Mallorca's spicy **sobrassada.**

Vegetarians may find they overdose on the ubiquitous *tortilla española* – Spanish omelette made with egg, potato and onion – but do look out for other vegetarian staples. Try wild mushrooms, or *setas*, cooked in garlic; stuffed aubergines; a hearty tomato soup – *oliaigua amb tomàquet* – traditionally accompanied with fresh figs in autumn. If opting for a *menú del día* (set course menu), vegetarians are unlikely to find a suitable main course, so pick two starters.

Traditional pastries include **ensaïmada,** a light swirl of cake traditionally served with a cup of thick hot chocolate.

Although restaurants, especially in resorts, almost always

cater for English tastes, you'll all have more fun with traditional island cooking. While Mallorca and Ibiza have fast food alternatives for children, Formentera and Menorca are certainly not ideal destinations for burger lovers: there isn't a single McDonald's on either.

Restaurants are on the whole very child-friendly, and waiters will happily find you a table in a corner with space for the pushchair. Even the smartest restaurants are usually happy to accommodate little ones at lunch. Some have **highchairs** available, but if you plan to eat out a lot, it is probably better to bring a portable one, see p. 20.

In high season, mainstream restaurants tend to open all day. Locals rarely eat before 2pm, and on a weekend their lunches begin even later and go on until past 5pm. In the evenings, tourists usually dine earlier, and from 10pm, locals and Spanish visitors sit down.

The 'Family-friendly Dining' sections in each chapter cover a range of restaurants in resorts and towns for all budgets. While eating out is cheaper than the UK, prices are not always as low as you might expect. A **set menu** is a good way to keep costs down: they usually include three courses, bread, wine and water, and start from as little as €7 (£4.70) per head. Many restaurants also offer lower-priced **children's menus,** but don't be afraid to ask for a child-sized portion of a main course dish. They are usually happy to oblige.

Made in Maó?

The French don't have the only claim to have invented mayonnaise. Menorcans believe the sauce has its origins on their island. During the French occupation of Menorca between 1756 and 1763, legend has it that a tired Duke of Richelieu headed to a farm with an empty stomach. Not knowing what to give the Duke, the Menorcan farmhand prepared him a sauce with egg yolk, salt and oil, and spread it on a piece of bread. So content was the Duke, he took the recipe with him back to France, naming it after the town of Maó (Mahón): *mayonnaise* was born. Other versions of the story claim that a frustrated chef produced the sauce – when his other recipe failed – for the banquet that Richelieu held to celebrate the French conquest of the island. Or that it was in fact Richelieu's local lover who introduced the Duke to the sauce, and as she came from Maó he named it after her. Whatever the origins of the sauce, Maó's residents really are known as *mahoneses*.

GETTING YOUR CHILDREN INTERESTED IN THE BALEARICS

Let your children play a role in preparing for your trip, to help spark their interest in what the islands have to offer. Using this book as a starting point, tell them about the attractions, from beaches, lighthouses and clifftop walks to farms, waterslides and animal parks.

Learning some **Spanish** will also make a big difference: locals are usually flattered when people make an effort. The **Appendix** (p. 257) has some phrases to get you and the children started. There are also several language courses aimed specifically at children. Websites like *www.little-linguist.co.uk* sell online.

For information on the Balearics' flora and fauna, visit the webpage of environmental group, GOB (*www.gobmallorca.com*). They publish several children's books about island animals, and at the Menorcan branch, *www.gobmenorca.com*, there are some in English. Try *The Tale of Spikes*, about a Menorcan hedgehog.

Older children will certainly be interested in the star-studded side of island life. Mallorca is a popular destination for celebrities, including Michael Douglas, Bill Clinton, Boris Becker and, going back a bit, Winston Churchill and Agatha Christie. Claudia Schiffer is also a familiar Mallorca face. The supermodel sold her luxurious villa in Camp de Mar to a Russian millionaire in July 2005 for a cool €11 million, one of the largest property deals in the Balearics' history. Ibiza, meanwhile, has long been associated with stars like Kate Moss.

FAST FACTS: THE BALEARICS

Area Codes See 'Telephone', below.

Baby Equipment Most hotels, apartments and villas can provide you with cots for a small extra charge. Supermarkets and chemists sell nappies, formula milk and jarred food, but not nappy bags. For specialist baby clothing or equipment, there are many baby shops across the islands, although clothing in particular is more expensive than in the UK.

Babysitters Most expensive and some moderate hotels arrange sitters for guests. Rates average €8–12 (£5.35–8) per hour.

Breastfeeding Breastfeeding in public is acceptable, but you may get stared at, especially if you're feeding an older infant. You may want to brazen it out, since breastfeeding is your natural right, or you might prefer to find an out-of-the-way spot.

Business Hours Shops outside large towns generally open at 9am or 10am (6am or 7am for bakeries), closing again at 1–1.30pm and then reopening between 5–6pm until 8.30pm. City-centre stores are open from 9am–9pm, Monday–Saturday. Supermarkets generally open from 9am until 9pm, with no break for lunch, opening on Sunday mornings between May and October. Banks open between 8am and 2pm, and close at weekends and bank holidays, although some banks open on Saturday mornings between October and May. Most have 24-hour ATMs. While bars and cafés open early, often from 6am, and stay open until past midnight, restaurants usually open from noon, and between May and October in resorts they stay open all afternoon into the evening. Public museums usually close on Sundays and / or Mondays and on public holidays, but most tourist sites open on public and school holidays. Many shops, restaurants and bars close completely from October to May in smaller resorts. Even in towns, many businesses close for up to a month after Christmas.

Car Hire See 'Getting Around', p. 30.

Chemists Staff at chemists (pharmacies), recognisable by a green cross, can provide first aid in minor emergencies. Rotas of pharmacies operating outside normal hours (9am–1.30pm and 5–8.30pm Monday–Friday; Saturday mornings only) are posted in every chemist window and in local papers. It's a good idea to take a first-aid course yourself; there's a CD-Rom (about £30) developed in collaboration with St John's Ambulance: see *www.firstaid forkids.com*.

Climate See 'When to Go & What to Pack', p. 19.

Credit Cards Keep a note of your credit card numbers in case they are lost or stolen. In the case of lost cards, telephone your cardholder. **American Express** ☎ *902 111 135;* **Diners** ☎ *901 101 011;* **Visa** and **MasterCard** ☎ *902 114 400.*

Currency See 'Money', p. 18.

Dentists For emergency dental treatment, go to your nearest hospital or health centre.

Doctors Some upmarket **hotels** have doctors on call, though they can be expensive. Emergency services are available 24 hours at health centres across the island. If you're staying in one place for a while, it's a good idea to **make a list of emergency contact details** and pin them up by the front door. Check to see if your host has already provided one in your welcome pack.

Driving Rules See 'Getting Around', p. 30.

Electricity Like the rest of continental Europe, electricity in Spain runs on 220-volt, 50-cycle AC. Visitors from the UK and Ireland need a two-pin European adapter (available at supermarkets) to use their own appliances; those from North America need a voltage transformer (unless the appliance has a dual voltage switch) and plug adapter. Some hotels can lend adapters, but don't rely on it.

Embassies & High Commissions The **British Consulate** in Mallorca can be contacted at Plaça Major 3D,

Palma (☎ *971 712 445.*) Mallorca also has an **Irish Honorary Consul General** (Sant Miquel 68, Palma ☎ *971 722504*) and a **US Consular Agency** (Av. Rei Jaume III 26 1, Palma ☎ *971 725 051*). Palma is also home to consulates for several other countries. On **Ibiza,** the **British Vice Consulate** is at Av. Isidoro Macabich 45, 1, Ibiza (☎ *971 301 818*). Ibiza also has a **German Consulate** (Antoni Jaume 2, Ibiza ☎ *971 315 763*), a **French Consulate** (Abad I Lasierra 35, Ibiza ☎ *971 301 216*), an **Italian Consulate** (Joan de Austria 5, Ibiza ☎ *971 315 428*) and a **Dutch Vice Consulate** (Via Púnica 2B, Ibiza ☎ *971 300 450*). On **Menorca,** there are consulates for the **UK** (Hon. Vice Consul, Camí de Biniatap 30, Horizonte, Es Castell ☎ *971 367 818*), **Germany** (Sant Andreu 32, Maó ☎ *971 361 668*), **France** (Deyà 30, Maó ☎ *971 354 387*) and the **Netherlands** (Àngel 12, Maó ☎ *971 354 363*).

Emergencies Staff in most hotels are trained to deal with emergencies, so call the front desk before you do anything else. Otherwise, for an **ambulance** call ☎ *112,* for the **police** ☎ *062,* for the **fire service** ☎ *112.*

Internet Access Of the growing number of Internet cafés in the Balearic Islands, try **Azul Internet Café** (C/Soledad 4, Palma, Mallorca ☎ *971 712 927*); **Ciber Tango** (Carrer de Sant Cristobal 20, S'Arenal de Llucmajor, Mallorca ☎ *971 442 826*); **Chill Internet Café** (Via

Púnica 49, Ibiza ☎ *971 399 736*); and **Informàtica Egocentric** (Vassallo 20, Maó, Menorca ☎ *971 355 690*).

Language In the Balearic Islands, both Spanish and Catalan are official languages. English is widely spoken.

Lost Property Unless you know where you dropped an item and can ask there, go to the nearest police station. For important documents such as passports, contact your consulate. For lost credit cards, see 'Credit Cards', above. If you think your car may have been towed away for being illegally parked, ask at the local police station.

Mail Each town has its own post office, easily spotted by its **yellow sign.** These are open from 8am–2pm in smaller towns and all day in large towns and cities. A letter or postcard weighing less than 20 grams requires a 57¢ stamp for destinations within the EU. Stamps can be bought from tobacconists, or *estancos*, and some souvenir shops. In many resorts, there are **yellow post boxes** near supermarkets and shops. When sending letters, it is advisable to write the return address (*Rte*) on the back of the envelope.

Maps Island maps can be picked up from many shops, town halls, tourist information offices and at car hire desks.

Newspapers & Magazines
Local daily papers include *Ultima Hora, Diario de Mallorca,* *Diario Menorca* and *Diario de Ibiza*. The English-language newspaper for the Balearics, *Majorca Daily Bulletin*, includes both local and international news. Otherwise, **English-language newspapers** from the UK and USA are widely available at newsstands and newsagents, without the supplements and at a premium price; the British *Guardian* has an international edition sold in Europe.

Police In **emergencies,** call ☎ *092*. For theft, you have to file a report with either the **National Police** or the **Civil Guard.** For straightforward reports, the police have recently introduced a new centralised number valid all over Spain, ☎ *902 102 112*, which enables you to file a report in either English, German, French, Spanish, Arabic or Japanese. You will need a form of identity to hand (such as your passport), and the call centre will give you a reference number for your case.

Post Offices See 'Mail', above.

Safety The usual common-sense tips apply. Don't leave money or valuables on display on your person, in your car or in your apartment or villa. Be wary of **pickpockets** in confined public spaces; don't allow yourself to be distracted by anyone while withdrawing money at a **cashpoint;** and don't walk alone in unlit open spaces such as parks (most of which are locked out of hours anyway) or even on seemingly innocuous residential streets after dark. Also see

'Travelling Safely with Children in the Balearics', p. 26.

Taxes A 16% national **value-added tax** (*IVA: impuesto al valor añadido*) is included in the price of most goods in Spain. It stands at 7% for accommodation and food. Many restaurants list their prices without IVA, so check whether or not it has been included. Non-EU residents can reclaim most of this if they spend €175 (£117.25) or more at a participating retailer.

Taxis Each town has its own taxi rank, and taxis can also be caught at airports and ports. See individual chapters, and 'Getting Around', p. 30.

Telephone Within Spain, all telephone numbers begin with 9 with either a two- or three-digit area code. Numbers starting with 6 are mobiles, and 902 numbers are charged at local rates.

To **call a Spanish number from abroad,** dial ☎ *00 34* from the UK (☎ *011 34* from the USA). To **dial the UK from Spain,** call the international code (☎ *00 44*) then the British number minus the first 0 of the area code; to call the USA dial ☎ *00 1* then the number. If you don't bring your mobile, there are plenty of payphones in towns and resorts. You will need a minimum of 20¢ to make a call.

Time Zone Spain is one hour ahead of **British time.** Clocks go forward by an hour for summer or 'daylight saving time', as in the UK, on the last Sunday in March, reverting on the last Sunday in October. Spain is six hours ahead of North American **Eastern Standard Time.**

Tipping Few restaurants include a service charge on your bill, so you may wish to follow common practice, and leave an extra tip (about 10% of the total).

Toilets & Baby Changing

There are few public toilets, so you're best off making a small purchase at a bar or café before using theirs. Public museums often have toilets, but few galleries do, and apart from in **El Corte Inglés** (see 'Fast Facts: Palma and the Rest of Mallorca', p. 49), baby changing facilities are few and far between. Newer and larger bars only are likely to have a fold-down changing table, so it's wise to carry a changing mat with you.

Water In towns, tap water is safe to drink, but in resorts it's safer to opt for bottled. If you ask for *agua* in a restaurant, you will be given bottled water unless you demand *agua potable*. Still water is *agua sin gas*, while sparkling is *agua con gas*.

Weather See 'When to Go & What to Pack', p. 19.

3 Palma and the Bay of Palma

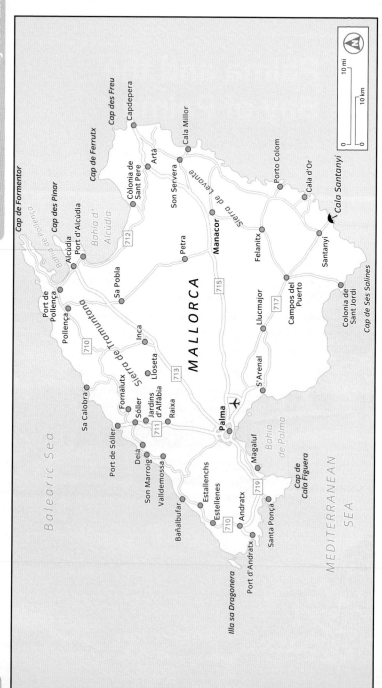

Cap de Formentor

Cap des Freu

Cap de Ferrutx

Cap de Pinar

Cap d'Alcúdia

Bahía d' Pollença

Bahía d' Alcúdia

Port de Pollença

Pollença

Alcúdia

Port d'Alcúdia

Capdepera

Cala Millor

Artà

Colònia de Sant Pere

Son Servera

Porto Colom

Cala d'Or

Cala Santanyí

712

Sa Pobla

Petra

Manacor

Felanitx

Santanyí

Colònia de Sant Jordi

Cap de Ses Salines

715

Llucmajor

Campos del Puerto

717

Inca

Lloseta

713

Sierra de Levante

MALLORCA

Port de Sóller

Sóller

Jardins d'Alfàbia

Fornalutx

Raixa

711

S'Arenal

Palma

Bahía de Palma

Sa Calobra

Sierra de Tramuntana

710

Deià

Son Marroig

Valldemossa

Estellenchs

Estellenes

Magaluf

Cap de Cala Figuera

Banyalbufar

Andratx

719

710

Santa Ponça

Port d'Andratx

Illa sa Dragonera

Balearic Sea

MEDITERRANEAN SEA

10 mi

10 km

0

0

In many ways this part of Mallorca represents the best and the worst of the island. Magnificent Palma with its maze-like medieval heart and shady boulevards; the ugly, over-developed coastlines of the bay.

Unlike Barcelona and Madrid on the mainland, both teeming with child- and teen-friendly parks, museums and activities, Palma doesn't at first seem to have a huge amount to offer, being more oriented these days to urban jet-setters and *fashionistas*. But keep scratching away at the surface and you'll find a host of pleasures to easily keep the gang happy for a long weekend.

Being outdoors is the way to go here, and activities range from exploring the ramparts of the old town's palaces and cathedral to bike rides along the seashore. A trip on the open-top double-decker bus on day one is an excellent way to get oriented. You can hop on and off at will. The Castell de Bellver for 360º panoramic views, and theatrical Poble Espanyol for a taste of the rest of Spain, are two sure-fire winners on the childrens' circuit. Sprinkle this with stops for tapas and ice-creams in a kaleidoscope of flavours, a couple of excursions to the beach, nearby theme parks and a train ride to Sóller, and you should escape boredom blues even without a car.

PALMA

Founded by the Romans, sacked by the Vandals, reconquered by the Byzantines and then colonised by the Moors, it was Palma's situation – a handy sail from Spain and front-on to North Africa – that made it one of the most strategically important sites in the Mediterranean by the time James I of Aragon showed to stake his claim in 1229 on what was then considered one of the most beautiful cities in Europe.

Palma retains its magic to this day, the pearl of the Mediterranean with a beautiful old town, a warren of maze-like streets and wide, palm-lined boulevards along the sea.

It is the capital of the whole of the Balearics and as cosmopolitan, if in miniature, as her bigger sisters, Madrid and Barcelona. Almost half the entire population of Mallorca lives in Palma, and it shows in the exuberance of the place. In recent years, Palma has become a hotspot on the destination list of the world's jet-set with movie stars and supermodels making their way here in search of a place to hide from the limelight. Yet despite the abundance of glamorous nightclubs and chi-chi cocktail bars, Palma retains that laid-back island feel.

The capital is located on the south coast of the island, at the centre of a wide bay. In many ways it's rather like Barcelona in miniature, boasting its own Passeig de Born (the chi-chi shopping quarter of the Catalan capital), Poble Espanyol (the theme park that mocks up emblematic Spanish cities) and a swanky port. Because it's fairly compact, Palma can easily be toured on foot, and by far the best way of enjoying the lively historic quarter is simply to wander around getting pleasantly lost. The suburbs that extend beyond the *Avingudes* (wide avenues that enclose the old city) have little to offer the visitor, though its certainly worth hopping aboard the *bus turisitic* (see p. 46) to explore the Castell de Bellver or up-and-coming Santa Catalina, one of the westernmost suburbs, with numerous bars and trendy restaurants. Be aware it's more an area to go for food or food shopping (Santa Catalina's market is a great place for picking up picnic fayre), than somewhere to find amusement for the children. The beaches are to the east and west of the town, with the best city beaches located around Cituat Jardi. Like Santa Catalina, the old fishing village of Portixol has undergone a dramatic face-lift with hot drinking spots opening every month. It's a lovely place to stroll along the pebble beach admiring the painted cottages that line the front. Allow a good half-hour to walk from the Port of Portixol to Cituat Jardi for the beach.

ESSENTIALS

Getting There

By Plane Son Sant Joan Airport (☏ *971 789 000*, *www.aena.es*) is just eight kilometres from the centre of Palma. Flights connect to mainland Spain including Barcelona, Madrid, Valencia and Malaga, as well as the UK and the rest of Europe daily. Many of the budget airlines fly here including easyJet, bmibaby, Monarch and Vueling. The number 1 bus leaves from right outside the terminal at the airport, to Plaça Espanya in the centre of Palma, every 15 minutes or so. It costs €1.85 (£1.25). A taxi costs around €25 (£16.75) into the centre.

By Ferry Ferries run regularly between Barcelona, Valencia and Denia on the mainland. The fast ferry from Barcelona takes just three hours and is a good option if you want to combine the Catalan capital with a little island-hopping. There are also daily passenger and car ferries connecting the other Balearic islands.

The port is located on the western edge of the city, about 10 minutes by taxi from the centre. Bus number 1 also goes there. Allow at least 30 minutes. Three ferry companies operate around the Balearics and to mainland Spain, including Trasmediterranea (*www. trasmediterranea.es*), Balearia (*www.balearia.com*) and Acciona (*www.acciona.ferries.org*). Try AFerryTo (*www.aferry.co.uk*) for an overview of the best available deals.

Journey time between Palma and Ibiza is about four hours. Palma to Maó is about five hours. To get to Formentera you must first go to Ibiza and then take a connecting ferry from the port in Ibiza Town to the smallest Balearic. It takes a further hour. See Chapter 11 for details.

By Car A rental car is far and away the best way to see the island, especially if you want to get off the beaten track and explore mountain villages and hidden beaches. You must be over 21 and have a valid driving licence to hire a car in Mallorca. Driving regulations are the same as for the rest of Spain: drive on the right, speed limit of 120 km/h on highways, 30 in built-up areas. Its safe, easy-going and pretty island roads make for happy motoring. Try Amigo Autos (℡ *971 498 399, www.amigo autos.com*) for cheap deals. Hertz (*www.hertz.co.uk*) and E-Sixt (*www.e-sixt.co.uk*) also have local offices.

By Bus Bus number 1 runs from the airport to Plaça Espanya. It continues to the ferry terminal, running along Avenidas Paseo Mallorca, Via Argentina and Paseo Maritimo. It leaves every 15 minutes. An information office (no phone) is located at the train station on

Plaça Espanya, where you can pick up timetables. The office is open Mon–Fri, 9am–8pm, Sat 9am–1.30pm; closed Sun and public holidays.

The Empresa Municipal de Transports (C/ Josep Anselm Clavé 5 ℡ *971 214 444. www. emtpalma.es*) has a good network of city buses. You can download main routes and timetables from their website, and it is recommended that you do so. Improvements to public transport mean that changes are frequent. Any information in a book like this is liable to become out of date fairly quickly.

Single city tickets cost €1.10 (£0.75), but if you plan to get around by bus it's more economical to use an EMT 10-journey discount card (€8 (£5.35)) available at tobacconists and EMT offices. Several people can use this card at the same time. It's valid for all urban lines. There are no concessions for non-resident children, though children under two go free.

Buses Aumasa (℡ *971 550 730*) covers the south-east coast. Autocares Mallorca (℡ *971 545 696*) covers the north-east: Port de Pollença and Alcúdia (about 1½ hours). Transabus (marked 'tib' ℡ *971 296 417*) covers the south-west part of Mallorca. Palma to Magaluf takes about an hour, leaving from the main bus station on C/Eusibi Estada. Contact the tourist office in Sóller (℡ *971 638 008*) for information on buses there. It takes about an hour by bus, but most people go by train (see 'The Little Train That Does', p. 74).

By Train There's only one train line in Palma (not including the toy-town train to Sóller), an enjoyable ride connecting Palma with Inca, Manacor and Sa Pobla. Contact **SFM Mallorca** (☎ 971 177 777, *http://tib.caib.es*).

Visitor Information

Innumerable websites about Mallorca offer up-to-the-minute information about what's on where, weather and general tourist information. Among the best are *www.seemallorca.com*; *www.mallorcaonline.com*; *www. a2zmallorca.com*; *www.balearnet. com*; *www.illebalears.com* and *www.guiadelocio.com/mallorca*. The excellent free glossy *Contemporary Balears* can be picked up in up-market hotels, restaurants, art galleries, muse-ums and some shops around town. It can also be found at the tourist office. The *Guia del Ocio* (*www.guiadelocio.com/mallorca*) is a listings magazine and Spain's answer to *Time Out*. It gives weekly information about what's

Palma Old Town

on, when and where. Although only available in Spanish, it's fairly easy to follow.

The main **tourist office** in Palma is at Casal Solleric, Passeig des Born 27 (☎ 971 729 634, *www.palmademallorca.es*. Open 9am–8pm daily) though there are others dotted around town: on the **Plaça Espanya** (☎ 971 754 329); **Plaça de la Reina** (no. 2 ☎ 971 712 216 and at the **airport** (☎ 971 789 556).

Hop On, Hop Off

The Bus Turístic (€13 (£8.70); valid for 24 hours, duration two hours) allows you to get on and off at all of the main sights including the Castell de Bellver, Poble Español, Passeig Marítim and cathedral. Information on-board is thin, but it's a good way to orient yourself and easily get to the places you're interested in. Buses leave from the top of the Passeig des Born every 20 minutes or so. Buy your ticket from the conductor. Note: these are not pushchair-friendly, particularly if you want to sit on the open-top deck.

A Perfect Palma Weekend

Day 1: Get dressed up and treat the munchkins to breakfast at Ca'n **Joan de s'Aigo** (C/Ca'n Sanç 10, ☎ *971 710 759*), a glamour-puss of an old-fashioned café in the heart of the old town. Furnished with red velvet armchairs and glittering chandeliers, it boasts more than 300 years of history, and because Mallorquín's think nothing of starting the day on hot chocolate, pastries and artesan ice-cream there's no reason why you shouldn't do the same.

Fortified thus, put your guidebook away and spend a couple of hours getting pleasantly lost in the **Casco Antiguo** (old town). Stop in at a couple of earmarked sights such as the **cathedral** (see p. 52) and **Es Baluard** (see p. 56) before heading out to the beach at **Ciutat Jardí** for sandcastles, swims and a fish lunch on the shore at **El Bungalow** (see p. 67).

Back in town hop on the sightseeing bus (see left) in time to see the sun setting over the city from the **Castell de Bellver** (see p. 54): it's one of the best views of all time.

Day 2: Catch the century-old **wooden train to Sóller** (see 'The Little Train That Does', p. 74). The hour-long journey takes you through beautiful Mallorcan farmland and orange groves before arriving in the chi-chi town. Explore the narrow, cobblestone streets and stop for ice-cream before jumping aboard the island's first tram to take you to the **Port de Sóller** for a day by the sea.

Spend the evening tapas-hopping through the streets of **Sa Llotja** back in Palma and watch the fire-jugglers and street performers on Plaça de Sa Llotja.

Getting Around

Once in Palma, the public bus system is good and increasing numbers of buses – but not all – have hydraulic lifts at the middle doors for easy access for pushchairs and wheelchairs. A single ticket costs €1.10 (£0.75). The **Empresa Municipal de Transportes Urbanos de Palma** (☎ *971 214 444 www.emtpalma. com*) is in charge of the city routes, while **Autocares Mallorca** (☎ *971 545 696 www. autocaresmallorca.com*) runs most of those to the rest of the island. There are also plenty of reasonably priced taxis. These can easily be hailed from the street or from taxi ranks outside the bus station and train station, on Plaça Espanya. One useful number is **Taxi Palma** ☎ *971 401 414*.

The best way to get off the beaten track and explore, however, is still to rent a car (see p. 45). Parking on the street isn't always easy, but there are plenty of multi-storey car parks. Check

PALMA TOWN

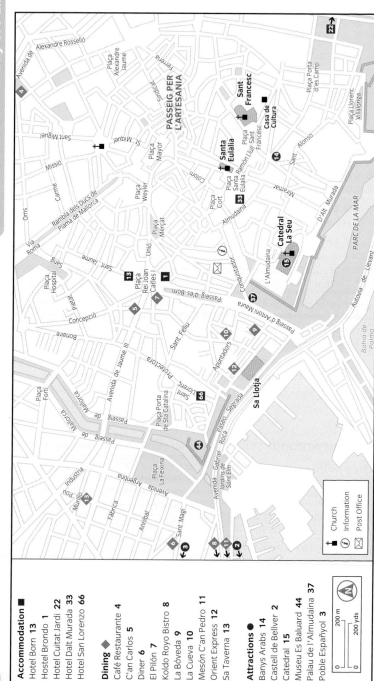

Accommodation ■
Hotel Born **13**
Hostel Brondo **1**
Hotel Cuitat Jardi **22**
Hotel Dalt Murada **33**
Hotel San Lorenzo **66**

Dining ◆
Café Restaurante **4**
C'an Carlos **5**
Diner **6**
El Pilón **7**
Koldo Royo Bistro **8**
La Bóveda **9**
La Cueva **10**
Mesón C'an Pedro **11**
Orient Express **12**
Sa Taverna **13**

Attractions ●
Banys Arabs **14**
Castell de Bellver **2**
Catedral **15**
Museu Es Baluard **44**
Palau de l'Almudaina **37**
Poble Espanyol **3**

+■ Church
ⓘ Information
⊠ Post Office

0   200 m
0   200 yds

with your hotel as to whether they have free parking or not. Higher-end hotels usually do.

Child-friendly Events

Check out local **arts and crafts markets** held year-long, from about 10am to 5pm every Monday, Friday and Saturday in the Plaça Major. Come December it transforms itself into a colourful **Christmas fair**, hawking toys, trinkets and decorations.

Arguably the most thrilling festival is **La Nit de Sant Joan** ★ (Saint John's night) on 24th June when everyone from eight to 80 stays out all night to watch bonfires on the beaches and fireworks in the Parc de la Mar. If you're looking to educate your tots in ways to be Spanish, this is a wonderful place to start.

Things are a little more sober during the celebration of **Mare de Déu de la Salut**, on 8th September. A solemn mass is held at the church of Sant Miquel, followed by a raucous children's festival which includes a street procession, music and folk dancing. Check with the tourist office in Palma for a schedule of events.

FAST FACTS: PALMA AND THE REST OF MALLORCA

Area Codes As in the rest of Spain, prefix ☏ *0034* from outside the country, followed by the full number. Mallorca numbers start ☏ *971*.

Baby Chairs Many restaurants offer highchairs though it is by no means guaranteed, especially outside of Palma and resort towns. Where possible this has been indicated in the restaurant entries throughout. Mallorcan restaurateurs are accommodating to babies and children and they will nearly always make room for a buggy or pram.

Baby Change Many women's toilets (*serveis/servicios*) in restaurants in Palma and the resorts have changing tables, especially fast-food places like Mcdonald's. The only other public area for changing is at **El Corte Ingles** (Avda Jaume III 15, Palma ☏ *971 770 177 www. elcorteingles.com*). **Public toilets** aren't common, but are usually clean. You'll find them at the main bus and train terminals in **Plaça Espanya**. Beaches generally only have Portaloos.

Business Hours Generally 10am–1.30pm and 4.30pm/ 5pm–8pm. Don't plan any commercial activity around lunchtime: streets empty and most shops close. Locals are quite religious about maintaining traditional Spanish hours, which means a long lunch followed, if possible, by a siesta. It is advisable to get into the same habit, especially in summer, when a power nap at lunchtime can revitalise the whole family. You'll also avoid the most dangerous rays at the beach.

Chemists Wherever you are in Spain, it is worth noting that chemists offer medication which in the UK would need a GP visit. They are the first port of call for people with minor ailments. Chemists take turns to open on a Sunday and after hours; if your local one is closed, a board outside will give you information about the closest. Chemists are identified by a glowing green cross outside and are found in most towns of a reasonable size. You won't generally find a chemist in small villages. In **Palma** go to C/ Jaume Ferran 77 (971 293 001); Pza. Juan Carlos I, 3 (971 711 534).

Consulate The **British Consulate** is at Plaça Major 3D, Palma (971 712 445 www.fco. gov.org. Open Mon–Fri Jul–Aug 8am–2pm; Mon–Fri Sep–Jun 9am–3pm).

Consumer Affairs If you need to make a complaint about a service you have received on the island (restaurant, hotel, whatever), contact the **Goven de les Illes Baleares** freephone number 900 166 000, or www. caib.es. The main office is at C/SAnt Gaità 3, Palma (971 176 262).

Credit Cards Most hotels and restaurants take **Visa** and **MasterCard. American Express** and **Diners** are not widely accepted.

Electricity The current in Mallorca is **220 volts** and **50Hz** with a two-pin plug. You will need an adaptor to use British appliances.

Medical Emergencies The general emergency number is 112 and is operated by multi-lingual staff. Urgent medical assistance is free at hospitals for all members of the EU, but you must be carrying an EHIC (see p. 24), which qualifies EU citizens for reciprocal health treatment. Public hospitals in Mallorca are: **Hospital Universitari Son Dureta** (Andrea Doria 55, Palma 971 175 000 www.hsd.es); **Fundació Hospital Son Llàtzer** (Ctra. Palma–Manacor, km 4 971 202 000. www.hsll.es); and **Fundació Hospital de Manacor** (Ctra. Palma–Alcúdia s/n 971 841 000 www.hospitaldemanacor.org).

Internet Access Keeping up with your email is a breeze, with Internet cafés in most main towns. In Palma try **Big Byte** (C/de Cerdà 2 971 452 477 www.bigbyte.com. Open 10am–8pm); **Azul Internet** (Calle Soledad 4 971 712 927 www. azulcomputergroup.com. Open Mon–Sat 10am–8pm). **Babaloo Internet** (C/ Verja 2, Palma 971 957 725 www.babaloo internet.com. Open 10am–8pm daily) also offers printing services.

Laundry You will find laundry facilities in most hotels and hostals, and in Palma there are a few Laundromats dotted around the old town. It's worth packing a small bottle of hand-washing liquid.

Newspapers and Magazines

In Palma, you can buy English newspapers at newsagents on the **Passeig des Born,** along the **harbour,** at the train station on **Plaça Espanya** and at the **airport.** You'll also find copies of British papers at the main resort hotels on the north-east and east coasts.

Nudity Bathing nude is legal in Mallorca, often at a certain section of the beach or on designated beaches. **Topless bathing** is common on most, including family ones. As a rule of thumb, the more remote the beach, the more likely you are to find people naked.

Petrol Petrol stations sell unleaded (95 and 98) petrol and diesel. They are dotted all over the island, but if you are motoring through the Tramuntana or Es Pla, make sure you have a full tank before you set off.

Parking Generally this isn't a problem, but **Palma** can be a nightmare and it's best to save yourself the hassle by heading straight for a multi-storey car park. These are indicated by blue signs with a 'P' through them, and cost about €1.50–2.00 (£1–1.35) an hour.

Photography **FotoLab30 S.L.** (C/ Juan Alcover, 32 Local A, Palma ☎ *971 775 302. Fax: 971 461 965 www.fotolab30.com*) is a professional camera shop that stocks everything you need, from lenses to carry cases. They also do developing.

Police The police station in **Palma** is located on Avda. Sant Ferran 42 (☎ *971 225 500*); in **Magaluf** on Camí Sa Porrassa 6 (☎ *971 131 710*); in **Valldemossa** on C/Rei Sanxo 1 (☎ *112*); in **Sóller** on C/Rectoria 7 (☎ *971 631 191*); in **Pollença** on C/Jonquet 61 (☎ *971 531 125*); in **Alcúdia** on Bastió de Sant Ferran s/n (☎ *971 545 066*); in **Inca** on C/Arta 11 (☎ *971 880 818*); in **Campos** on Plaça Major 1 (☎ *971 651 626*); in **Artà** on Plaça Espanya 1 (☎ *971 829 595*); in **Manacor** on Avda. Del Parc s/n (☎ *971 550 048*); in **Cala Rajada** on C/Roses s/n (☎ *971 565 463*).

Post Office In **Palma** the post office is on C/Constitució 6 (☎ *971 228 882*). Post boxes are yellow in Spain and most towns and villages have one. In **Palma Nova,** the post office is on C/Na Boira 2 (☎ *971 680 006*); in **Valldemossa** on C/Pintora Pilar Muntaner 3 (no phone); in **Sóller** on C/Rectoria 7 (☎ *971 631 191*); in **Pollença** on C/Jonquet 61 (☎ *971 531 125*); in **Alcúdia** on Avda. dels Pinceps d'Espanya 5 (☎ *971 545 440*); in **Inca** on Plaça Angel 12 (☎ *971 500 423*); in **Campos** on C/Parròquia 1 (☎ *971 650 164*); in **Artà** on C/Ciutat 26 (☎ *971 836 127*); and in **Cala Rajada** on C/Magallanes s/n (☎ *971 818 622*).

Safety The biggest crime problem in Mallorca is bag-snatching, typically in the **Casco Antiguo** in Palma, and around the coastal strip of the Bay of

Palma, particularly **Magaluf** and **S'Arenal**. Elsewhere crime isn't much of a problem. That said, don't be complacent. Keep belongings out of sight in the car, and keep expensive cameras out of sight on your person. If you get lost, stop in a café to consult a map, especially in the city. Browsing on the street makes you look vulnerable.

Tipping Tipping is not considered compulsory (the Spanish often only leave a few coppers), but it is considered polite for foreigners to leave 5–10% in bars and restaurants.

Time Zone GMT + 1.

WHAT TO SEE & DO

Historic Buildings & Monuments

On an island like Mallorca most sights are suitable for anyone from eight months to 80 years. It's more a question of what gets their creative juices flowing. On the whole most children seem to enjoy roaming around castles and convents, and older children may get jaded by endless churches. If you want to visit galleries and museums, excite the children first with a little bit of background on Picasso and Miró, both well represented here. And remember that even though you are fascinated by obscure modern art, they may not be. Balance your days with a mix of culture and good old-fashioned fun in the form of beaches, water parks and animal magic: Palma has it all.

Catedral de Palma ★ ★

ALL AGES No doubt the jewel in Palma's crown, this magnificent pile is one of the biggest and most extravagant Gothic cathedrals in the world, and took four centuries to complete. It was converted from a mosque in 1229, although it took a further four centuries to complete the Christian face-lift, and it was not until the Catalan architect Antoni Gaudì stepped in at the turn of

Palma Cathedral at Night

the century that it acquired its heavenly interior. Inside, the 44-metre-high nave would be enough to induce vertigo were it not for the celestial light that streams through Gaudì's carefully planned windows. It's just as impressive viewed from without: a glorious, honey-coloured building that seems to float above its foundations, aided by the fact that it's also the only cathedral in the world that enjoys the distinction of having its image reflected in the sea.

C/Palau Reial 29 ☎ 971 723 130. Open Nov–Mar 10am–3.15pm; Apr & May 10am–5.15pm; Jun–Oct 10am–6.15pm; Sat 10am–2.15pm; Closed Sun & holidays. Entry €3.50 (£2.35). Under 11s free.

Banys Arabs **ALL AGES** So little of Palma's Moorish past remains that it helps to see something physical in order to get an idea of why its last Arab ruler was so devastated when the town was razed. Palma was, after all, once considered the most beautiful of all European cities. Today, these eleventh century Arabic baths, while crumbling, still give a glimpse of the era, boasting stately columns and elegant archways supporting a central dome where light poured through 25 tiny skylights. The steam rooms and relaxation areas are still in evidence, as are the pretty landscaped gardens, shaded by palms and orange trees. It makes for a very pleasant reprieve from the heat of the city, 21st-century life a mere murmur at the door.

C/Serra 7 ☎ 971 721 549. Open Apr–Nov 9am–7.30pm; Dec–May 9am–6pm. €1.50 (£1) adults and children. Under 11s free.

Palau de l'Almudaina ★

ALL AGES There has been a castle or palace on this spot since the Romans first arrived in 123 BC, and to all intents and purposes the palace's role continues to this day to be one of hosting and entertaining dignitaries. It is still the official royal residence in Palma and offers a fascinating peek into the chequered history of Spain. The Mudéjar ceilings in the Paseo de Ronda corridor hark back to the Moorish occupation, while the Hall of Kings is decorated with portraits of nine of the island's subsequent kings. Curiously, you can see chapels alongside Arab baths; Gothic arches against stone sculptures; gargoyles grinning down on ornate tapestries depicting knights in battle. For

Outside the Palau de l'Almudaina.

The Castell de Bellver HH **AGES 6 AND UP** (C/Camilo José Cela 17 ☎ *971 730 657*. Open Apr–Sep 8am–8.30pm, Oct–Mar 8am–7.15pm, Apr, May, Jun, Sep 10am–7pm; Jul, Aug 10am–2pm, 4pm–9pm. €1.80 (£1.20) for adults and children. Children under two free) commands a lofty position above the bay of Palma, flanked on either side by pine woods and framed to the west by the hazy outline of the Tramuntana mountains fading into the mist. It is a magnificent sight and offers far and away the most spectacular view of Palma. Built by Jaume II in the early 14th century, it was originally conceived as a summer residence for Mallorcan kings, but war and civil unrest on the mainland led to it being turned over for use as a prison during the 18th century. Graffiti by those early prisoners can still be seen etched into the walls. Today, it has a happier use as the home of the city history museum and the **Despuig Collection of Classical Sculpture.** Its cylindrical shape also makes it a wonderful space for occasional summer events such as the **Bellver Classical Music Festival** held in July. See ***www.simfonia-de-balears.com*** for the latest schedule, and contact the castle direct for information on other events through the year. Programmes are put together every three months or so.

Castell de Bellver

The Aquarium

children who can't resist a real-life working castle, especially those with an active imagination, this one is a real treat.

C/Palau Reial s/n ☎ *971 214 134.* ***www.patromonionacional.es****. Open Apr–Sep Mon–Fri 10am–5.45pm; Sat 10am–1.15pm; Oct–Mar Mon–Fri 10am–1.15pm, 4pm–6pm; Sat 10am–1.15pm. €3.20 (£2.15); children under 11 €2.30 (£1.55). Free Wed.*

On the Beach

Although the Bay of Palma covers many miles, the best beaches are those just outside Palma itself, particularly around Ciutat Jardi (take bus route 15). It offers a clean, wide strand and plenty of places for cheap lunchtime fayre. It's also good for watersports.

A shade more on the glamorous side, the beaches at Illetas (about 15 minutes on the number 3 bus from Plaza España in the direction of Magaluf) are a series of three small beaches separated by rocks. The Virtual Club (*www.virtualclub.es*) allows guests to sunbathe in style with

Palma's Aquarium

★★★ **ALL AGES** (Exit 8, Palma–Llucmajor Highway, Palma)

Far and away the most impressive animal kingdom in the Balearics, and indeed the rest of Spain, the newly inaugurated **Palma Aquarium** ☎ *971 264 275. Fax: 971 264 132 www.palmaaquarium.com*. Open Spring 2007) is a prime example of how to get it right. It offers a full range of experiences based around biological, cultural and historical themes and is managed by marine biologists. An iconic building, it has an organic quality to it that draws visitors across shimmering pools, through tropical rock gardens and beneath waterfalls as a backdrop to the incredible diversity of aquatic life on display, including giant sunfish and white-tipped sharks. Among other activities scuba diving is available for the more adventurous.

Polynesian-style grass shades, loungers, reasonably-priced cocktail bar and restaurant, massage and watersports for a membership fee of €8 (£5.35) a day.

But if it's a real beach holiday you're looking for, your best bet is to get out of town in a hire car, or base yourself on the **south** or **north** coasts of the island. See Chapters 5 and 7 for some ideas.

Museums, Galleries & Crafts Spaces

Es Baluard ★ ★ ★ AGES 11 AND UP

For budding artists in the family, no course of study is complete without a peek into the world of Pablo Picasso. Here, you can enjoy his works alongside that of his friend and contemporary Joan Miró, who lived on Mallorca from 1955 until his death in 1983. But what gives this gallery space such appeal is the architecture. It's a stunning building, the kind of place that crops up in Bond movies, seamlessly marrying the Gothic structure of the old town walls with contemporary design. Think cool white concrete, blonde wood and light zooming in at you from all directions, designed in such a way as to enable visitors to enjoy the space from the rooftop. Add to that a fantastic café serving imaginative mid-priced meals, and the fact it stays open until midnight; and even for children, this is one of Mallorca's top attractions.

Museu de Arte Moderno y Contemporáneo/Contemporary Art Museum, Pl. Porta Santa Catalina ☏ 971 908 200 www.esbaluard.org. Jun–Oct 10am–midnight daily; Nov–May 10am–8pm, closed Mon. €6 (£4) adults; €4.50 (£3) under-12s.

Fundación La Caixa

AGES 11 AND UP The permanent exhibition is by Catalan artist Anglada Camarassa, but the temporary exhibits here (often photography) can occasionally be excellent. Either way, it's

Arts & Crafts

Itineraris ★ (Divulgalia, S.L., C/ Sant Domingo 11 ☎ *971 720 720. Fax: 971 720 721 www.itineraris.org*) runs several different walking tours through Palma, uncovering its Roman, Muslim, Jewish and Christian heritage and setting the scene for its modern incarnation as one of Europe's most cosmopolitan cities. You'll peek into old palaces, learn some of the city's less known legends, uncover ghosts and secrets and mysteries. Tours cost €10 (£6.70) for adults; children under 12 go free. See their website for a full list. Tours start from outside the *ajuntament* (town hall) on Plaça Cort in the old quarter. They are conducted in English, Spanish and German. Call ahead to check the language for the tour you wish to join.

Cycling around Palma is a good way to get around. On the whole it's pretty flat, unless you intend cycling up to the Castell de Bellver, and there is an excellent network of **bicycle lanes** running along by the sea from Ciutat Jardi to the port area. That said, it's not recommended that you attempt getting around the old town by bicycle: crowds and cobbles make the going tough. **Palma on Bike** (Plaça Salvador Coll 8 ☎ *971 711 754 www.palmaonbike.com*) offers bike tours in English and Spanish as well as rentals from €10 (£6.70) a day, no concessions, or €25 (£16.75) for three days.

worth a dip in to admire the modernist decor. Call ahead or check the website for up-to-the-minute information on exhibitions.

Gran Hotel, Plaça Weyler 3. ☎ 971 178 500. www.fundacio.lacaixa.es. Open 10am–9pm. Sun & holidays 10am–2pm. Closed Mon. Free admission.

Poble Espanyol ★ ALL AGES

Cheesy as it sounds, this custom built 'Spanish Town' located just below the Castell de Bellver (about 20 minutes from the centre via *bus turistic* or taxi) does for Spain what film sets do for Hollywood, and in its tinseltown way attempts to take visitors on a journey around the whole of the country in an afternoon. Along the way you'll see more than 100 of Spain's celebrated monuments replicated across a labyrinth of maze-like streets and faux cobbled plazas. Among them are the Alhambra in Granada, El Greco in Toledo and the Ermita de Sant Antonio in Madrid. Combined with various craftsmen at work and flamenco shows, it all makes for a jolly afternoon out, provided it's taken with a pinch of salt. Children generally love it and sometimes get dressed up in traditional garb too. Note that food and drink in the bars and restaurants here is a good deal more expensive than anything in town.

C/de Poble Espanyol 39 ☎ 971 737 070. Open daily 9am–6pm. Shops closed Sun and holidays. €5 (£3.35) adults, €3 (£2) children under 11.

Museu de Pepas FIND

AGES 5 AND UP This curious antique doll museum is sure to delight mums and their daughters (though probably not their sons). It's a treasure box of more than 500 dolls collected from all over Spain, France and Germany, ranging from the downright gorgeous to the out-and-out weird. As wacky museums go, this is something of a find, and the kind of place in which to savour a special bonding moment.

C/Palau Reial 29. ☎ 971 729 850. Open Tue–Sun 10am–6pm. Adults €4 (£2.70), children €3 (£2), free to under-twos.

Palma Craft District ☆ FIND

ALL AGES This passage of artesan stores in the heart of the Sa Gerreria district is perfect if you want to stock up on textiles, jewellery, ceramics, glass, wood, metal and leather goods – all those things that you could spend a week pursuing across the island but can get in one swoop here. The area is also home to the **Sa Gerreria School of Arts and Crafts,** which means there's plenty to look at from Mallorca's most talented craftsmen and -women. Items range from textiles and pottery, to glass, jewellery and ornaments all made on the premises. It's a good place to pick up gifts. A new guided walk run by the school takes place every Monday

morning at 10.30am (Note: this is subject to change) providing a pleasant amble around the area's streets and some of the better shops. At the time of writing, it was free.

Passeig per l'Artesania s/n, C/Bosc 7, Palma ☎ 971 720 720 for tour information. Shops open Mon–Sat 9am–1.30pm, 7pm–8pm.

Outings for Active Families

Jungle Parc AGES 6 AND UP

Suspended on rope in the tree-tops between three and 10 metres high, the 'flying fox'-type activity at the Jungle Parc is a great activity for blowing off steam, especially if the children have been cooped up on long journeys. In a nutshell you trail through the treetops across rope bridges and in a series of canopy paths that involve climbing and sliding, but hopefully not falling. Children younger than 12 must be accompanied by an adult. Wear comfortable clothes and trainers.

Avenida Jaime 1, 40A, Santa Ponça ☎ 630 948 295. www.jungleparc.es. Open daily, 10am–8pm. Entrance €13 (£8.70), no concessions. By car take the MA-1 from Palma; there's no direct bus.

Golf Fantasia AGES 6 AND UP

This 54-hole golf-based theme park is the stuff of dreams for golf obsessed adults, and an ideal place to introduce the youngsters. Set amid a lush backdrop of sparkling waterfalls, exotic plants, lakes and mysterious

Palma's council takes the continual beautification of its city seriously, and as such, an ongoing project to provide more green areas and revamp popular promenades like the **Passeig des Born** are in full swing. The latter is due to be completed during 2007. In the meantime, Palma does not want for quality recreational zones. Most notable is the **Parc de la Mar** ★ which skirts around the front in full view of the cathedral and the bay, encompassing shady terraces and pavement cafes, as well as children's play areas. It's a good place to take a break from sightseeing if your hotel isn't within easy reach.

caverns it's a fun day out for all the family, even the non-golfers who just want to hone their pitch-and-putt in a non-serious environment.

C/Tenis 3, Palma Nova ☎ 971 135 040. Fax: 971 680 392 www.golf-fantasia.com. Car: PM-1 from Palma. Bus: 20.

Hippocampes Divers

AGES 10 AND UP A new dive centre based out at Illetas, this state-of-the-art facility has a Caribbean look and feel to it, and offers snorkel trips as well as more advanced diving. Discover Scuba (€75 (£50.25)) is an excellent testing ground for finding out whether an open water certification is right for you.

Balneario la Solana, Paseo de Illetas 56, Illetas ☎ 971 707 779, Mobile: 677 741 975 www.hippocampes. com. Snorkel trips €20 (£13.40). Bus: 3. Car: PM-1 from Palma.

Shopping

Palma is a shopper's paradise with excellent shopping to be found on **C/Sant Miguel** and around the **Passeig des Born**. **Petit Planet** ★ (C/Sant Jaume 23 ☎ 971 723 613) stocks cute childrens clothes for ages 0–12 in gorgeous colours and fabrics. **Bagatela** (C/Passeig del Born 24 ☎ 971 715 312) is great for picking up local arts and crafts, like the ghostly white-painted figurines marked with stripes of colour called Siurells, blown glass and ceramic ware. **Picornell Cereria del Call** (C/del Call 7 ☎ 971 715 727) dates back to 1785 and stocks

Sobrassada Shop, Palma

gorgeous decorative, votive and scented candles. **Joyas Forteza** ★ (C/Colon 2 ☎ 971 715 866) may just be the place to buy your little darling her first string of pearls. Specialists in typical Mallorquín jewellery they stock a superb range of Mallorcan grey pearls as well as diamonds and other precious stones. For artesan cheeses, sausages, wine and other picnic fodder, look no further than charming **Ágape** (C/Argenetía 12 ☎ 971 725 213). Cute, typical Balearic flat sandals in a rainbow of colours for all ages are available from **Picarol** (C/Forn del Raco 1 ☎ 971 711 196), or from **Espardenyeria Isern** (C/Llotgeta 6 ☎ 971 717 385) in the old town.

Live Entertainment

In terms of theatre, cabaret, music and shows, Palma has yet to catch up with its rivals on the mainland. Nearly all performances are in Spanish, although occasionally they can be colourful enough to hold the attention of younger children.

The weekly listings magazine *Guia del Ocio* (*www.guiadelocio. com/mallorca*) is an invaluable resource for what's on where. It's in Spanish only, but fairly easy to figure out. Discounts for children depend on the show and you should always check with the production company first.

The best known theatre is the **Teatre Principal de Palma**, (Carrer del la Riera 2A ☎ 971 713 346. Fax: 971 725 542 *www. teatreprincipal.com*) where you

can often catch qood quality *zarsuela* (Spanish opera). It can be great fun even if you don't understand the lingo.

For opera, dance, classical and pop concerts check out the latest at the **Auditorium** (Passeig Marítim 18 ☎ 971 735 328. *www. auditoriumpalma.com*. Tickets €25–50 (£16.75–33.50) depending on where you sit. No concessions).

Some of the better and more extravagant shows are actually at the theme parks, such as the wacky and completely over-the-top **Els Pirates** ★ (the Pirates) adventure show in Magaluf (Ctra. La Porrassa ☎ 971 130 411 Fax: 971 130 083 *www.pirates adventure.com*. Cost €43–48 (£28.80–32.15) incl. dinner for both children and adults). Buy tickets on the door or from the tourist office. The show is set aboard a life-size pirate ship bursting with hearty roars, swashbuckling sword-fights and daredevil feats, with acrobatics and pyrotechnics. It's well equipped for children with a barbecued sausages and spit-roasted chicken dinner thrown in.

Nothing beats a **live football** ★ game for the sheer adrenalin rush and Mallorca's football team, RCD (Real Club Deportivo) Mallorca, are fairly easy to catch at home. A new stadium is currently on the drawing board (no date as yet), but for now matches are held at the Son Moix Stadium on Cami dels Reis. Tickets range from €19–€30 (£12.70–20) and are

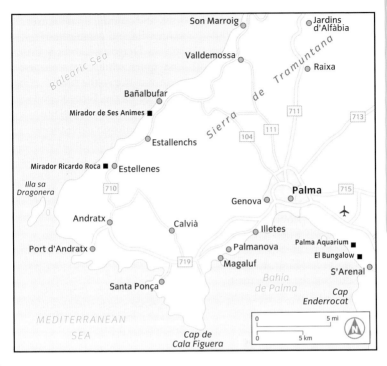

available from the RCD Mallorca website (*www.rcdmallorca.es*; ☎ 971 221 221). There are no special prices for children.

MAGALUF & S'ARENAL

Little-Britain-on-Sea, **Magaluf** is a veritable colony of ex-pats who came to the island in the 1970s in search of sun, sea and sangria. In exchange they brought pints of beer, fish and chips and buckets and spades. Decades later Magaluf is as brash as ever, though it has cleaned up somewhat in recent years, with a general revamping of the hotels,

stricter licensing laws and some lipstick and powder on the seafront. The beach does get crowded and for those desperate for a reprieve, Cap de Cala

Windmill near Magaluf

Figuera is a lovely spot just down the coast where tiny coves and fishing ports are a welcome antidote to the party scene. For children, however, Magaluf can be bliss: a great place to make English-speaking friends and take full advantage of the amusement parks situated in the immediate vicinity. It also boasts the biggest disco in Europe, **BCM** (Avda. De S'Olivera 14. ℡ *971 132 609 www.bcm-planet dance.com*. €15 (£10.05) adults. No children under 18), which pulls in 4000 people a night.

S'Arenal is where Germans with the same idea as those Brits settled. It's less high-rise than Magaluf but the song remains the same: bratwurst and sauerkraut are more commonplace than *patatas bravas* and olives; the predominant language is German; and most of the entertainment comes in the form of row-upon-row of beach shops hawking blow-up crocodiles and sun hats. The beach is decent enough and there are plenty of water sports on offer. The area also has its fair share of theme parks, including the excellent new **Aquarium** (see p. 55). Like Magaluf, it's also fairly easy to escape simply by driving further east down to **Cala Pi** – a cute and often deserted fjord popular with windsurfers.

Two Fun Days Out Near Magaluf

Aqualand ALL AGES While for most parents water parks can represent a hellish day out,

Aqualand really is a cut above the rest, continually renewing itself and coming up with ever more wild and wonderful rides, such as Dragoland, to keep little ones quiet, while even teenagers return in awe of the thrills provided by the Tornado and Boomerang rides. Aqualand specialises in adrenalin thrills ranging from high speed tubes, flumes and rapids, to death slides and black holes. A family menu for four consists of pizza and soft drinks and costs €19.90 (£13.35).

Ctra. Cala Figuera, Magaluf-Calviá ℡ *971 130 811. Fax: 971 131 336. www.aqualand.es. Open daily May, Jun, Sep and Oct, 10am–5pm, Jul and Aug 10am–6pm. Closed Nov through Apr. Adults €18.50 (£12.40). Children under 12 €13.50 (£9.10). Children age 0–3 go free.*

Marineland ALL AGES This magical world of cute, friendly dolphins and sea lions is hugely popular with young children, though adults might dislike the idea of these magnificent creatures in captivity. As such places go, Marineland is a responsible outfit with good conditions for the animals and some excellent research and educational programmes. Other exhibits include turtles, puffins, penguins, sharks, iguanas, seahorses, and tropical aquatic creatures like frogs and snakes. Additional bonuses include a mini-waterpark for tiny tots, and access to a clean beach. But when it comes to extra special treats, nothing beats joining in the **Dolphin School**, ★

which allows closer contact with these magnificent creatures and the chance to learn more about the way they interact with each other. Be aware that reservations must be made for this experience and, sadly, Marineland is notoriously unreliable in terms of setting this up in English (it's easier if you speak some Spanish). Contact Gloria Fernández or Paco Gutiérrez directly on ☎ 971 675 125.

Costa d'En Blanes, Calviá ☎ 971 675 125. Fax: 971 675 554. www. marineland.es. Open Mar–Nov daily 9.30am–6pm. Adults €19.90 (£13.35), children under 12 €13.90 (£9.30), children 0–4 free.

FAMILY-FRIENDLY ACCOMMODATION

Hotel San Lorenzo ★ ★ ★

You've got to love a town where even the trendiest boutique accommodation welcomes the kiddies with open arms; and the sexy San Lorenzo is an absolute boon for yummy mummies and dandy daddies. A converted 17th century town house in the old quarter, its best features include an Art-Deco bar brought all the way from Paris, and an oasis-like swimming pool surrounded by lush plant life built into the inner-courtyard. It has only nine individually decorated rooms ranging from those with private terrace and fireplace, to others designed as a duplex which works well for those travelling with young children. The junior suite has a fold-out bed, suitable for two children.

C/San Lorenzo 14, Palma ☎ 971 728 200. Fax: 971 711 901 www.hotel sanlorenzo.com. Double €165–235 (£110.55–157.45). Duplex suite with fireplace and terrace €250 (£167.50). Extra bed €35 (£23.45). Cot €15 (£10.05). Continental breakfast €9 (£6). Nine rooms. V, MC. Amenities: A/C, breakfast room, swimming pool, sun terrace. In room: satellite TV, minibar, free WiFi.

Hotel Dalt Murada ★ ★ A

splendid 16th century mansion converted into a smart, atmospheric hotel in 2001, this is a great place for indulging old-fashioned fantasies. The sweeping staircase, carved ceiling cornices and antique-stuffed rooms delight young and old alike. With just 14 rooms, the Dalt Murada has a welcoming, homely atmosphere and laid-back vibe with polished-wood panels, high ceilings, dark wood beams, and authentic tiled floors. The three double bedrooms and five suites are built around an inner courtyard and garden, some with four-poster beds, others with glass chandeliers.

C/Almudaina 6A, Palma ☎ 971 425 300. Fax: 971 719 708 www. daltmurada.com. €140 (£93.80) double, €336 (£225.10) penthouse suite with cathedral views and jacuzzi; €30 (£20.10) for extra child's bed, cot free. Breakfast included. 14 rooms. V, MC. Amenities: garden, patio, dining room. In room: A/C, hydromassage shower, satelite TV, Internet, minibar.

Hotel Born ★ ★ FIND In a class

of its own, the Hotel Born has

Hotel Born

neither luxury nor glamour, instead boasting a genuinely aristocratic feel minus any of the pretension. Located in a 16th century mansion, the place oozes character from its gorgeous, marble-tiled, palm-tree-shaded courtyard where breakfast is served in the mornings, to the gallery that overlooks it and the Regency-style bedrooms. There's no swimming pool, mini-golf or play areas, but then again, few places in Palma are as likely to excite your youngster's imagination. Comfortable, relaxed and a bargain to boot, this old-fashioned guest house is one of Palma's classics.

*C/Sant Jaume 4, Palma ☎ 971 712 942, Fax: 971 718 618. **www.hotelborn.com**. €73 (£48.90) double, €105 (£70.35) suite. Extra bed €35 (£23.45). Cot free. 20 rooms. Breakfast €9 (£6). V, MC. Amenities: patio, breakfast area. In room: A/C, heating, satellite TV, telephone.*

Hostal Brondo ★ **VALUE** A characterful Mallorcan town house converted into a charming, small-scale guest house, the Hostal Brondo has legions of fans, large and small. Friendly and service oriented, staff here are always on hand with the personal touch and insider suggestions for travellers looking to get off the beaten track. Rooms are basic but clean and comfortable; some are en-suite, and priced accordingly. No breakfast is served here, but there are plenty of cafes in the neighbourhood, making a game of starting every morning in a different place and judging them on the fluffiness of their *ensaimadas*. The big draw is the Brondo's incredibly cheap prices and its location, smack bang in the heart of the old city.

*C/ C'an Brondo 1, Palma ☎ 971 719 043 **www.hostalbrondo.net**. €45 (£30.15) double without bathroom, €60 (£40.20) double with bathroom, triple room with three single beds €60 (£40.20) without bathroom, triple room with double bed and single bed with bathroom €65 (£43.55), studio apartment to sleep four with full catering facilities €120 (£80.40). 10 rooms. No breakfast. V, MC. Amenities: TV lounge, ceiling fan.*

Hotel Ciutat Jardi ★ ★ **FIND** A great option for families looking to get off the tourist track, yet remain within striking distance of the action. Located just across the road from the beach, the four-star Ciutat Jardi also boasts its own well-kept swimming pool and rooftop terrace. The fact it's family run shines through in the friendly, accommodating atmosphere. It's a great option for those travelling with older children who want a little bit of independence thanks to its safe, edge-of-town location. Bicycle and roller-skate hire is available from reception, with the centre of Palma just 10 minutes away, past the trendy bars and restaurants of Portixol en route.

C/ Illa de Malta 14, Ciutat Jardi, Palma ☎ 971 746 070. Fax: 971 570 527 www.hciutatj.com. Double €140–270 (£93.80–180.90). Extra bed €35 (£23.45). Cot free. Breakfast included. 20 rooms. All credit cards. Closed Dec 21st–Jan 16th. Amenities A/C, DVD, piano room, breakfast room, children's play area, garden, swimming pool, massage. In room: A/C, heating, DVD, whirlpool bath, minibar.

Hotel Sol Melia Magaluf **VALUE**

A bucket-and-spade classic, this three-star hotel is a good budget option with clean and comfortable, if basic, rooms. It doesn't have air conditioning, which can be a drag during the heat-blasting months of July and August, though it does have ceiling fans which do just fine in spring and autumn. What it lacks in modern refinements it makes up for in terms of how much fun your brood can have here. Running around, shouting and generally having a rare old time are all smiled upon: there are two outdoor pools, mini-golf and endless games and activities organised by staff. It also serves decent quality, buffet-style, all-you-can-eat meals with a good range of different dishes for around €15 (£10.05), and its

close proximity to the beach and other attractions in Magaluf can't be faulted. Perhaps its biggest asset of all, however, is the friendliness and general willingness of staff to help. It's a family hotel in the truest sense of the word.

Avda. Magaluf s/n, Magaluf ☎ 971 131 300. Fax: 971 131 940 www.solmelia.com. €50–130 (£33.50–87.10) double half-board, children between 2–11 50% discount. 422 rooms. V, MC. Amenities: 2 bars, 1 restaurant, 2 swimming pools, ceiling fan, laundry, Internet service, car rental, daytime and evening entertainment. In room: A/C, heating, TV, telephone.

FAMILY-FRIENDLY DINING

Restaurants

Koldo Royo Bistro ★ ★ ★ The newest addition to the empire of Mallorca's most famous chef, Koldo Royo, recently opened its doors to adults and children with an appreciation for life's culinary treasures. The elegant surrounds combined with a chilled out atmosphere ensure everyone feels at home, though the focus is very much on the food. A special childrens menu is available for €13 (£8.70), with daily and weekly menus for €20 (£13.40) and €26 (£17.40). All highlight the signature dishes of the main restaurant on the first floor, wowing budding gourmands with their innovative use of colour, fun presentation and unexpected flavour combinations. Expect such creations as stuffed tomatoes with chive oil, haricot bean stew with salt cod, and strawberry soup.

C/Ingeniero Gabriel Roca 3, Paseo Maritimo, Palma ☎ 971 732 435. Fax: 971 738 647 www.koldoroyo.com. All credit cards. Booking essential. Set menu 3 courses and wine €25 (£16.75). Childrens menu €13 (£8.70). Highchairs.

Diner ☆ FIND

A child-tastic winner that has nothing to do with Mallorca, and everything to do with Uncle Sam. It is of course a true, American-style diner offering tip-top eggs over-easy with hash browns, juicy burgers, peanut butter and jelly sandwiches, soda fountains and *Happy Days*-style décor.

C/Sant Magí 23, Palma ☎ 971 736 222. No credit cards. No reservations. Burger €5.50 (£3.70), peanut butter and jelly sandwich €3.50 (£2.35), eggs with hash browns €5.50 (£3.70). Highchairs.

Café Restaurante + NTRL

VALUE The windows on to the Plaça Espanya and the coveted terrace seats require early arrival or booking in advance to secure, but it's worth it: this is a prime people-watching spot as well as one of the healthiest lunch options in town. Inside, a large, cheery dining room is staffed by cheerful waiters who bustle back and forth with the day's lunches. The formula is simple: a menu of sandwiches and 20 or so constructed salads. Or, you can do it yourself choosing from a base of leaves, pasta or rice, and building your own toppings from a massive range. You get five toppings for €6.50 (£4.35). A bargain.

Plaça de España 8 bajos, Palma ☎ 971 722 232 www.masntrl.com. Reservations recommended. All credit cards. 5 ingredient salad €6.50 (£4.35). Highchairs.

Ca'n Carlos ☆

One of few places in the centre of trendy Palma where food-lovers get a taste of real home cooking. Think granny's kitchen, Mallorca style. All meals come with a stack of the ubiquitous *pa amb oli* (crusty brown Mallorcan bread with tomatoes and oil), mortars piled with *alioli* (garlicky mayonnaise) and meaty olives, followed by traditional dishes such as *sobrassada* (a rich sausage paté liberally spiked with paprika), *tumbet* (a salad of roast peppers, aubergines,

Ca'n Carlos

courgettes and potatoes in olive oil) and the wonderfully onomatopoeic *arros brut* or 'dirty rice', cooked with chicken, pork and vegetables.

C/Aigua 5, Palma, ☎ 971 713 869. Closed Sun. Reservations recommended. No credit cards. Starters €5–10 (£3.35–6.70); mains €9–15 (£6–10.05).

Orient Express ★ ★ VALUE

Decked out to resemble the interior of an old-fashioned train carriage, this tiny Palma eatery is a locals' favourite where regular patrons opt for the deliciously light, wafer thin French-style crepes rather than island classics. Typically Mallorcan it is not; however, it's a good place to encourage children to be a bit more adventurous, with a good choice of fun tapas like ostrich carpaccio, prawn and cheese kebabs, and garlicky baby squid. Best of all it's one of those places where you arrive a stranger, but leave a friend. A true gem: a hop, skip and a jump away from the well-worn tourist trail.

Sa Llonja del Mar 6, La Llonja, Palma ☎ 971 711 183. Reservations recommended. All credit cards. Starters €5–10 (£3.35–6.70); mains €9–15 (£6–10.05).

El Bungalow ★ ★ ★

Handily placed in Ciutat Jardi, this charming fisherman's cottage on the beach is everything seaside dining should be: boat-fresh fish and seafood with the sparkling Mediterranean lapping at your toes. While more out of the way than some of the glitzy fish restaurants in town, it's worth making the trip out for a long lazy lunch where children can play in the sand while adults munch on clams and mussels, whole sea bass baked in salt and some of the island's best paellas, washed down with crisp, cold white wine. When reserving, be sure to ask for a table on the seaside terrace; the other side doesn't have the views. And go with plenty of time: the Spanish sentiment *no hay prisa*, there's no hurry, is very much the rule here.

C/Esculls 2, Ciutat Jardi, Palma ☎ 971 262 738. Reservations essential. All credit cards. Starters €7.50–15 (£5–10.05); mains €11–25 (£7.40–16.75).

Mesón Ca'n Pedro ★ VALUE

A classic Sunday lunch spot and a fine way to crown off a weekend in Palma, Ca'n Pedro is one of the island's best loved restaurants. The numbers speak for themselves, with over 1000 meals served every day to a rabble of jostling, jovial extended Mallorcan families who come to feast on juicy spit-roasted chicken; succulent, falling-off-the-bone baby lamb; hearty snail casseroles; and crisp fried potatoes with lashings of alioli (garlic mayonnaise). All washed down with jugs of wine mixed with *gaseosa* (lemonade); as parents get snoozily sloshed, children join in the raucous ambience. Note, the restaurant is split in two, Ca'n Pedro I and Ca'n Pedro II. The upper level, Ca'n Pedro II, is the better in terms of tables and views, and also serves fresh fish.

C/ Rector Vives 4 and 14, Genova, Palma 🕿 *971 702 162 www.mesoncanpedro.com. Reservations essential. All credit cards. Grilled meat, chips and roast vegetables about €25 (£16.75). Highchairs.*

Tapas Bars

La Bóveda ✩ ✩ VALUE The undisputed king of Palma's tapas bars, La Bóveda is a raucous place where eating with your hands is de rigueur and a member of staff is employed with the sole purpose of slicing wafer-thin rounds of delicious *pata negra* (black pig) jamón. There's something here to please even the fussiest of eaters, ranging from beautiful fresh mushrooms to scrambled eggs with prawns. Get the children making their own *pa amb oli.*

C/Botería 3, Palma 🕿 *971 714 863. No reservations. No credit cards. Tapas €1–4.50 (£0.70–3) each, €15 (£10.05) for small plate jamón.*

La Cueva This cave-like bar specialises in hearty, traditional dishes such as rabbit stew (children are surprisingly amenable to rabbit, unless of course they have their very own 'Fluffy' back home), or terracotta dishes of *albondigas* (meat balls) for the less adventurous.

C/Apuntadors 5, Palma 🕿 *971 724 422. No reservations. No credit cards. Tapas €1–4.50 (£0.70–3).*

Sa Taverna A cute bar specialising in *pa amb oli* – bread with olive oil and tomatoes – and a huge range of toppings. Children love the mix and match appeal of the meal and the laid-back atmosphere.

Carrer Pou 12, Palma 🕿 *971 454 826. No reservations. No credit cards. Tapas €1–4.50 (£0.70–3).*

El Pilón ✩ ✩ A lively little place where kids can watch the chefs at work in the huge, open plan kitchen. For the brave, there's excellent *pulpo a la gallega* (octopus served in chunks on a wooden platter and sprinkled with Spanish pimenton paprika); and shell-on prawns to eat with your hands.

C/Cifre 4, Palma 🕿 *971 717 590. No reservations. No credit cards. Tapas €1–4.50 (£0.70–3). Prawns and pulpo €9-15 (£6–10.05).*

4 West Mallorca and the Serra de Tramuntana

MALLORCA WEST

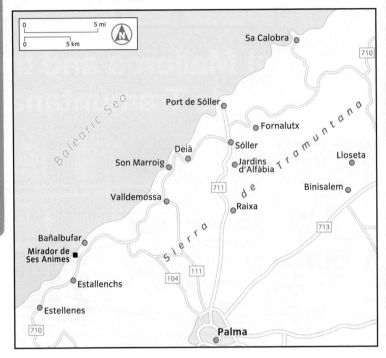

Easily the most spectacular stretch of Mallorca's varied coastline, the Serra de Tramuntana rises up in great terracotta- and ochre-hued terraces speckled with olive groves and pine trees. At their base you'll find secret beaches and hidden coves (usually accessible via a series of hairpin bends, which is worth considering if your children suffer from car-sickness), while the interior unravels in a series of honey-coloured villages like the aptly-named Valldemossa ('beautiful valley') and Deià (second home to Hollywood stars and Europe's glitterati), luxury hotels and some of the finest walks on the island.

Since the 1800s the area has been adopted as a muse by travelling artists, writers and musicians – Frederic Chopin and Robert Graves among them – and it's easy to see why as you travel through the unspoiled hinterland. No doubt about it, this is one of the most magical areas in all of Spain.

ESSENTIALS

Getting There & Around

To explore the rugged west coast of Mallorca a **rented car** (see p. 30) is recommended, though the 1930s train will get you from the centre of Palma to the region's capital of Sóller in an hour (see 'The Little Train That Does', p. 74). Public transport, while fairly reliable, does limit you. For more information on bus routes and timetables (summer and winter schedules are different) contact **Conselleria Transports** in Placa d'Espanya in Palma (📞 971 753 445). The Palma-Sóller bus service stops in Deià, three times a day in high season. A one-way ticket is €4.50 (£3), €2.50 (£1.70) for children under 11. The bus stops at the main plaza in Valldemossa, and at the only car park in Deià. It takes about one hour to get to Deià (with no traffic; potentially longer in high season), and about two hours to Sóller by this scenic route.

The main town of the south-west part of the region, **Valldemossa,** is just 20 minutes' drive away from the centre of Palma along the PM-111. While to the north-west, **Sóller** can be reached in about 45 minutes along the C-711. You could easily combine the two in a day-trip, making stops en route to take in a couple of the key sights, lunch or a picnic, swims or a walk.

One of the most popular boat trips on the island sets sail from **Port de Sóller** and follows the north-west cliffs around to the postcard-perfect bay of **Sa Calobra.** During high season it goes several times a day and costs €15 (£10.05) for adults, €10 (£6.70) children under 11. Tickets can be bought direct from the boat in the port. Please note that prices and timetables change every year. Information is available from Conselleria Transports (see left) and tickets can be combined with the train ride (see 'The Little Train That Does', p. 74).

Visitor Information

The main **tourist office** for this region is in **Valldemossa** (Avenida de Palma 7 📞 *971 612 106*) where you can pick up hiking and biking maps, as well as information on guided excursions in the Tramuntana. In **Sóller,** there's an OIT at Plaça Espanya s/n (📞 *971 638 008*).

Child-friendly Events

The **Sunday morning market, 10am–2pm,** in Valldemossa on the main square is a fun and atmospheric place to start the day. Pick up local arts, crafts and food.

Sa Mostra (*www.sollernet.com/ samostra/*; *www.samostra.org*) is an international folklore festival held in Sóller for one week every July. It first started in 1980 and has since risen to become one of the finest festivals of its kind in the world, attracting folk singers and performers from as far away as India, Nigeria and Puerto Rico.

Fire-breathing demons feature at the Sant Bartolomeu ★ on August 24th in Sóller. It's a frenzy of flames and fireworks, demonic dancing and chanting in which decorum is thrown to the wind and practical jokes, men dressing as women and women as men, outlandish costumes and general merrymaking and mayhem are de rigueur. The festival is practised across the island and in much of Catalonia, but the one in Sóller is the biggest and the best, with the town's residents spending up to three months getting ready.

WHAT TO SEE & DO

Children's Top Attractions

● Snorkelling off the treasure-island beach of Sa Calobra, see p. 76.

● Playing hide and seek among the monasteries and palaces of Valldemossa, see right.

● Dressing for lunch at L'Olivo, see p. 84.

● Eating home-made ice-cream in Sóller, see p. 86.

● Canyoning at Aventur Parc, see p. 81.

● Catching the little wooden train from Palma to Sóller, see 'The Little Train That Does', p. 74

The West's Towns

Considered one of the must-do sights and a mere 20-minute drive from Palma on the PM-111 (the Palma-Sóller bus also stops here), Valldemossa ★★ is everything you could want from a fairytale town: pretty sandstone houses with peonies and gerberas spilling out of window boxes and cute country stores selling local produce, as well as a colourful Sunday market. The stately Sanxo Palace and Carthusian monasteries – lived in by monks of the order of St Bruno of France in the 11th century – (see 'Historic Buildings, Parks and Gardens', p. 77) are world-class sights fully deserving of their UNESCO World Heritage status. The Port of Valldemossa has a handy shingle beach if all you want is a quick swim or a snorkel, while the soaring mountains all around make for perfect picnic spots and nature walks. Simply follow any of the well-marked and maintained walking trails out of town to find your own little nook far from the madding crowd. With a young family in tow, it doesn't come better than Valldemossa.

Another 20-minute drive away on the C-710 (Palma-Soller bus), over the ridge of the mountains, is Deià ★. The town was popularised by travelling artists and writers in the 1800s, and has since become a magnet for Hollywood stars, royalty and European glitterati. Michael Douglas and Catherine Zeta Jones; Claudia Schiffer and

A Day-trip for the First-time Visitor

Easily achieved by bus from the Estación Autobuses on C/Eusebi Estada in Palma, but infinitely more comfortable if you have your own hire car, this route is just 35 km long, but feels like more because of the way the roads outside Palma twist and turn. First stop is the postcard town of **Valldemossa** (see p. 72) where George Sand and her lover Frederic Chopin infamously spent a miserable winter in the 1830s. Visitors who have read Sand's damning account 'A Winter in Majorca' will be pleased to learn that things have improved no end, and it's now one of the most charming spots on the island. Be sure to visit the **Carthusian monastery** (see p. 72) and **King Sanxo's Palace** (see p. 77) before continuing on to **Deià** (see p. 72), more rugged and exposed, where elaborate mansions and charming cottages cling precariously to the mountainside. It is here that the great and the good (Michael Douglas and Catherine Zeta Jones to name two) have made their second homes and, if you're lucky, you may spot your idol in one of the village's many high-end restaurants. Stop at the newly inaugurated **Robert Graves Museum** (see p. 79) before heading off for a refreshing swim at the **Cala Deià** (see p. 76) – a shingle beach where Graves reportedly hosted all-night, nude swimming parties. Either stop in town for a late lunch, or continue on to **Port de Sollér** (see p. 75) where the pickings are considerably cheaper and the views over the bowl-shaped bay stunning.

Train to Sóller

The Little Train That Does

The train lopes its way out of it's own little station on Plaça Espanya (you can't miss it), in Palma, with the Tramuntana to the left. The clouds hang heavy above this blue-grey peaks like puffs of candy floss. Past dusty station houses and scruffy farmyards, the train soon leaves the city behind and chugs on to the island's fertile plains dotted with olive groves and almond orchards, past squat villages the colour of dust, the air scented with figs. The train speeds along at about 20 km/h, rattling away until it reaches the foothills. Here pine trees provide a shady canopy before heading into a dank, musty tunnel. Like travelling deep into the centre of the earth, even adults can't help but be thrilled. On the other side, the landscape changes to sheer cliffs and narrow gorges, outcrops shrouded in mist and the summer haze, where the little train stops for views above Sóller before pulling into the station. While it's certainly good fun and a great option for those without a hire car, it gets very crowded in high season and you need to plan properly. There are no trains between 2pm and 6.30pm, which you'll want to bear in mind if children are prone to grizzle and need afternoon naps. See www.sollernet.com for timetables. Ferrocarril de Sóller, C/Eusebio Estada 1 (Palma stop: ☎ 971 752 051, Sóller stop: ☎ 971 630 130). Adult return ticket €14 (£9.40), child under 12 return ticket €10 (£6.70). Trains go about five times a day in summer, and tour times in winter, both ways.

Michael Schumacher; ex-Mr Bond Pierce Brosnan have all bought houses here in recent years, and it's not uncommon to spot them lingering over lunch in one of the town's classy restaurants.

No wonder they like it. Deià is a spectacular little place that clings to the mountainside like a limpet. It's worth spending at least a morning or afternoon here exploring the charming village with its earth-coloured houses and pine-forest green blinds. In truth there's nothing much to see, aside from the **Robert Graves Museum** (see 'The Top Museums', p. 79) on the outskirts, but people come by the thousand to catch a glimpse of the thing that has inspired so many artists and writers: a place so beautiful it catches your breath.

'Tourists are good animals, though they vary according to nationalities,' Graves once remarked. 'The most easily domesticated, the Majorcans agree, are my English compatriots.' It's good to know then, that English travellers and their children will be made welcome.

Note: coaches are not allowed to stop in Deià and parking is limited to prevent overcrowding. If you go to any of the museums you can walk back into town along the road, or pay (€5

Deià Village

(£3.35)) in the car park at the port and take the half-hour, steep hike back up towards the village. Unless, you have the forearms of a giant, this might not be the best option with pushchairs.

Heading back down the mountains towards the coast, **Sóller** is Mallorca's very own Orange County. It nestles snugly in a bowl, surrounded on all sides by vertiginous mountains and a distant view of the sea on the horizon. A genteel town of statuesque *modernista* architecture, art galleries, boutiques and pavement cafes, it has little traffic and the air is cool, but while locals are perfectly happy to welcome your little ones,

there isn't a great deal for them to do here. Think of it as a morning excursion, rather than a base, if you have easily-bored teenagers.

Port de Sóller on the other hand has a more laid-back air and a slightly scruffy ambience that makes it popular with families. Like all seaside towns visitors will find clusters of souvenir shops rimming the water's edge. And because it's hemmed in by mountains, the sand beach is great for tots, with some shade provided by palm trees and calm, lagoon-like water. The journey by **tram** from Sóller is an additional €4 (£2.70) for adults, €2.50 (£1.70) for children under 11, and leaves

Public Art

The villages of the Serra de Tramuntana have attracted a number of artists and writers over the years, drawn to the eye-popping landscapes and hidden-away charms. **Sóller,** for example, is so art-friendly that you can enjoy works bequeathed to the town by Joan Miró and Pablo Picasso for free at the train station above Plaça Constitució. For more contemporary works by international artists still living in the village, check out **Can Puig** (Costa d'En Llorenç ✆ *971 634 091*).

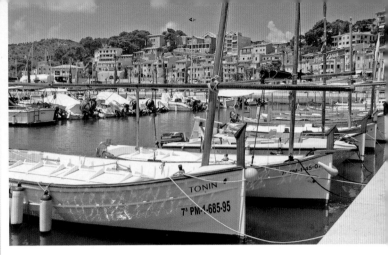

Port de Sóller

from the train station (☎ *971 630 130*). Even if you don't choose to stay, it's a good place to come for a quick dip and lunch somewhere like the fabulous **Ca's Mariner** (see 'Family-friendly Dining', p. 84), or one of the many kid- and teen-friendly pizzerias and burger bars.

Beaches

Part of the west coast's attraction – exactly what has kept it unspoilt – is the fact that it isn't big on beaches. The coastline here is too sheer, rocky and lacking in sand to make for good sandcastle or sunbathing territory.

The best and most accessible beach is the pint-sized, shingle cay at **Deià** with its ramshackle, round-stone boat houses, rickety staircases leading down to the sea and crystalline water. The car park costs €5 (£3.35) for the day.

The less romantic, narrow strip of sand that rims **Port de Sóller** is a good option for younger children because of the way the harbour is cupped by mountains, ensuring the water is always calm and shallow.

But the best beach of all is one that requires a boat ride from Port de Sóller (Barcos Azules, Passeig Es Través 3, Port de Sóller ☎ *971 630 170* www.barcosazules. com €20 (£13.40) per person): **Sa Calobra** ★ ★ ★ It's the stuff of movies with towering granite cliffs that glow golden in the sunlight, sparkling turquoise water and bottle-green umbrella pines providing pockets of shade for those who get there early. It has no facilities, so be prepared if you're going with very young children, and be sure to check on departure times for the boat. In high season they head in and out every couple of hours or so, but it varies every year. For older children this can be a veritable treasure island, especially if all they really want to do is mess about in the water. Snorkelling is excellent here. Take plenty of drinking water, a large picnic, books, snorkelling gear, a parasol shade and plenty of sunscreen, and this may just prove to be one of Mallorca's best days out. Note: it can get very busy in high season (July and August).

Historic Buildings, Parks & Gardens

Real Cartuja de Jesús de Nazaret ★ ★ ★ AGES 5 AND UP

This magnificent sandstone Carthusian monastery dates back to the 17th and 18th centuries and presides regally over the sleepy town of Valldemossa. It was made famous by its illustrious guests, the composer Frederic Chopin and writer George Sand, who took over the cells the monks had abandoned only three years earlier, during the winter of 1838–39. By all accounts they had a thoroughly horrid time, Chopin with tuberculosis and Sand with a generally miserable outlook, but it makes for fascinating territory in the present day. The vastness of the place makes it great for *Famous Five*-inspired adventures, and while its history suggests a more sober outlook, it provides children with a wonderland for exploration. The church boasts a jewel-encrusted bishop's throne, the pharmacy a Harry Potter-type emporium filled with dusty bottles and fascinating potions. The two cells left undisturbed since Sand and Chopin's departure are filled with the ghosts of the past, most notably in the form of personal letters, locks of hair and Chopin's piano. For

adults, the astonishing collection of modern art here, including works by Miró, Picasso, Francis Bacon and Henry Moore, can do nothing but inspire. An all-round winner for family entertainment.

Real Cartuja de Valldemossa 📞 971 612 106. Open Mar–Oct 9.30am–6pm, Sun 10am–1pm; Nov–Feb 9.30am–4.30pm, Sun 10am–1pm. €7.50 (£5) adults; free for under-10s.

King Sanxo's Palace

AGES 6 AND UP Originally built as a winter residence for the Mallorcan monarchy, it was turned over for use as Valldemossa's first Carthusian monastery in the 14th century, after the kingdom of Mallorca became part of the Spanish crown. The monks who had lived there since 1399 were finally expelled in 1835 after the secularisation of church property. During those 450 years, as their religious community grew, a second monastery, the Royal Carthusian Monastery, was built next door, and the palace once again became the residence of aristocracy. The interior is

The Monastery, Valldemossa

full-to-bursting with antiques, tapestries and plush rugs and is now the oldest part of the Carthusian monastery complex – though much of the original building has been restored.

Plaça de la Cartoixa, Valldemossa. 971 612 106. Open Mar–Oct Mon–Sat and holidays 9.30am–6pm, Sun 10am–1pm. Nov–Feb Mon–Sat and holidays 9.30am–4.30pm, closed Sun. Entry included in the price for the Real Cartuja.

La Granja ★ AGES 5 AND UP

This 3,000-square metre mansion spans nearly 1000 years of history, from the 10th to the 20th centuries. There is plenty to see: formal tiled dining rooms, Burberry-style parlours, and heavily draped bedrooms. The music room is alive with sounds, while re-enactments of the life of the servants of the aristocracy take place around you. The gardens ramble over 20000 square metres with fountains, ponds and ancient trees. You also get to taste traditional Mallorcan cheeses and jams as part of the tour, as well as enjoy local artesan traditions like *sobrassada* sausage (minced pork mixed with paprika), goat's milk cheese, and candle and shoe making. Twice a week a special horse dressage show is staged with folk music and dancing. Call in advance for upcoming schedules.

Carretera Esporles-Puigpunyent km 2, Esporles 971 610 031 Fax: 971 619 305 www.lagranja.net. Open daily 10am–7pm (summer), 10am–6pm (winter). €11 (£7.40) adults, €4.50 (£3) children. Restaurant serves traditional dishes 971 610 032 for reservations.

Museu Balear de Ciències Naturals I Jardí Botànic

ALL AGES Beautifully laid out and impressively planted, this gargantuan garden gives a good overview of Mallorca's endemic species, and provides a welcome retreat from the crowds in high season. There are several walkways, as well as corners for picnics and lazing in the shade. It's well set up for children with numerous exhibits, interactive displays and photos showcasing everything from endangered species to medicinal plants and how to use them.

Carretera Palma-Sóller km 30 971 634 064 www.jardibotanicdesoller. org. €5 (£3.35). Children under 12 free. Open Tue–Sat 10am–6pm, Sun and holidays 10am–2pm. Closed Mon.

Sóller Cemetery FIND

AGES 7 AND UP For the ghoul inside every little boy and girl, this cemetery is the most spectacular on the island boasting a fascinating collection of funerary tributes ranging from macabre angel statues to ornate mausoleums. The tombs are loaded with symbolism – a garland of roses to represent the circle of life and regeneration; a bat wing for night; an hourglass for time passing; and it can be fun – in an *Addams Family* kind of a way – to play the game of trying to figure it all out. The grave of Robert Graves is also here. He believed that the church was built on the site of an ancient temple to the moon goddess.

Follow signs from C/Luna, Sóller. No phone. Free entry. Open 10am–sundown.

Jardi Botanic, Sóller

The Top Museums

Robert Graves Museum ★ ★

AGES 7 AND UP This long-overdue tribute to the poet who put Deià on the map was finally opened in July 2006, and is an absolute must for anyone who wants to understand Mallorca's artistic appeal. Situated in Ca N'Alluny 'faraway house' where he lived with his family between 1932 and 1985, the exhibition has been put together with the help of Graves' son, William, and it exudes atmosphere. Still littered with the paraphernalia of an artist at work – a typewriter, bundles of notebooks, letters from Gertrude Stein and William Churchill, and, most bizarrely, a mistaken newspaper announcement of his death during the Second World War – it provides a wonderfully true expression of the artist's life.

Walking the West

Hiking is a great alternative to the more obvious Mallorcan beach holiday, and the Serra de Tramuntana offers some of Spain's most spectacular mountain scenery, perfect for spring and autumn breaks. The main peaks include the **Puig Mayor** (1445m), **Massanella** (1340m) and **L'Ofre** (1080m). There are coastal paths to follow from Sóller to Deià, or a more challenging route that goes from the **Gorg Blau to Lluc** (a wild and lonely monastery high in the mountains). Whatever route you choose, you can guarantee some of the best scenery in Spain, pine-scented fresh air and a Mediterranean breeze to blow away the cobwebs. Valerie Crespi-Green's book *Sunflower Guides: Mallorca* has detailed information on roughly 20 walks on the island, as well as good ideas for picnics. **Tramuntana Tours** (see 'For Active Families' p. 81) runs guided walks with little extras, like help identifying local flora and fauna.

Ca N'Alluny, Ctra Deià-Sóller s/n, Deià. ☎ 971 636 185. www.fundaciorobertgraves.com. Open Tue to Sat 10am–5pm, Sun 10am–3pm, Mon closed. €5 (£3.35), no concessions.

Museu de la Mar AGES 5 AND UP

Located on top of a cliff wedged between the lagoon-like harbour of Port de Sóller and the big blue Mediterranean sea, this museum is noteworthy as much for its views as for the contents. It's a manageable uphill climb even for the most reticent of toddlers, and well worth it. The museum itself charts the rising importance of Port de Sóller for shipping fish, oranges and olives, and gives a sense of the history of the place. While today it's a mere 45-minute drive from Palma, in the old days Sóller was completely cut off from the capital, yet thrived on its own thanks to the bounty of its orange-filled valleys.

C/ Santa Caterina d'Alexandria, Port de Sóller ☎ 971 632 204. Open 10am–2pm, 5pm–8pm (summer); 10am–2pm, 3pm–6pm winter; closed Mon. Free entry.

Ca'n Det Olive Press

AGES 5 AND UP One of only three remaining working olive mills on the island, Ca'n Det dates back to at least the 16th century and still uses the traditional millstones and wicker mats to extract the olive oil that the Romans considered liquid gold. Children are surprisingly absorbed by watching the process from start to finish, and a visit may even encourage picky eaters to try some. Visits by appointment only: they speak English and if you're alone, they'll arrange a time when other people are coming too.

Explotacions agricoles Can Det S.L., C/Ozonas 8, Soller ☎ 971 630 303. €7.50 (£5), €4 (£2.70) children under 11.

Some Family Entertainment

Stars in Concert ★ Running since 1963, this unimaginatively titled show was inspired by 'Legends' in Las Vegas. Stars in Concert is a star-spangled line-up of tribute bands from Elvis and Tom Jones to the Blues Brothers, along with a re-enaction of the masked dancers and sequinned costumes of the Venice Carnival. The theatre is located inside a grand old country estate, and by itself makes the visit special. The restaurant offers several different menus as well as à la carte, and an uninspiring children's menu of chicken nuggets or fish fingers and chips for €22.50 (£15.10) per child. An adult's classic menu includes cheese, paté, suckling pig, pudding and wine; it costs €40 (£26.80). The gourmet 'platinum' menu costs €90 (£60.30). In all cases the show is included.

Ctra. de Sóller km 10.8, Palma ☎ 971 617 533. Fax: 971 617 069 www.sonamar.com. Shows nightly. Book direct.

For Active Families

Tramuntana Tours ★★

AGES 11 AND UP For bike hire, walking tours, snorkelling excursions, or even deep-sea fishing, this small company in Sóller offers a wide range of fun-filled options. The cycling, for example, ranges from fairly easy routes following the roads, to off-roading through the mountains. You can join a group or ask for a tailor-made adventure; all equipment is provided. See their website for prices which vary by tour, from €400 (£268) for a half-day pleasure boat trip (max. six persons) to €8 (€5.35) a day for a simple run-around shopping bicycle. Children's bikes and mountain bikes are also available.

C/ de la Luna 72, Sóller ☎ 971 632 423 www.tramuntanatours.com.

Octopus Diving Centre ★

AGES 10 AND UP A fun and friendly option for water babies, Octopus does two boat dives in a day (10am and 4pm) for €28 (£18.75). Non-divers can tag along if there's room, for €15 (£10.05). Octopus also offers different packages of up to 10 dives, which work out to be a bargain if you're in town for a week or so.

This is a place to indulge all your Jacques Cousteau fantasies and start to understand the magic of the underwater world. While the water of the Med may not offer the drama of the Caribbean or the Red Sea, around the Balearics it's particularly clear, with spectacular visibility, healthy flora and fauna and even, if you're very lucky, the chance to swim with octopi. Open water courses start at €360 (£241.20) and last for four days. Opening hours change according to season and the weather. Call in advance to check the diving schedule.

C/Canonge Oliver 13, Port de Sóller ☎ 971 633 133. Mobile: 608 631 756.

Aventur ★ **AGES 8 AND UP** This

adventure park for children aged eight or over has lots of adrenalin-pumping activities ranging from abseiling and hiking to canyoning (a mix of climbing, hiking and rampaging through rivers) and climbing. A new refreshing mountain offers the chance to cool off in crystal-clear waters.

Ctra. Puigpunyent-Palma s/n ☎ 971 616 622. Open daily, all year, 10am–7pm. Wear comfortable clothes, trainers and bring a camera. €15 (£10.05) adults, €7.50 (£5) children under 11.

FAMILY-FRIENDLY ACCOMMODATION

This side of the island is typically expensive; it's where millionaires and film stars buy up second (or even third) homes. That said, there are bargains to be had for those willing to search.

Hotel Eden ★ **VALUE** Located right on the seafront in Port de Sóller, this family-friendly hotel is a bargain in an area that can otherwise be hideously expensive. Bedrooms are typically three-star standard with brightly coloured soft furnishings, tiled floors and Formica furniture, but it's clean and comfortable, if a little lacking in character. The advantage of staying here, aside from the location, is that it's a small, safe town where your teenagers can roam at will, and small children can enjoy a clean beach with shallow water. A spacious lobby leads to a good-sized swimming pool where the children can make new friends while parents take advantage of the well-stocked cocktail bar.

Es Través 26, Port de Sóller ☎ 971 631 600. Fax: 971 633 656 www.hotel eden.com. 152 rooms. €76 (£50.90) (with breakfast), €116 (£77.70) (full-board) double standard. €84 (£56.30) (with breakfast), €124 (£83.10) (full-board) double superior. Prices per room. Children 2–12 get a 50% discount. V MC. Amenities: WiFi, ADSL, restaurant, bar, lounge, swimming pool, solarium, garden. In room: A/C, central heating, telephone, safe, satellite TV, fridge, hairdryer.

La Residencia ★ For the ultimate once-in-a-lifetime family getaway, look no further than La Residencia, beloved of vacationing stars, athletes and politicians. This super-luxury hotel has everything from paradise-like gardens and to-die-for views, to light, airy interiors and just about every leisure activity you can dream of. Dreams such as these don't come cheap: you can bank on spending at least €325 (£217.75) a night for a double room, even in low season. It's worth keeping an eye out for special Christmas and New Year packages, though, as bargains can be had. Bedrooms are flooded with sunshine by day, cosy at night with crisp linens tastefully decorated with a mix of well chosen antiques and contemporary design pieces. Food at the gourmet **El Olivo** (see 'Family-friendly Dining', p. 84) is one of the best dining experiences in Spain.

C/Son Canals s/n, Deià ☎ 971 639 011. Fax: 971 639 370 www.hotel laresidencia.com. 36 single & double rooms, 17 junior suites, 2 superior suites with rooftop terrace and private swimming pool. Rates double standard €245–420 (£164.15–281.40), double superior €325–525 (£217.75–351.75), junior suite €425–675 (£284.75–452.25), superior suite €650–850 (£435.50–569.50), children under 12 get a 30% discount. Breakfast included. Children under 10 only between 1st July and 18th Aug, 20th–31st Oct, Christmas and New Year. Amenities: 3 restaurants: El Olivo (gourmet), Son Tony (Mediterranean bistro), Pool Restaurant (snacks), spa, gym, 2 tennis courts and private coaching, yoga, tai chi, aqua aerobics, 1 indoor swimming pool, 2 outdoor swimming pools, boat excursions, hot air balloon flights. In room: A/C, heating, bath, shower, Internet, video, satellite TV, family games, telephone.

Pensión Miramar ★★ VALUE

A reassuring deal in a village of millionaires, this 19th century farmhouse boasts those same magnificent views over the golden rooftops as the competition at a fraction of the cost. Traditional bottle-green blinds frame the windows, décor is simple but clean and comfortable, and the atmosphere is friendly and laid-back. There's even a small dining room serving simple, country fayre and verdant terraces for taking coffee and enjoying the peace and quiet. *C'an Oliver, Deià 971 639 084 www.pensionmiramar.com. 9 rooms. Double €28–€38 (£18.75–25.45). Extra bed €15 (£10.05). Cot free. Breakfast €7 (£4.70). Amenities: patio-garden, restaurant. In room: ceiling fan, heating.*

Hotel Valldemossa

At the top end of the scale in Valldemossa, this hotel consists of two 19th century houses joined by a series of staircases and terraces: great fun for the children to explore while weary parents take the weight off their feet. It was renovated in 2004, adding all the super-duper 21st century touches that take the grind out of modern-day travel, including a luxury spa and expensive gourmet restaurant, which to its credit offers an imaginative vegetarian menu. However, the original features have been lovingly maintained, and there's plenty of communal living space and acres of garden. The place is stuffed with antiques and original artworks, with individually decorated rooms and a true family atmosphere. Think of them as your posh friends in the country. *Ctra. Vieja de Vallemossa s/n, Valldemossa 971 612 626. Fax: 971 612 625 www.valldemossa hotel.com. 3 double rooms. 9 suites. V, MC. Double €210 (£140.70) summer, €170 (£113.90) winter. Suite €410 (£274.70) summer, €340 (£227.80) winter. Breakfast included. Amenities: indoor and outdoor swimming pools, spa, bar, gourmet restaurant. In room: A/C, heating, Internet, satellite TV, DVD, mini-bar.*

Es Petit Hotel ★★ FIND

A true gem in the centre of Valldemossa, this family inn has just eight light, airy and simply decorated rooms. The best have private terraces with views over the village, and all come with crisp, white cotton sheets against a brightly painted wall, simple farmhouse furniture and exposed beams. There's a large communal terrace and a small garden for coffee and drinks, a winter room with a blazing fireplace and a small

Tiled Mural, Valldemossa

dining room. What it lacks in luxuries it makes up for in laid-back, friendly atmosphere.

C/Uetan, Valldemossa ☎ 971 612 479. Fax: 971 612 848 www.espetit hotel-valldemossa.com. Double €90–€115 (£60.30–77.10) in high season. Additional bed €46 (£30.80). Breakfast included. V, MC. Amenities: restaurant, garden, lounge area. In room: A/C, heating, satellite TV, telephone, free Internet.

Sa Torre de Santa Eugenia ★

With its remote inland location, Sa Torre makes a great alternative hotel for active families. Fully-equipped apartments decorated in rustic chic style form the basis of the accommodation, each with a double bedroom, kitchen, dining/living room with fireplace giving visitors plenty of independence and a private terrace. There's also an excellent country restaurant run by the brothers of the López Pinto Ivars family (Pedro and Victoriano), bar service and two swimming pools nestled in herb-scented gardens. Victoriano doubles up as a fun and knowledgeable guide to the Serra de Tramuntana mountains.

C/Alqueries 70, Santa Eugenia ☎ 971 144 011. Fax: 971 144 112. www.sa-torre.com. V, MC. Apartment €125 (£83.75), additional bed €15 (£10.05), breakfast €12 (£8). Amenities: bathtub and shower, cleaning service, 2 swimming pools, bar and towel service, reading room, restaurant, laundry, private parking.

La Muleta VALUE

The sanctuaries, refuges and rustic guest houses of Mallorca make a great option for adventurous families on a budget. La Muleta is one of the best, with fantastic Mediterranean views and easy access to Sóller, Deià and Valldemossa. It has basic rooms, cabins (requiring your own sleeping bags), a basic bar and restaurant, cooking facilities and endless walks for breathing in the Mediterranean air. Sometimes it's the simple things that work best.

Far des Cap Gros, Port de Sóller ☎ 971 173 700 €25 (£16.75) per person per night, children under 11 €15 (£10.05) per night. Cot free. Family rooms available by arrangement. No credit cards. Breakfast in the restaurant from €3.50 (£2.35) for tostadas. Reservations must be made at least five days in advance.

FAMILY-FRIENDLY DINING

L'Olivo ★★★

MODERN MEDITERRANEAN Housed in a handsome 16th century olive press, the aptly named El Olivo is one of the best dining experiences in Spain. Its soaring rafters and whitewash make it a light and airy dining experience by day, romantic and intimate by night. But when you're going with the family the best thing to do is book a spot on the terrace for a long, lazy lunch. Adventurous children get a buzz out of the high design and interesting flavours of the modern Mediterranean fayre, and seem to revel in the chance to play grown-up for a while. While the pork cheeks and sweetbreads may prove a little much for most, even little ones enjoy delights like poppy-seed noodles with orange sauce, seasonal mushrooms on parsley mash and roast chicken in a salt crust. The set price lunch menu of €45 (£30.15) for a meal of this calibre won't bust the bank; expect to spend €60 (£40.20) upwards to go à la carte.

C/Son Canals s/n, Deià 📞 *971 639 011. Fax: 971 639 370. Set lunch menu €45 (£30.15). All credit cards. Booking essential. Over-10s only.*

Ca's Mariner ★ ★ FIND VALUE

FISH & SEAFOOD A staunchly family-run restaurant, unlike many of the eateries that line the bay of Sóller, Ca's Mariner has just four tables lined up along the pavement with great views over the bay, as well as a pleasant fisherman-themed dining room. While these pavement tables tend to get grabbed by visitors, inside is packed with locals who come to feast on the specialities of superlative fish and seafood and slow-roasted goat kid. Service can be a little brusque at times, but that's just part of the place's authenticity. There's no special tourist treatment here, just superb home cooking and the island's best produce. Try the *caldereta* (stew) of lobster; giant prawns from the

Seafood at Ca's Mariner

bay; *bandeja de marisco* (a selection of seafood including clams, mussels, three different kinds of shrimp and razor clams); or *parrillada de pescado* (mixed grill of fresh fish).

C/Santa Catalina 12, Port de Sóller 📞 *971 634 727. Main courses €14.50–€25 (£9.70–16.75). V, MC. Reservations recommended. High chair.*

Domenico PIZZA & PASTA This

excellent family restaurant serves proper thin-based, chewy pizzas and home-made pasta and puddings in a convivial and laid-back atmosphere. The butter coloured dining room and flower-filled patio give it a happy air, making it a fun place for birthday parties and family gatherings. Easygoing staff are happy to adapt to your needs, and those of your children, so parents can relax.

C/Dr Marina 44, Port de Sóller 📞 *971 633 155. Main courses €11–19 (£7.40–12.75). Highchairs available. V, MC. Reservations recommended.*

Casa Jaume UPMARKET MALLORCAN

This charming buttercup yellow dining room on Deià's main street leads out to a gorgeous hanging terrace at the back, with views over the village's innumerable posh houses and fruit orchards. Chef Biel Payeras Salas provides a welcome halfway house in a village where dining options are either haute cuisine and prohibitively expensive, or basic sandwiches and pizzas. His dishes are generally solid Mallorcan with a twist, like succulent roast chicken with a hearty forcemeat stuffing made to the recipe his grand-mother used in 1965; roast fish of the day; *tumbet* – a Mallorquín take on *ratatouille*; and more adventurous dishes like stuffed eggplant and zucchini. Watch out for *Frito Mallorquín*: while *frito* generally implies anything fried, this is a classic island dish of fried lungs, kidneys, liver and any other edible innards the cook can lay his hands on.

C/Arxiduc Lluis Salvador 22, Deià ℂ 971 639 029. Main courses €12.50–€33 (£8.40–22.10). V, MC. Reservations recommended.

El Barrigon ★ TAPAS A classic on the tapas scene, this atmos-pheric bar is a great place for meeting people and enjoying the social whirl. Photo-packed walls are testament to the artists and writers who have visited the region over the years, and enjoyed the *bonhomie* of El Barrigon. With more than 60 different tapas to choose from there should be something for everyone, ranging from aubergines stuffed with goat's cheese to chicken croquettes and slivers of *pata negra jamón*. Live jazz concerts are held in the pretty garden on Saturday evenings throughout the summer.

C/ Archiduque Luis Salvador 19, Deià ℂ 971 639 139. About €15–€20 (£10.05–13.40) per person for several shared tapas and wine. No credit cards. No reservations.

Son Tomas ★ ★ FIND
MARKET COOKING Banyalbufar is a lovely little village of terraced mountainsides and great views, and it is well worth stopping off here for lunch as part of a drive through the Tramuntana. This family-run restaurant has been going for 23 years, serving a loyal clientele with fresh and often home-grown products. With indoor and outdoor seating it's a good place to ensure the children are getting their five portions of fruit and vegetables a day. Expect dishes such as fish *tumbet* (a Mallorcan salad of tomatoes and peppers) and orange cake with vanilla ice-cream. Take-away paella and *fideuas* (the pasta equivalent) are also avail-able with advance warning.

C/Baronia 17, Banyalbufar ℂ 971 618 149. Fax: 971 618 135. Main courses €11–20 (£7.40–13.40).V, MC. Reservations recommended.

An Ice-cream Stop

Sa Fàbrica de Gelats ★ ★ No matter where you eat in Sóller, save room for ice-cream here. People travel from all over the island for its excellent home-made ice-creams and sorbets. Though it has more than 40 different varieties to choose from, the most popular is the orange ice-cream made from the valley's finest fruits.

C/Cristòbal Colon, Sóller ℂ 971 631 708. 1 scoop €1 (£0.67). No credit cards.

MALLORCA NORTH-EAST

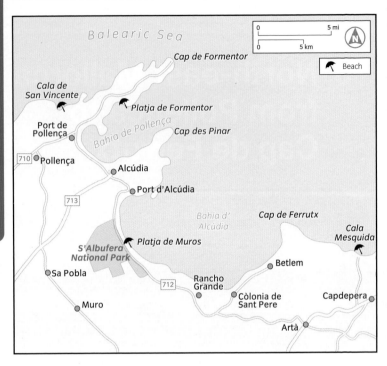

Balearic Sea

Cap de Formentor

Cala de San Vincente

Platja de Formentor

Port de Pollença

Bahia de Pollença

Cap des Pinar

710 Pollença

Alcúdia

713

Port d'Alcúdia

Bahia d' Alcúdia

Cap de Ferrutx

Cala Mesquida

S'Albufera National Park

Platja de Muros

Betlem

Sa Pobla

Rancho Grande

712

Capdepera

Muro

Còlonia de Sant Pere

Artà

0   5 mi
0   5 km

Beach

The north-east corner of Mallorca is the undisputed favourite when it comes to family beach holidays. The **Bahia d'Alcúdia** has eight kilometres of clean, golden sand – a beach-bum's paradise with everything from white-knuckle banana-boat rides to serious sports like windsurfing and scuba diving. And yet, the water is generally calm enough to make it a winning experience for toddling first-timers, too. Sadly, if you look inland the view is not quite so idyllic, given the explosion of resort-type development along this stretch of coast. On the whole though, it provides a safe and comfortable environment for tiny tots, and a plethora of entertainment options, from shopping and fairground rides to resort discos, for teens. The tourist-led infrastructure also means there are plenty of showers, public toilets and restaurants.

Added attractions include the **Albufera** wetlands – a former lagoon separated from the sea by pine-backed sand dunes – for family bike rides and bird watching.

The area also has a couple of decent theme parks, like **Rancho Grande,** and some lovely towns and villages inland: **Pollença, Sa Pobla** and **Alcúdia** itself, the old Roman capital of the island. On the down side, in high season traffic along the road from Alcúdia to Artà can make town-to-town exploring a bit of a nightmare.

ESSENTIALS

Getting There & Around

While it's always possible to get around the region without one, a **rental car** (see chapter 2) will make the going much smoother and stop you getting stuck in the resorts.

There are four **buses** a day from Palma, run by **Autocares Mallorca** (971 545 696 *www. autocaresmallorca.com*), but they do tend to be packed in high season. Getting on and off with a pushchair isn't easy, though if your children are older they'll be comfortable enough. Buses run by the same company also connect Pollença to Alcúdia and Alcúdia to Cala Rajada (see Chapter 6) on the east coast, running about once an hour in high season. Always check the timetable in advance as this is subject to change. Journey time varies according to traffic density, but from Palma allow at least 1½ hours. **Shuttle buses** run along the bay from the **Port de Alcúdia** to the posher resort town of **Playa de Muro** every 20 minutes or so. They get hideously crowded in high season, and getting on with a pushchair is a struggle. Bus stops are located at regular intervals all the way along the C-712 which runs between these resort towns.

Taxis aren't always easy to find and you are generally better off to book one through your hotel, rather than rely on flagging one down: try **Alcúdia Taxi** (971 549 497). Most drivers speak English.

Finally, you could opt for **bike hire,** available from most resorts and hotels. There is usually a bike lane that circles the resort, but do bear in mind traffic is heavy in the summer. **Pro Cycle Hire** (Port de Pollença. 971 866 857. About €5 (£3.35) a day) has good quality childrens' and adult bikes.

If you're staying in one of the resort hotels, they should arrange transfer from the airport for you. You can also take a taxi from the airport to Alcúdia for a set rate of €80 (£53.60). Taxis don't generally have child seats, so be sure to book in advance if you need one. **Palma Taxis** (971 401 414) and **Radio Taxis** (971 755 440) both provide reliable services.

Alcúdia is also the closest point on Mallorca to the neighbouring island of Menorca and the charming town of **Ciutadella** (see p. 175). On a clear day you can even see it. **Iscomar** (Muelle Comercial s/n, Alcúdia 971 549 854) runs a daily **ferry service** from Alcúdia to Ciutadella, which takes about two-and-a-half hours and costs €59 (£39.55) per person for a day-return ticket. Advance bookings are recommended in high season.

Visitor Information

Alcúdia has mushroomed to the extent that it now has three tourist offices: **OIT Municipal Port d'Alcúdia** (Ctra Arta 68 /Fax: 971 892 615); **OIT Municipal Port d'Alcúdia** (Passeig Marítim s/n /Fax:

971 547 257); and **OIT Oficina del Centre Històric** (Carrer Major 17. ☎ 971 897 100. Fax: 971 546 515).

In **Port de Pollença** the tourist office is on the seafront by the bus station (☎ 971 865 467 Fax: 971 866 746. oitport@aj pollenca.net). And in the inland town of **Pollença** it's in the old quarter at C/Santo Domingo 17 (☎ 971 535 077. Fax: 971 535 077. **oit@ajpollenca.net**).

In Port de Pollença **Multi-Hire** (C/Méndez Núñez 23 ☎ 971 864 080 www.multi-hire.com) rents out just about everything: wheelchairs and crutches; baby strollers and car seats; mountain bikes and child helmets; DVD players and PlayStations; high-chairs and cool boxes. All prices are online, ranging from €5 (£3.35) a day for a highchair to €8 (£3.35) a day for a wooden cot.

Orientation

The north-west corner of Mallorca takes in the magnificent bays of **Pollença** and **Alcúdia**, as well as the more petite beaches of **Colonia de Sant Pere.** The C-712 runs along the edge of the Bahia d'Alcúdia all the way to **Artà**, wedged between the sparkling Mediterranean and gentle rolling countryside.

Two fingers enclose the bays on the uppermost north-eastern tip of the island rather like a hook; the **Cap de Formentor** and the **Cap de Ferrutx** offer a more wild and rugged landscape than the area's sandy beaches, and both make good hiking destinations for older children, though it will prove a bit much for anyone under 10. Overall, the north-west has a winning combination of resort towns and

Port de Pollença

ancient, medieval villages; gently rolling hills and dramatic cliffs. In many ways, this is the perfect family destination: there's something to suit everyone.

Child-friendly Events

The **Fiesta of Moors and Christians** ★ takes place on 2nd August in Pollença and is not to be missed if you happen to be on the island around this time. It commemorates a battle that took place here in 1550, in which 1500 townspeople fought off the attack of the pirate Dragut. Traditionally Christians dress in white, while Dragut's supporters are multi-coloured. The entire town turns out to take part.

In Alcúdia the **Fiesta de Les Llanternes** ★ on 24th August is designed with tots in mind. The town's littlest children parade through the streets at night carrying Chinese lanterns made out of melons (from the harvest). Combined with the traditional Mallorcan folk songs that they sing, this is one of the cutest sights in all of Spain.

WHAT TO SEE & DO

Towns & Cities

Arriving in **Pollença** ★ one could very easily feel the need to go no further. It has the kind of idyllic charm of a fairytale holiday in the country: a beautiful and lively town plaza with cafes spilling on to the pavement, lots of good places to eat and several impressive churches and convents. The **Port de Pollença,** by contrast, has a more holiday feel, and for many is preferable to the bigger resort of Alcúdia. The beach at **Cala San Vincente** is nicer than that in the town, but be aware of the sometimes strong undertow in the sea.

The biggest town on the north-east coast, **Alcúdia,** is unexpectedly pretty, enclosed within wheat-coloured walls. Confusingly named Pollentia by the Romans who made it their capital, the best way to get to grips with it is to take advantage of the Tourist Office's free two-hour **walking tour** (see 'Walking Shoes', p. 93). For many visitors its biggest attraction is simply wandering the streets. The **crafts market** `OVERRATED` on Tuesday and Sunday mornings attracts hordes, though most of what's on sale is tat: fake handbags, plastic belts, tacky toys. *Siurells*, local linen and lace are your best bets. Just be sure to stop in one of Alcúdia's many pavement cafes to soak up the atmosphere. Come in August and the streets are festooned in festival apparel.

The **Port de Alcúdia** on the other hand is the Torremolinos of Mallorca's north, awash with unsightly, unchecked development. On the upside, it's not quite so full-on as Magaluf (see Chapter 3), and is certainly more family oriented. If you can bear it, it's a good place to be if you have teenagers.

Keep on travelling around the curve of the bay, and eventually you come to **Colónia de Sant Pere,** a diminutive fishing village

Children's Top Attractions

- A day-trip to **Ciutadella,** Menorca, see Chapter 9.
- Bike-riding through the wetlands of **Albufera,** see p. 94.
- Playing cowboys and indians at **Rancho Grande,** see p. 94.
- Visiting the colourful **demons** of Sa Pobla, see p. 96.

on the far side of the Badia de Alcúdia with sweeping views of the mountains that enclose it. The tiny beaches are backed by squat cliffs: it gives a taste of what Mallorca was like before tourism. There are a handful of beach bars along the front, from cheap and cheerful **Café Bahia** (Paseo del Mar s/n ☏ *971 581 234*), which serves sandwiches, spit-roasted chickens and barbecued sardines, to the more elaborate **Sa Xarxa** (see 'Family-friendly Dining', below). Continue driving on towards **Betlem** and camper vans avail themselves of the flat areas jutting out to sea. It's popular with a handful of die-hard surfers.

Heading inland, **Artà** occupies the centre of the north-east tip of the island (about 45 minutes' drive from Palma). It is a lovely town, the polar opposite of the seaside resorts. The gentle hills of the streets and the honey-coloured houses, plus the added attraction of some excellent boutique accommodation and restaurants, make it a good base if your family is still young enough not to need too much entertaining. Even if they do, the Artà coastline is home to two of the island's best beaches, **Cala Torta** and **Cala Mesquida** (see p. 93);

and the close proximity of the east coast's slightly classier resort towns make it a good base for exploring by car. See Chapter 6 for some ideas. There's not a huge amount to do here, though it does have a couple of very handsome buildings (such as the **Santuari de Sant Salvador;** see p. 111) and a small, school-project-style museum, the **MuseuRegional d'Artà** (Carrer d'Estrella 4 ☏ *971 835 017*), show-casing mainly religious artefacts and ceramics and jewellery uncovered from archaeological sites around the island.

Heading back towards Pollença on the inland road PM-343, the sleepy little village of **Sa Pobla** has a couple of quirky charms. The **Demon Museum** (see 'The North-East's Top Museum', p. 96) is probably the highlight, but the old centre also has some striking *mod-ernista* buildings and a handful of local art galleries.

Beaches & Resorts

After a spectacular drive along dramatic ridges shaded by pines, with sea on either side, the **Platja de Formentor** ★ has an exclusive, paradise-island feel to it. These days, unless you are

Artà

staying at the Hotel Formentor here, you have to leave your car in the car park (€5 (£3.35) a day) at the western end of the beach and walk until you find a patch of sand of your own. Although the strand itself is narrow, the sand is of the finest powder quality and pearl white adorned with overhanging pines dappling the turquoise water. The hotel is in charge of all the fun facilities here, whether it's up-market snacks or windsurfing and sailing opportunities, and there's no classier place to do it. Otherwise you'll need to be fairly self sufficient: pack a picnic and bring plenty of drinking water.

At the other extreme, the **Bahia d'Alcúdia** is an 8km long, wide stretch of golden sand with all the facilities you could dream of – from burgers and ice-cream to scuba diving and banana boats. They come at a fraction of the cost of Formentors, and for teens in search of new friends this may well be the more popular option.

Cala Torta and **Cala Mesquida** on the north-east tip of the island are wilder, virgin parts of the coast. Both are well signposted from the C-715 leaving Artà, but expect a good 10-minute walk along a worn cliff path to get to the beaches themselves. This isn't anything

Walking Shoes

The tourist office in Alcúdia offers free, two-hour walking tours around the old town every Wednesday at noon. It's well worth it as a means of getting oriented among the narrow, twisting streets and hearing tales of the town's Moorish, Byzantine and Roman predecessors. Contact the OIT Oficina del Centre Històric at Carrer Major 17 (📞 *971 897 100. Fax: 971 546 515*).

Formentor

too strenuous, and all but the most grizzly children shouldn't have a problem. Babies can be carried comfortably. The beaches offer a mix of sand and shingle backed by shallow scrubby cliffs. There's no shade, but it does offer more in the way of exploring if your brood aren't for just lying in the sun all day. Again, you need to be well prepared with picnic fodder and drinks, but if you like beachcombing, snorkelling and generally getting off the beaten track, these are the beaches for you.

Trips Out For All The Family

S'Albufera Parc Natural ★★

ALL AGES What few people know about S'Albufera is that visits are limited to 30 people in the park at any one time. So, while in high season that means a little bit of forward planning (and booking), it also makes for guaranteed peace and quiet. It's the largest wetland park in the Balearics, sewn together by a network of seasonal streams and rivers, paths and bridges. It's teeming with different birds, including ducks, heron, cranes and spoonbills, as well as smaller critters like frogs and lizards. It's a magical place for easy family bike rides, or simply ambling around watching the wildlife. The visitors centre is an excellent resource for more information on the flora and fauna of the park.

Parc Natural de S'Albufera de Mallorca, Llista de Correus, Can Picafort ☎ 971 892 250. Fax: 971 892 158. Open Apr 1st–Sep 30th 9am–6pm; Oct 1st–Mar 31st 9am–5pm. To visit the park, you must obtain a visiting permit, free from the reception centre.

Rancho Grande ★ AGES 5 AND UP

Unleash your inner cowboy at this Mallorcan hoe-down. Rather than resorting to the plastic madness of other resorts, the creators of this Arizona-style ranch don cowboy hats and chaps and invite visitors on an alternative journey through the Parc Natural S'Albufera (see p. 94). Horseback treks traverse forest and skirt lagoons, while the Tramuntana rises like a true Western backdrop. For those who don't, or won't, ride there are old-style Pocahontas wagons and a menagerie of tame "farm" animals including ostriches, donkeys and goats. Afterwards, just like real cowboys, a BBQ is stoked into action, sangria is poured and the good folks of the prairie join together on long trestle tables for an evening of music and line-dancing. Yeee-haa!

Son Serra de Marina ☎ *971 854 121. Fax: 971 854 163* **www.ranchogrande mallorca.com**. *Moonlight riding and barbecue adults €57 (£38.20), children €40 (£26.80). 1-hour riding lesson €13 (£8.70). Full-day riding excursion inc. lunch €100 (£67).*

Plaza de Toros Alcúdia

ALL AGES Unusually for Mallorca, the bull ring (which was both a continuation of the town walls

Fighting Bulls

and a lookout post) celebrated its 100-year anniversary in 1993. It still hosts a *corrida* (fight) twice a year: 25th July for the feast of Sant Jaime and 15th August for the town's annual festival. The matadors are the great and the good from all over Spain.

Taquilla Plaza de Toros, Alcúdia ☎ *971 547 903. €3.50 (£2.35), children under 3 free.*

Fun On (& in) the Water

Alcúdia Hidropark **ALL AGES**

With its giant water slides, swimming and boating pools, and three mini-golf courses in

---

A Drive to Cap de Ferrutx

From Artà take the C-712 northwards to Colonia de Sant Pere at the easternmost heel of the Bahia d'Alcúdia. Drive right past the town and the road eventually peters out and becomes a dirt track; a bit like journeying to the edge of the world. The track eases through woods and along the cliffs offering fantastic views across the Mediterranean, as well as a couple of secluded beaches. It's a lovely place to stop for a picnic as patches of woodland provide ample shade.

If your crew are only motivated by a destination, wear them out by scrambling to the top of **Ermita de Betlem** (well-signposted just outside of Colonia de Sant Pere), a tiny chapel at the top of a steep hill, founded in 1805.

The North-East's Top Museum

Children love nothing more than a spook or a ghoul, and the collection of benign 'demons' at the Museu de Sant Antoni I el Dimoni ★ (The Demon Museum) AGES 7 AND UP in Sa Pobla is one of the island's underrated attractions. Stepping out for village festivals and the feast of Sant Antoni, the Mallorcan *Dimoni* is a colourful folkloric character: a beast that paints our base urges in glorious technicolour. Those of Sa Pobla are a delightfully ugly bunch, with curling tusks, grotesque pink tongues, vampire teeth and horns, and comical ears and noses.

The Old Train Station, Sa Pobla. ☏ 971 540 394. Open Tue–Sat 10am–2pm, 4pm–8pm. Admission free. Not suitable for younger, easily-scared children.

landscaped grounds, this is a good option when children tire of the beach. It's smaller than its monster counterparts in Magaluf, but has a reasonable selection of attractions ranging from wave pools, tube slides and flumes for older children, to kiddies' play-pools and mini-slides. It also has two large swimming pools for those with a more pedestrian approach, though these do get crowded. And it has golf. Food-wise we're talking pizza, burgers and hot dogs with chips, plus lots of fizzy drinks, but there is a picnic area if you want to avoid the sugar rush.

Hidropark Alcúdia, Avenida Tucán s/n, Port de Alcúdia ☏ 971 891 672. Fax: 971 891 827 www.hidropark. com. Adults €16 (£10.70), children 3–11 €8 (£5.35), children under 3 free. Open May 1st–Oct 31st, 10.30am–6pm daily.

Robinson Cat AGES 7 AND UP

Fancy an action-packed Mediterranean excursion aboard a Crusoe-inspired boat? The catamaran is a good choice for those who like a little luxury, and the chance to sunbathe across the nets and watch the water whizz by below. Their (slower) fishing boat is a better option for land-lubbers who aren't quite sure how they're going to take to the big blue. Either way, this is a lovely way to see the north coast from the sea, and make new friends while you're at it.

Port de Pollença s/n ☏ 639 332 236. Full-day boat trip 9.30am–6pm, adults €45 (£30.15), children €28 (£18.75). 5-hour sailing catamaran trip €40 (£26.80) adults, €25 (£16.75) children. Both include fishing, snorkelling, music, lunch, drinks and swimming.

Scuba Mallorca AGES 8 AND UP

A great place for absolute beginners and already certified divers, Scuba Mallorca is run by fun-living Brits who are well-geared to serving children. With gin-clear waters and comfortable temperatures, this is a great place to get to grips with the underwater world. This stretch offers a huge variety of sites filled with technicolour Mediterranean fish,

TIP ›› Shopping ‹‹

On the whole if you want to shop, you want to be in Palma (see p. 59 for Palma's shopping highlights). The towns and villages tend to offer pretty much the same, island-wide: souvenir stores, local food and wine, and handicrafts make the most interesting gifts. **Alcúdia, Pollença** and **Artà** are all good for up-market boutiques selling this stuff. Remember that once outside of Palma, most places close for siesta between 1.30pm and 5pm, so it's best to keep that time for the beach. One place worth a look is **Sacs** (C/Major 24, Alcúdia. ☎ *971 548 617*). Not to be confused with Saks of Piccadilly, this is nonetheless a good place to pick up a few trinkets, especially *Siurells* – typical Mallorcan white whistle-ornaments flecked with green and red stripes. They cost anywhere from €5 (£3.35) upwards.

colourful coral and mysterious underwater caves and grottoes. No experience is necessary, so it's a good place to try-dive, or embark on PADI certification. Because of its huge popularity, it is recommended you book at least five days in advance in high season. Scuba Mallorca can also help with accommodation for folks who want to make theirs a full-on diving holiday.

Alcúdia Market

C/El Cano 23, Port de Pollença ☎ *971 868 087. Mobile: 616 324 422. www.scubamallorca.com. 1-tank shore dive €40 (£26.80), 2-tank boat dive €70 (£46.90), snorkelling €20 (£13.40), discover scuba diving (for non-divers) €70 (£46.90), bubblemakers course (for children aged 8–10) €65 (£43.55).*

FAMILY-FRIENDLY ACCOMMODATION

Hotel Marina Delfín Verde ★

VALUE For a large-scale resort hotel, the Delfín Verde has done rather well in terms of styling, with soaring windows in a lobby furnished with wicker armchairs and a generally more up-market atmosphere than one might expect for the price. It's also completely family-oriented, suiting teens, tweens and toddlers as well as mum and dad. The rooms aren't quite so stylish, but they are perfectly comfortable, reasonably sized and most have a terrace. The hotel runs regular offers, so it's worth making a call or checking the website in advance for value deals.

Calle la Gavina 4, Port de Alcúdia
℡ 971 891 732. Fax: 971 891 756.
www.marinabalear.com. 171
rooms. All-inclusive offers for a family
of 4 available from €198 (£132.70)
per night in high season. Amenities:
buffet restaurant, bar, swimming
pool, childrens' pool, table-football,
children's play park, ping-pong,
sun-loungers, disco, evening enter-
tainment, highchairs. In room: A/C,
heating, telephone, TV.

Hotel Illa D'Or A lovely four-star right on the beach in Port de Pollença, the Illa D'Or is something of a landmark and despite being open since 1929, it continues to get rave reviews. It was completely renovated in 2004, giving it a slick, modern edge while maintaining its original features. Light airy bedrooms, a marble lobby and lushly planted gardens give it a boutique feel despite its size, and the apartments are a good option for anyone wanting more independence. It's a true family place, often with whole generations of the same family staying together. Its greatest asset, though, is location, location, location, with the turquoise waters of the Med laying on fairytale views.

Paseo Colon 265, Port de Pollença
℡ 971 865 100. Fax: 971 864 213.
www.hoposa.es, 120 rooms. Superior
double €100–202 (£67–135.35),
beds for children 50% reduction.
Apartments for 4 from €202 (£135.35).
Substantial reductions in Nov, Feb
and Mar. Amenities: restaurant, indoor
pool, outdoor pool, childrens' pool,
gym, sauna, jacuzzi, tennis court. In
room: A/C, heating, telephone, TV.

Aparthotel Duva ★ ★ `VALUE`
With part of the complex recently refurbished (it's worth asking to be in this newer section), this aparthotel offers some of the best family accommodation on the island. The newer, self-catering apartments are sleek, modern and spacious with separate lounge and kitchen areas, a master bedroom, luxury bathrooms and large terraces overlooking the hills. Rooms are a little more basic and don't have the slick finish, but nevertheless make a comfortable base. Aside from which, plentiful play and sports areas mean that children are kept happy and entertained from sun-up to sundown. Though not right on the beach, there's plenty of green space – even ducks in a pond – and a shuttle bus and cycle lanes to the beach in Port de Pollença. The food's decent, the staff unfailingly friendly and helpful and

Pool at Aparthotel Duva

the atmosphere fun and relaxed. A real winner.

Ctra. Port de Pollença km 58, Pollença ☎ 971 868 132. Fax: 971 867 316 www.duva-pollensa.com. Full board €30–70 (£20.10–46.90) per person. Children 2–12 50% reduction. Under 12s free. Self-catering apartments €45–115 (£30.15–77.10) sleeping 2–4. Amenities: bar, restaurant, swimming pool, gym, spa, tennis courts, paddle tennis, beach volleyball, kids' club, horse riding, paella making demonstration, bingo, mini disco. In room: satellite TV, telephone, air-conditioning, heating, balcony, free WiFi.

Son Brull The ochre walls of this posh rural accommodation set in a stately 18th century monastery have a somewhat sombre aspect from outside, but reveal a glamorous and comfortable interior within. Despite the designer trip, children and teenagers are welcome and seem to revel in their new-found, jet-set status. Handsomely draped day-beds overlooking the pool and fields beyond give Son Brull the feel of a rural supper club – the kind of place one is more likely to see in Barcelona or Palma than out in the *campo*. Bedrooms are all large with dark wood frames, tadelact (polished cement) floors, long drapes and plain white walls. The effect is calming rather than austere, and complemented by well-chosen art works and occasional blooms. Impeccable service gives this an edge over similar places.

Ctra. Palma-Pollença PM220 km 49.8, Pollença ☎ 971 535 353. Fax: 971 531 068. www.sonbrull.com. 23 rooms. Superior double €206–292 (£138–195.60). Deluxe €309–348

(£207–233.15). *Junior suite €412–504 (£276–337.70). Deluxe with terrace €515–637 (£345.10–426.80). Junior suite with terrace €618–743 (£414.10–497.80). Extra bed €70–108 (£46.90–72.35). Cot €20 (£13.40). Half-board €41–40 (£27.50–26.80) supplement. Amenities: gourmet restaurant serving avant-garde Mallorcan fayre, U-bar in the old olive press playing chillout music, spa, swimming pool, WiFi zones, nearby golf, cooking experiences and wine tastings. In room: A/C, heating, satellite TV, DVD player, music, non-smoking rooms, WiFi.*

Hotel Cala Sant Vicenç ★

For a similar experience at half the price, the Hotel Cala Sant Vicenç, a sturdy terracotta mansion with arcaded white windows overlooking the bay, is less plush than Son Brull but no less comfortable. It may even be a better bet for families with younger children. A good-sized pool is surrounded by mature gardens. The rooms make use of rustic furniture, with cooling blue linens and bags of space.

C/Maressers 2, Cala Sant Vicenç, Pollença ☎ 971 530 250. Fax: 971 532 084. www.hotelcala.com. Standard €127–204 (£85.10–136.70). Superior €163–246 (£109.20–164.80). Junior suite €202–289 (£135.35–193.60). Extra bed €79–104.30 (£52.90–69.90). Cot €17.50 (£11.75). Half-board supplement €49 (£32.80). Amenities: Restaurant Cavall Bernat for high-end cuisine, Trattoria Cala Sant Vicenç for low-key nights out, poolside grill, swimming pool, gym, sauna and beauty area. In room: A/C, heating, satellite TV.

Sa Duaia ★ ★ ★ FIND This

spectacular, windswept spot feels like the edge of the world: it's a remote and untouched corner of the island, surrounded by umber mountains, with rippling wild grasses reflecting the waves (and views of Mallorca) in the foreground. Book well in advance to secure accommodation, as it's particularly popular with Spanish families. It has a decent-sized swimming pool, wild and romantic terraces that could easily have been plucked from the Arizona desert with their cactus and palm trees, and an excellent, rustic restaurant serving wood-roasted meats with all the trimmings. Traditional dishes include rabbit with onions, goat kid and snails. For children, it has the unusual distinction of displaying its menus on laptop screens so fussy eaters can see a photograph of their options before they commit to one. It's also good for active families, offering mountain-biking and trekking excursions.

Ctra. Artà–Cala Torta km 8, Artà ☎ 651 826 416. Fax: 971 810 033 www.sa duaia.com. 6 rooms. Double €22–31 (£14.75–20.75). Junior Suite €63–95 (£42.20–63.65). 4-person apartment €74–109 (£49.60–73). 6-person villa with swimming pool €140–210 (£93.80–140.70). 10% discount on stays of more than 3 days. 20% discount on stays of more than 10 days. Breakfast €6 (£4). Main courses €13.50–20.50 (£9.10–13.75). Amenities: restaurant, bar, swimming pool, gardens. In Room: A/C, heating, TV.

Hotel Parc Natural ★ As the name suggests, this resort-style hotel is sandwiched between the beaches of Alcúdia and the wetlands of the Albufera Natural Park, facing the beach of Playa de Muro, making it a top spot for an active holiday. The service stands out: staff go out of their way to ensure your stay goes without a hitch. All of the spacious bedrooms have terraces with views over the garden (cheaper) or the sea. To keep the children amused, there's plenty of blow-off-steam action in the form of swimming, bikes and other sports, while parents get to indulge in a little R&R. It's a good compromise if you want something a cut above the usual resort-style package. As with many of the large chain hotels on the islands, it's worth looking online or making a call to check for deals. They can be amazingly good value.

Family Entertainment in Port de Alcúdia

Shows, *espectaculos* **as the Spanish call them, mainly take place** within the resorts themselves. Those at the **Hotel Marina Delfin Verde** (see p. 97) have been singled out for their varied programme ranging from *Lord of the Dance* to racy comedians. It's not everybody's cup of tea, but over the course of a week you should find something to suit, and on the whole the standard is above average. Entertainment is usually free for guests; occasionally a minimal price is added for non-guests, usually less than €10 (£6.70). Book direct with the hotel.

Ctra. Alcúdia–Artà s/n, Playa de Muro
☏ *971 820 017* **www.grupotel.com**.
*142 rooms. Double from €105
(£70.35). V, MC, AE. Amenities:
restaurant, bar, large swimming pool
with childrens paddling pool, massage, bicycles, sports programmes,
beach volleyball, gym, ping-pong,
live music, disco. In room: heating,
A/C, telephone, satellite TV with
music channel, safe, mini-bar, balcony with garden or sea view.*

FAMILY-FRIENDLY DINING

Mirador de la Victoria ★ Set
amid a pine-forest, this place has
an element of the fairytale about
it, and great views over the bay of
Pollença. It's great for families
with a kiddies' play park nearby.
The extensive menu features paellas, fresh fish and grilled meats, as
well as more elaborate dishes of
rabbit with onions and snails,
and lip-smacking fig ice-cream.
Combine it with the adjacent
beach and you have the makings
of a great family day out.

Ctra. Cabo Pinar Alcúdia, Alcúdia
☏ *971 547 173. Fax: 971 547 173.
Lunchtime menú €13.50 (£9.10).
Main courses €11–20 (£7.40–13.40).
Highchairs. All credit cards.
Reservations recommended.*

**Restaurante y Pizzeria Ca
n'Olesa** A charming lunch or
dinner spot with the best views
of the plaza, the menu here is
a mixed bag of authentic
Mallorquín cooking and good,
thin-crusted, chewy pizzas with
a range of interesting toppings
from *bresaola* (cured beef) and

ruccola, to simpler tomato,
buffalo mozzarella, basil and
oregano. Express an interest in
local wines and the delightful
staff will be happy to advise.

Plaça Major 12, Pollença ☏ *971 532
908. Mains €8–21 (£5.35–14.10).
Highchairs. V, MC. Reservations
recommended.*

Balaixa ★ ★ ▣▣▣ The beautiful
old Mallorcan farmhouse has
buckets of charm as well as
lots of nooks and crannies and
garden terraces for games of
hide and seek. Result? Romance
for mums and dads, fun and
games for the children. The
swimming pool is an added
bonus for lunch, and the fayre is
solid Mediterranean with something to please everyone.

*Ctra. Puerto Pollença, Port de
Pollença* ☏ *971 530 659* **www.
balaixa.com**. *Three-course lunch
with wine €15 (£10.05). V, MC.
Reservations recommended.*

Ca'n Pacienci Another beautiful stone farmhouse tucked away
down an unpaved lane, this
tasteful country restaurant offers
an unusual repertoire mixing
top-notch potted crab and
grilled asparagus with exotic
twists like Thai beef salad,
Peking Duck and Goan prawn
curry. The surrounds by contrast
have a lovely old-world feel, with
a sheltered terrace surrounded by
flower-clad stone walls, exposed
wood beams and beautiful brick
fireplaces. A great choice if
you're looking for somewhere
special and a little bit different,
for adventurous eaters.

Ctra. Port de Pollença km 54, Port de Pollença ☏ 971 530 787. Open Mon–Sat, evenings only. Mains €18–25 (£12.10–16.75). V, MC. Reservations recommended.

Al Fresco ★ A great option for picnics when you can't make your own, Al Fresco serves a wide range of freshly-made sandwiches on various breads, as well as salads, *panini* (toasted sandwiches) and substantial mains like fish and chips, pasta, curries and paellas. All to take away.

C/Méndez Nuñez 10, Port de Pollença ☏ 971 865 904. Sandwiches from €4 (£2.70). No credit cards, no reservations.

Sa Plaça As the name suggests, this friendly little bistro commands a top spot on the central square, and despite the rather formal, wedding-reception-style decor, has a laid-back air. It's a good place for lunch, offering a mix of salads, steaks and tapas, as well as a dedicated childrens' menu.

Plaça Constitució 8, Alcúdia ☏ 971 548 793. Main courses €6–12 (£4–8). V, MC. Reservations recommended.

Piero Rossi ★★ FIND If you ask the children, Piero Rossi ranks as a favourite for friendly service and finger-licking pizza cooked in a wood-fired oven. It's at its best in summer when meals are served by candlelight on the terrace. The balance for families is just right, offering sophisticated

palates the full gamut of carpaccios, salads, home-made pasta, meat and fish dishes. It's also excellent value for money: most meals cost around €25–35 (£16.75–23.50) for three courses including wine. A children's menu is available.

Ctra. Alcanada 3, Port d'Alcúdia ☏ 971 548 611. Highchairs. Three courses including wine €25–35 (£16.75–23.50). V, MC. Reservations recommended.

Sa Xarxa ★★★ An established favourite among locals and in-the-know tourists, Sa Xarxa's tables spill off the narrow, wrap-around terrace and on to the pine-shaded pavement. At first it seems like all the other *chiringuitos*, but close inspection reveals a more sophisticated restaurant where a cosy interior is decked with fishing paraphernalia and lit by candles. By night it's great for romantic dinners; by day a favourite family haunt. The specials here, as one would expect, are grilled, boat-fresh fish like meaty *Cap Roig* (scorpion fish), *gallo* (John Dory) and locally caught prawns, as well as whole *dorado* (gilt-head bream) baked in salt, Argentinian steaks and toothsome home-made tapas. Worth travelling for. If you can, time your arrival for sunset over the Bahia d'Alcúdia.

Passeo del Mar s/n, Colonia de Sant Pere ☏ 971 589 251 www.sa-xarxa. com. Mains €15–20 (£10.05–13.40). V, MC. Reservations essential.

6 East Mallorca from Cala Rajada to Santanyí

MALLORCA EAST

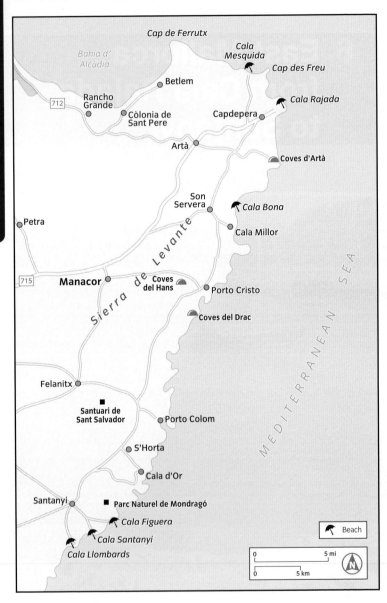

Cap de Ferrutx

Cala Mesquida

Cap des Freu

Bahía d' Alcúdia

Betlem

Rancho Grande

712

Còlonia de Sant Pere

Cala Rajada

Capdepera

Artà

Coves d'Artà

Son Servera

Cala Bona

Cala Millor

Petra

715

Manacor

Coves del Hans

Sierra de Levante

Porto Cristo

Coves del Drac

MEDITERRANEAN SEA

Felanitx

Santuari de Sant Salvador

Porto Colom

S'Horta

Cala d'Or

Santanyí

Parc Naturel de Mondragó

Cala Figuera

Cala Santanyí

Cala Llombards

Beach

| 0 | | 5 mi |
| 0 | 5 km | |

N

The east of Mallorca consists mainly of template resort towns – think Benidorm and Torremolinos on the mainland – with a handful of authentic fishing towns like Porto Cristo sprinkled in between. The bulk of the coast is neither as beautiful as the south, nor as family-friendly as the beaches of the north, nor as dramatic as the west. That makes it generally cheaper than the rest of the island, if lacking in genuine *Mallorquín* character; nearly every place has a British feel, though the resorts themselves are all family-focussed. That said, in areas like Cala de Mondragó you can still find virgin beaches, especially if you're prepared to hike. Still, your children may well have more fun making new friends in the chock-full entertainment schedules here than they will soaking up the atmosphere in more scenic towns.

The east is also home to Mallorca's most stunning caves, each of them vying for the top position. Whether you choose to visit just one, or see a few, eastern Mallorca's grottoes always impress.

ESSENTIALS

Getting There & Around

If you don't have a hire car, buses from Palma to the east coast and the **Calas de Mallorca** – a string of small beaches and resorts that occupy the southern stretch of this coast – number up to 10 a day in high season, but they do get crowded. In high season you can expect journey times to take around two hours from Palma, while hopping up and down the coast between resorts can take anything from 30 minutes to two hours. Frequent shuttle buses run up and down the coast every day. See *http://tib.caib.es/index.en.htm* or phone ☎ *971 177 777* for up-to-the-minute information on schedules.

Most buses are not particularly pushchair-friendly, and this is made worse when they're busy. Tickets cost €1.50 (£1) one-way between resorts, and €4.50 (£3) one way from Palma to main towns like Cala Rajada and Porto Cristo. Lines 400 and 500 cover the east coast. The 411 goes from Palma to Cala Rajada,

the 412 from Palma to Porto Cristo. There is no train covering this part of the island. As for elsewhere, the ideal way of getting around is by hire car. See p. 30.

Many of the resorts will simply bus you in from the airport, and there's no shortage of excursions once you are ensconced in your new abode. These range from club nights for older teens, where a supervised bus visits the area's best discos (usually including alcoholic drinks), to trips to the island's theme parks.

Boats from Cala Rajada to **Ciutadella,** Menorca, take one hour and run twice a day with **Cape Balear** (☎ *902 100 444, www.capebalear.es*). It is fairly expensive: €60 (£40.20) one-way for adults with a 50% discount for children under 12, but it is a quick and convenient way to get a taste of one of the highlights of the smaller islands.

Visitor Information

There are tourist offices in every town and village along the east coast. The bigger ones are **OIT**

Cala Ferrera – Felanitx (Avda. de s'Horta 35, Cala Ferrera ☎ 971 659 760; turisme@felanitx.org), **OIT Cales de Mallorca** (Centre Cívic, Passeig de Manacor, Cales de Mallorca ☎ 971 834 144. *Fax: 971 833 179 www.manacor.org*), **OIT Porto Cristo** (Passeig del Moll s/n, Porto Cristo ☎ 971 815 103. *Fax: 971 849 105 www. manacor.org*), **OIT Cala Bona - Son Servera** (Passeig del Moll s/n, Cala Bona ☎ 971 585 864 *www.sonservera.com*) and **Municipal TIO Cala Ratjada – Capdepera** (C/Castellet 5, Cala Rajada ☎ 971 563 033. *Fax: 971 565 256. www.ajcapdepera.net*). Also useful is the website *www. firstsunmallorca.com*.

Orientation

The east coast is backed by the Serra de Llevant, a pleasing if less dramatic mountain range that mirrors the Tramuntana in the west. This smaller-scale, farm country has its own rewards in terms of aesthetics: dotted with windmills and easily scalable heights, there's plenty of outdoor fun to be had.

The main road that snakes its way across the bottom of these hills is the PM-610, with various tributaries running off it to get to the *calas* (small bays and beaches).

Most of the towns and villages are purpose-built resorts, and can seem a little soulless. It's often described as 'Little Britain in the Sun'. But there are a couple of authentic towns, notably **Porto Cristo** and **Cala Rajada,** which succeed in reconnecting you with Spanish life.

Child-friendly Events

The festival of **Pa Virgen del Carmen** on July 16th kicks off in port towns all over the island, but the one in **Cala Rajada** is particularly colourful: a procession of

Playing on the Beach, Porto Cristo

boats, gaily decorated in bunting, ribbons and flags, that floats through the harbour.

Equally colourful, but this time floating across the sky, the annual **Regata Internacional 'Bahia de Cala Millor'** takes place over the last five days of October. It attracts hot-air balloon aficionados from all over Europe, the US and Africa, and makes for one of the most bewitching spectacles on the island. Contact **Mallorca Balloons** (PO Box 11, Cala Ratajada ☎ *971 565 332/971 818 182. Fax: 971 565 332 www. mallorcaballoons.com*) for more information about the regatta, as well as balloon rides for your family, see p. 112.

WHAT TO SEE & DO

No trip to Mallorca is complete without visiting the island's impressive network of caves and grottoes, most of which are located near the east coast. These limestone caverns, sculpted over millennia by dripping rain and seawater, provide a fairytale landscape that delights young and old alike. Should the rain fall in Mallorca it's definitely something to have up your sleeve and the **Cuevas des Hams** and **Cuevas del Drach** are both well worth a visit.

If spending the day underground isn't quite your cup of tea, take time out in the **Parc Natural de Mondragó**. Declared a Natural Park in 1992, the wetlands, forest, sand dunes and virgin beaches make this one of the loveliest coastal parks on the island, just perfect for combining easy walks with sandcastles and swimming.

Resorts & Towns

With more class than most of the east coast's resorts, **Cala Rajada** nevertheless still has its fair share of *biergartens*. It's traditionally more popular with German tourists than Brits, though is gradually being 'discovered' by us. It's a reasonable seaside base for exploring this part of the island, with more to entertain the children than, say, **Artà**; although being tucked away on the tip can make it seem rather cut off, especially if you're keen to get to the bigger theme-park attractions near

Children's Top Attractions

- Exploring mysterious **caves and grottoes,** see p. 109.
- Building sandcastles at the **Parc Natural de Mondragó,** see p. 108.
- Standing on top of the world at the **Santuari de Sant Salvador,** see p. 111.
- Hot-air ballooning around **Cala Rajada,** see p. 112.

A Natural Gem

While pretty much every town and resort along this stretch has a beach, you need to head north or south (see Chapters 5 and 7) for the truly lovely ones. With one exception: the **Parc Natural de Mondragó** ★★ (℡ *971 181 022*), 8 km east of Santanyí, is one of Mallorca's best-kept secrets. Finding your perfect patch of sand means a walk through pine trees and sand dunes, dodging basking lizards and chirruping birds, and drinking in stunning views along the way. Take picnic fodder, sunscreen and some shade with you, and find a secluded spot in the dunes or the pines for a long, lazy family day out.

There are a couple of basic *chiringuitos* (beach bars) on the main beaches, which both boast idyllic white powder sand and impossibly blue water. But it's the smaller coves that make for the best snorkelling and rock pool exploration. To get here approach either from Cala Figuera to the south, or from Porto Petro to the north. Both towns have small tributary roads heading straight for the park. It's well signposted from either direction, but you will need to park the car and walk to the beaches. Unfortunately, there's no public transport.

Palma. That said, it has an intimate, comfortable feel about it that makes it a great place for a relaxing family holiday, especially if your children are young enough not to need too much entertaining. The best beaches are on the outskirts.

Cala Bona is a wholly more agreeable option than brash, brutish **Cala Millor** just along the coast. Here, a small fishing port forms the focal point of the village, with a number of restaurants and bars clustered around its fringes. There's not a great deal to do, but it is extremely popular with young families who want to avoid the full-on resort packages. The atmosphere at night, when everyone takes to the streets to promenade the

short distance around the port, is particularly engaging.

About half-way down the east coast, there's no shortage of things to do in **Porto Cristo.** While there is something quite old-fashioned about using it as a base, it's worth keeping in mind for a rainy day. Quiet streets are shaded by tunnels of pine, the harbour is bustling with various water-based activities, and it has several small, sandy beaches. It is also home to Mallorca's rather grim **Aquarium** (see 'Animal Magic', p. 110 for information on Mallorca's amazing new aquarium, just outside Palma), but that doesn't stop younger children from finding it endlessly fascinating. Still, the star attraction remains those caves.

Cala Mondragó Beach

Caverns & Grottoes & Caves

Cuevas del Drach ★★★

AGES 5 AND UP The 'Dragon's Cavern' is hands-down one of Mallorca's top sights. A world-class attraction comprising a strange and mysterious underground labyrinth of stalactites and stalagmites dripping from the ceiling and rising from the floor like great wax sculptures: a Buddha, fairies, witches and warlocks can all be made out, among other creatures and mythical scenes. It's as fantastical and mesmerising as any Disney movie, and takes a good hour to get around. It also boasts the world's largest underground lake, named after its discoverer Edouard Martel in the late 19th century. A boat ride is unmissable. The only downside is its popularity, with thousands of sightseers turning out every day for a tour. Get there early to avoid long queuing times.

Carretera Cuevas, Porto Cristo
℡ 971 820 753. Fax: 971 815 089.
Open Nov–Mar, 10.45am–3.30pm daily; Apr–Oct, 10am–5pm daily. Closed Dec 25th and Jan 1st. Adults €9.50 (£6.40), children under 7 free.

Cuevas del Hams ★ **ALL AGES**

While not so immediately spectacular as the Cuevas del Drach, a recently opened new cave, specifically with

Entrance to Cuevas del Drach

smaller children in mind, makes this a perfect precursor to the mother caves just up the road. These were discovered by Pedro Caldentey in 1905 and are generally more tot-friendly: the formations are revealed with multi-coloured lights and given fantastical names like the Sea of Venice and Fairy Land. Another advantage here is that groups are small and guides are well-informed.

Ctra. Porto Cristo-Manacor s/n ℂ *971 820 988* **www.cuevas-hams.com**. *Open Apr–Oct, 10am–6pm, Nov–Mar, 10:30am–5pm. Adults €10 (£6.70), children under 12 free.*

Animal Magic

Aquarium de Mallorca

OVERRATED Mallorca's (for now) only aquarium is oddly depressing: a dark, dingy place with small, murky tanks – some cracked – providing tenement-like homes for miserable-looking fish. It's tempting not to put it in at all, but alas, little ones find it endlessly fascinating. Until the new one opens in Palma at the start of the 2007 season, Porto Cristo's offering boasts exotic fish from the Great Barrier Reef in the land of Oz, to Japanese Koi and Amazonian flesh-eating piranhas. Covering two floors, the 115 or so species even include locals like ugly, wobbly-jowled mero and arm-thick moray eels.

C/Gambi 7 – Apartado 61, Porto Cristo ℂ *971 820 971. Open Apr–Oct, 9:30am–5pm, Nov–Mar, 11am–3pm. €5.50 (£3.70), €3 (£2) children under 11, free for under 2s. 150 metres from the Cuevas del Drach.*

A Bit of Culture

Another of the east coast's hidden gems, the Jardins Casa March ★

AGES 5 AND UP or March House Gardens, in Cala Rajada, were once owned by the mega-rich Mallorcan banker Juan March. His passion was art, and his bequest to the area is among the most famous and admired in Spain, mainly for its impressive sculptures by Rodin and Henry Moore. While this all sounds rather grown-up, it's also a lovely garden to run around in, and a good place to let off some steam in an enclosed environment, especially if you're visiting out of season and it's too cool for the beach. In July, a series of evening concerts are held in the park, making for a charmed evening under the stars with a picnic and a bottle of wine. Anyone wishing more information on these, or to visit the collection during the day, needs to pre-book with the tourist office in the town (Municipal T.I.O. Cala Rajada – Capdepera, Cala Rajada ℂ *971 563 033. Fax: 971 565 256* **www.ajcapdepera.net**. €5 (£3.35), children under 12 €3 (£2). Ticket prices vary depending on the concert.

Castle in the Clouds

About 15 minutes' drive east of Felanitx, just off the PM-401, is a steep, vertigo-inducing climb up to the *Refugio* of the **Santuari de Sant Salvador** ★★★ **AGES 12 AND UP** You'll need to be fairly fit to tackle it. While most kids seem to zoom to the top like mountain goats, parents may well find themselves lagging behind. Allow at least one-and-half hours and carry at least a litre of water per person. If that's not put you off, the effort is well worth it, and you can feel extra saintly as the cars bomb past, because at the top you'll find what may be the best view on the entire island. The whole of Mallorca is spread out below you: to the east, **Porto Colom** and the rippling hills of the Serra de Levante; to the south-east flat, alluvial plains stretching as far as the eye can see and ending in a hazy blur, with **Cabrera** (see Chapter 7) a low, black silhouette on a silver sea; to the west, on a clear day, the Tramuntana (the Serra de Levante's bigger mirror image; see Chapter 4) rise majestically, forming a natural frontier to the rest of the world; to the north the bay of **Alcúdia** (see Chapter 5) shimmers silver. The only sound is the whistle of the wind as it whips through the pine-encrusted mount; a sigh of loneliness. Perched on top of the highest point of the Serra de Levante, the sanctuary here was built in the 14th century, and remained home to the monks until 1992. It sprawls over two hilltops, the first crowned with a larger-than-life figure of Christ and the sanctuary itself, the second marked with a concrete cross facing north. Both sunset and sunrise are memorable, and basic accommodation is available (Puig de Sant Salvador, Felanitx ☎ *971 827 282*. Double €30 (£20.10)) should you wish to spend the night. There is no public transport to the top, but there is plenty of parking. Super-fit families can cycle it.

Safari Zoo This small animal park has everything from farm-yard beasties to exotic critters: zebras, hippos, tigers, crocs, baboons and rhinos. The three-kilometre circuit can be done by train or car, and as places of this ilk go, it's well put together. Note that the lion and tiger show is only on during high season, April to November.

Ctra Porto Cristo-Cala Millor, Sa Coma ☎ 971 810 909. Fax: 971 810 484. Open year round 9am–7pm. Adults €12 (£8), children under 12 €7 (£4.70).

Adventures for Active Families

Albatros Diving AGES 8 AND UP

You can't miss the turquoise-painted shop front at the east coast's premier dive outfit (they have another branch at Cala Figuera). Bubblemaker programmes for children aged 8–10 give tots a taste of underwater magic by taking them to a shallow bay a few metres away. There they'll get a chance to see a few fish, octopus and shells.

For older children, 'try dives' are a good way to find out what they think before embarking on an expensive open water course. The area is not so hot on fish action, but it does have a pleasing network of caves and grottoes, corals and polyps, eels and other underwater wiggling things. Night dives and other specialist courses are also available.

Port de Cala Bona 18 ☎ *971 586 807. Mobile: 653 477 560 www.albatros-diving.com. PADI Open Water Dive course €320 (£214.40) (4 days). Try Dive/Bubblemaker €80 (£53.60). Supervised snorkelling trip by speedboat €30 (£20.10).*

Hot-air Ballooning ★ ALL AGES

Floating peacefully above the island is a magical and memorable way to see it. This bird's eye view is about as close as the family will ever get to sprouting wings, and there's nothing quite like hanging out in a basket beneath a brightly coloured canopy. The fleet now has eight different balloons – designed for different-sized groups – including one that can take a massive 16 people, making it the biggest hot air balloon in Spain.

Mallorca Balloons, PO Box 11, Cala Rajada ☎ *971 565 332 / 818 182. Fax: 971 565 332. Open Mar–Oct, 9am–1pm, 4.30pm–7.30pm. Adults €120 (£80.40) for 30 minutes, children aged up to 11 €60 (£40.20) for 30 minutes. Not suitable for anyone with vertigo.*

Glass-bottomed Boat Rides

ALL AGES A little less sedate, the glass-bottomed boat service zips up and down the east coast, with

Albatros Diving

jumping on and off points just like the open-top tourist buses in Palma. It stops in pretty much every port from Cala Rajada to Calas de Mallorca. Trips last about 90 minutes and enable children to explore the underwater world through the safety of pressurised glass.

Port de Porto Cristo s/n ☎ *639 654 848. Adults and children €12 (£8) one-way.*

FAMILY-FRIENDLY ACCOMMODATION

Hostal Ca's Bombu VALUE Set a block or two back from the sea, Ca's Bombu is a particularly good overnight option if you plan to get the ferry to Ciutadella (Menorca) early the next morning. A family-oriented, friendly place, this was the first hotel to open in Cala Rajada and dates back to 1885, as evidenced by the older section of the hotel with its wood panelling and black-and-white marble floors. The bedrooms have less character, but are clean and comfortable. The bonus is a good-sized swimming pool set around a pretty, bougainvillea-filled terrace.

C/Leonor Servera 86, Cala Rajada ☎ 971 563 203. Fax: 971 563 246 www.casbombu.com. 50 rooms. Double, €36 (£24.10). Singles, €24 (£16.10). Single, Room with extra bed €41–47 (£27.50–31.50). Breakfast included. V, MC. Amenities: restaurant, bar, swimming pool. In room: very basic with fan.

Aparthotel Bonaire ★ A modern and unashamedly family-friendly resort hotel best for those seeking a relaxing poolside holiday. Friendly and energetic young staff provide constant supervised entertainment for children of all ages and plenty of activities for adults, too. A small natural beach is just 200 metres away, and the larger Cala Millor a walk of two kilometres. Note that out of season the atmosphere changes dramatically, with a more elderly clientele and many bars and restaurants closed. Throughout 2007, the Aparthotel Bonaire is offering a 10% discount to celebrate its 10-year anniversary.

Ctra. Cala Bona-Costa de los Pinos s/n, Cala Bona ☎ 971 813 733 www.protur-hotels.com. Apartments from €100 (£67) a night. Amenities: outdoor and indoor pools, gardens, gym, hairdressing salon, crèche (in summer season), children's club and entertainment, evening entertainment, Internet access, games and sports matches. In room: A/C, balcony, lounge, kitchenette with microwave, direct telephone, satellite TV, safe.

Hotel Felip VALUE If you're going to stay in Porto Cristo, you might as well be overlooking the port and beach: the old-school Hotel Felip fits the bill nicely. Black-and-white marble floors, a long wooden bar and pastel-striped sofas and armchairs give it a faintly *fin de siècle* vibe, entirely appropriate to its 100-year history. It is nothing of the sort of course, and the smallish rooms come with all mod cons, if the decor is somewhat dated. It's great for families with youngish children who get to make new friends round the swimming pool.

C/Burdils 41, Porto Cristo ☎ 971 820 750. Fax: 971 820 594 www.thbhotels.com. 88 rooms. Double €34.50–65.50 (£23.10–43.90) incl. breakfast; an extra bed is available at 15% off the full price. Children aged 0–12 get a 50% discount off the full price. Cots free. Amenities: restaurant, bar, swimming pool, garden. In room: hairdryer, bath, balcony, satellite TV, A/C, heating, mini-bar, safe, Internet access.

Blau Porto Petro Beach Resort & Spa ★★ A five-star hotel that goes all out for the kiddies, this newly built goliath is located on the edge of the Mondragó nature reserve, and fronts a wide sweep of deep blue Med. The Blau chain is geared towards children, though it is probably better suited to young ones than teens, offering a wide range of services and activities to keep tots happy. Its Kids' Club consistently ranks as one of the best on the island, and it's a good way to do a family holiday in style. Added bonus points include a gourmet restaurant,

Ran de Mar, which has a children's play area, and special allotted times in the spa for children. It is expensive, but if you want to treat yourself, as well as the children, the extra pennies are worth it. As with many chain hotels on the island, room prices can vary wildly depending on season and availability, so be sure to ask about special offers.

Avenida des Far 12, Porto Petro 📞 *971 648 282. Fax: 971 648 283* *www.blau-hotels.com. Suite for 2 adults & 2 children €205–605 (£137.35–405.35). Amenities: free parking, 24-hour concierge, 4 restaurants, 3 bars, children's pool, free child-minding during the day, babysitters at night, swimming lessons Jun-Sep. In room: A/C, balcony/ terrace, ADSL, telephone, cable TV, mini-bar, kettle, separate shower and bath, hairdryer, 24-hour room service, turn-down service.*

Son Mas ★★★ FIND Located four kilometres inland from the beach, Son Mas is a true country retreat, yet within striking distance of the action. Located in a 17th century mill-house, the renovation is sympathetic and tasteful, opening up the building to let in natural light while preserving original features. Cotton drapes, exposed beams, wood floors and stone add up to give it an elegant yet relaxed air that is truly a cut above the usual family accommodation. It's a home-from-home for anyone looking for something a little special. Children are welcome and there's plenty of open space for running around, as well as a couple of added extras: the infinity

pool overlooking the Serra de Levante and superb food.

Camino de Son Mas, Porto Cristo 📞 *971 558 755. Fax: 971 558 756 16 rooms, suites only. Suite €237–260 (£158.80–174.20). Extra bed €59–65 (£39.50–43.55). V, MC. Amenities: large outdoor infinity pool, heated indoor pool, sauna and Jacuzzi, various communal areas and lounges, restaurant, children's menu at €17.50 (£11.75). In room: air-conditioning, satellite TV, direct telephone, Internet connection, safe, mini-bar, full bathrooms with bath and shower, separate toilet, hairdryer.*

FAMILY-FRIENDLY DINING

The east coast towns offer pretty much the same fayre as each other, at similar prices: from grilled fish and meat, to pizzas and pasta. As a rule, anything with a view of the port or sea will be more touristy than something a street or two back.

Cala Rajada

Es Recó Des Moll ★ FIND One street back from the port, Es Reco does superb fresh fish and seafood in a genuine *Mallorquín* environment. The grey-blue shutters and simple decor give it a laid-back air, while friendly staff welcome your brood with open arms. While children get to feast on home-cooked croquettes and the like, adults can try unusual treats like prawns with *gulas* (baby eels), *pulpitos* (baby octopus) and grilled *navajas* (razor clams). The daily catch is chalked

Es Recó Des Moll, Cala Rajada

up on the board outside, with prawns,
mussels, clams and local fish all sold by weight. There are steaks and *Mallorquín* specials for non-fish lovers, and it also has a solid, mainly Spanish, wine list.

C/Ca's Bombu 2, Cala Rajada ☎ 971 564 849. No outside seating. Mains €8–21 (£5.35–14.10). V, MC. Open 1pm–4pm, 8.30pm–11pm. Closed Sun and Mon.

Bar Café Sa Cova In a cute spot right against the water's edge, this has long been a favourite among German families (the owners are German) and their children for its good value, eat-as-much-as-you-can casual dining. Several different breakfasts, lunch and dinner are served, under various themes: a BBQ on Thursdays offering sausages, kebabs, salad, fish, baked potatoes; brunch; paella on Sundays; tapas on Mondays. You can't really go wrong.

Cala Lliteras s/n, Cala Rajada ☎ 606 949 403 www.sa-cova.com. Open daily 9.30am–11pm. Happy hour

6pm–8pm. BBQ €14 (£9.40) per head; paella €7 (£4.70) per head; brunch 10am–4pm, €12 (£8) per head. No credit cards.

Cala Bona

Ca'n Julia ★★ FIND If your travels do take you to Cala Bona or Cala Millor, it's worth heading out of town in the evening for dinner at Ca'n Julia, a locals' spot in an old townhouse in the neighbouring village of Son Servera. Gracious, happy hosts have converted their garden into an outdoor dining room and grill, serving home-cooked meals with gusto. It's all excellent, and even the pickiest eaters seem to enter into it with enthusiasm. Choose from sumptuous paellas or mountains of crisp, fried *chipirones* (baby squid); BBQ chicken, kebabs and steaks; or the house special, a slow-cooked shoulder of lamb, bathed in tomatoes and mountain herbs. The only thing to avoid is the house wine, which tastes like it has sat in carafes for too long. Splash out on a decent Mallorcan bottle instead.

C/Juan Massanet 42, Son Servera 📞 *971 567 413. Closed Mon. Mains €6–11 (£4–7.40). No credit cards. Open 1.30pm–3.30pm, 8.30pm–11pm.*

Fonoll Marí A rustic restaurant on the main drag, Fonoll Marí is named after an edible succulent that grows on the cliffs here, and is pickled to serve with cheese and charcuterie. The food is nicely cooked, traditional Mallorcan fayre, with a twist on the usual offerings. Try the sole with almond sauce.

C/Passeig del Moll 24, Cala Bona 📞 *971 813 641. Mains €8.50–14.50 (£5.70–9.70). V, MC. Open 1pm–4pm, 8.30pm–11pm. Closed Sun.*

Porto Cristo

Siroco Away from the main drag, Siroco occupies a pleasant spot overlooking Es Riuet – the hook-shaped section of canal that runs off the main harbour – offering the usual selection of paella, fish, seafood and decent children's plates at standards a touch higher than elsewhere in town.

C/Verí s/n, Porto Cristo 📞 *971 822 444. Mains €11–16.50 (£7.40–11.10). V, MC. Open daily 1pm–4pm, 8.30pm–11pm.*

Pambolieria Cap D'Es Toi

VALUE Also away from the main drag – this time facing the back of the town – this canalside bistro specialises in the ubiquitous *pa amb oli*, as well as some slightly more inventive offerings. Here you can get pear and Roquefort, or celery, walnut and apple salads, alongside the usual pizzas, pastas and fish dishes. In fact, the selection is huge, so you're bound to find something to satisfy the children. They also get their own kids' menu for under €5 (£3.35). A bargain.

Passeig es Riuet s/n, Porto Cristo 📞 *971 822 578. Mains €7–14 (£4.70–9.40). V, MC. Open daily 1pm–4pm, 8.30pm–11pm.*

Cala Bona

MALLORCA SOUTH

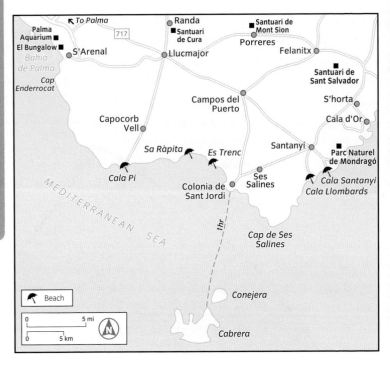

To Palma
Palma Aquarium ■
El Bungalow ■
S'Arenal
Bahía de Palma
Cap Enderrocat
717
Randa
Santuari de Cura ■
Llucmajor
Porreres
Santuari de Mont Sion ■
Felanitx
Santuari de Sant Salvador ■
Campos del Puerto
S'horta
Cala d'Or
Capocorb Vell ●
Sa Ràpita
Es Trenc
Santanyí
Parc Naturel de Mondragó ■
Cala Pi
Colonia de Sant Jordi
Ses Salines
Cala Santanyí
Cala Llombards
MEDITERRANEAN SEA
1hr
Cap de Ses Salines
Conejera
Beach
0   5 mi
0   5 km
Cabrera

The southern coast of Mallorca seems to belong to another island: flat, windswept, with fields of wheat and old-fashioned windmills lining the horizon. It remains Mallorca's least visited coastline, with few big beaches to draw the crowds. For that reason it's nearly always possible to escape the masses here, even in high season. The only exception is long, sandy **Es Trenc** beach, which draws locals and visitors from the interior, and even Palma.

Es Trenc aside, the coast is mostly tiny coves, and has avoided much of the overblown development of the east and north. The coves that run up the island's south-east edge, after **Cap de Ses Salines,** are the most attractive. **Còlonia de Sant Jordi,** just beyond Es Trenc to the south-east, is the area's largest resort. The planned developments on the edge of town aren't terribly appealing, but its port is charming. This is the place to get a boat to the archipelago nature reserve, **Cabrera.**

Inland is a pine-covered wilderness. Its few, well-spread villages, hamlets and farmsteads offer little other than some prehistoric sites, but they do house some of Mallorca's loveliest and most secluded country hotels.

ESSENTIALS

Getting There & Around

Your own transport, whether car or bike, is invaluable, especially if you're staying in one of the south's remote country houses or farmhouse hotels, or plan to do much moving around. For local bike hire, contact Juan at **Hostal Colonial** (see 'Family-friendly Accommodation', p. 127). For car hire, see p. 30.

Buses also serve the area and cost between €1.45 (£0.95) and €4.50 (£3) for a single journey. With the odd exception they do not have special pushchair ramps and overhead lockers, so be prepared to heave-ho if you have a baby on board. Palma to Campos takes about an hour, Palma to Santanyí about one-and-a-half hours, and Palma to Cala Pi about one hour. The following routes serve the region:

 500 Palma–S'Arenal–Llucmajor–Campos

● 501 Palma–S'Arenal–Polígono Llucmajor–Llucmajor–Campos–Santanyí–S'Alquieria–Calonge–Cala Ferrera–Cala d'Or–Cala Egos–Porto Petro–S'horta

● 502 Palma–S'Arenal–Polígono Llucmajor–Llucmajor–Campos–El Palmer–Còlonia de Sant Jordi–Ses Salines–Els Llombards–Cala Santanyí–Cala Figuera–Santanyí

● 515 Llucmajor–Son Bieló–S'Estanyol–Sa Ràpita–Campos

● 520 Palma–Hospital Son Llàtzer–S'Arenal–Las Palmeras–Delta Maioris–Sa Torre–Badia Blava–Badia Gran–El Dorado–Cala Pi

Timetables change frequently, so check for up-to-date information on ☏ 971 177 777, or online at *http://tib.caib.es/terrestre/autobusos.en.htm*.

Old Windmill

Visitor Information

In **Llucmajor** you'll find tourist information at Plaza Reina María Cristina s/n (📞 *971 440 414*); in **Santanyí** at Av. Cala Llonga, Cala D'Or (📞 *971 657 463*). The tourism office in **Còlonia de Sant Jordi** is at Centre Cívic, C/Dr Barraquer 5 (📞 *971 656 073*; open 8am–2pm Mon–Sat).

Orientation

The South is bisected by the C717 which runs from Palma to Porta Petro on the south-east coast, linking the area's few main settlements: from west to east, **Llucmajor, Campos** and **Santanyí**. The roads to the coast radiate out from this, making beach-hopping a bit of a round-about journey. **Cala Pi** is the westernmost attractive point, a tiny cove with self-catering apartments and second homes. In the middle part of the coast is the long, wild **Es Trenc** beach. Following the coast to the south you come to **Còlonia de Sant Jordi,** the area's main resort. Then there's the windswept southernmost point of Mallorca, **Cap de Ses Salines.** The coast turns north-east from here, and there's not much to see until the start of the east coast proper with the pretty coves and little resorts and fishing villages of **Cala Llombards, Cala Santanyí** and **Cala Figuera.**

WHAT TO SEE & DO

Child-friendly Events

Many of Mallorca's coastal towns and villages, like **Sa Rapita** and **Cala Figuera,** celebrate the festival of the **Virgen del Carmen** (*Mare de Déu del Carme* in Mallorquín), on the Sunday nearest to 16th July. The whole village decorates boats and takes a statue of the Virgin out for a jaunt on the water.

On the second Sunday in August, Llucmajor's **fiestas de Santa Candida,** celebrating the patron saint, feature religious processions and rituals. There are also pagan-flavoured festivities: concerts, dancing and parades of traditional figures – large giant statues and oversized, grotesque heads are carried through the streets by locals, to the accompaniment of traditional music.

Children's Top 5 Attractions

- The boat trip to **Cabrera,** see p. 124.
- Snorkelling off **Cala Llombards,** see p. 123.
- Shopping for presents at **Santanyí market,** see 'Towns down South', p. 121.
- Playing cowboys and Indians at **Botanícactus,** see p. 124.
- Star-gazing at **Finca Sant Blai,** see p. 128.

On 24th August **Ses Salines** celebrates **Sant Bartomeu's Day** with a big public paella, among other festivities. Take turns queuing up for your portion.

Towns Down South

The pleasant village of **Santanyí**, hewn from honey sandstone in 1300, maintains its historic character. It sits about 50 km south-east of Palma along the C717, just a few kilometres from the island's south-east coast and lovely little coves like **Cala Figuera**.

As you drive into town you'll spot the ancient sandstone gateway (**Sa Porta Murada**). Try to get a parking space just outside this. Walk through and enter a maze of narrow streets lined with squat cottages, which lead to the oblong-shaped main square, where there are plenty of eating and drinking opportunities. Head here on Saturday for the **weekly market** ★ when Pl. Major (the main square) and surrounding streets are filled with local bounty and traditional handicrafts like the 'cloth of tongues' (*roba de llengues*). Little girls who like pretty and shiny things will love the jewellery and accessory shop **Reina Rana** ★ (Pl. Major 15 ☎ 971 642 075; closed Sat afternoon and Sun). For lunch, try **Bar Sa Font** at Pl. Mayor 27 (☎ 971 163 492) for a wide variety of tasty crepes and hearty servings of *pa amb oli*.

Còlonia de Sant Jordi is the main resort on the south coast, with not unpleasant (though not that appealing either) holiday apartment developments on its outer reaches. The small port retains some charm, with local fishing boats adding colour and good restaurants serving fresh, locally caught fish. There's family-friendly accommodation, too (see p. 128). It has a small sand and rock beach, **Cala Galiota**: entering town from Campos, take the road straight into town, Av del Marques del Palmer, and take the ninth turning on the left, C/Major. Turn

Sa Porta Murada, Santanyí

left on to C/Ponent to get to the port, right on C/Puntassa to get to Cala Galiota. There's a car park at the beach.

Beaches & Resorts

The beaches and resorts listed below run west to east along the southern coast.

Cala Pi This is one of the older, more tasteful resorts on Mallorca, with low-rise developments hugging cliffs overlooking a tiny cove. The beach is sandy but small, with sunloungers and parasols for hire. The aquamarine waters and pretty little blue fishing boats are terribly photogenic. It's possible to climb up for a clifftop walk to nearby, rocky **Cala Bertran** (great for snorkelling) by following the steps hidden behind the beach's boathouses. Park in the Cala Pi car park and follow the signs to the beach (*platja*), accessed by a small set of steps. If you head towards the beach-houses and walk in front of them in the

direction of the sea you should find some steps to the right just before the last row of boat-houses. Climb the steps up to the roof of one of the houses, then take the rough-hewn stone steps up a steep, short climb to the clifftop path. Follow the path to the left. It leads down a slope and then rises and enters a gap in a stone wall. From here you can see the *atalayas* – military lookout towers that date back over 400 years. The path then divides – take the right path to Cala Bertran, a few minutes' walk away.

Es Trenc ★★ This virgin stretch of white powdery sand has its position in a national park to thank for being saved from developers. In summer it can be very crowded with poinsettia parasols jostling right up to the shore, but 3.5 km of sand means you can always find a space and it's particularly good for children because of its sandcastle potential and calm, shallow water.

Cala Pi

To find it, driving out of Sa Rapita towards Campos, you'll come to a badly-signed turn on the right. Take this, down a bumpy road through meadows, passing some old windmills. At the next junction turn right to Ses Covetes. You'll start seeing cars parked by the side of the road as you approach the beach, trying to avoid paying the car park fee further up (€4 (£2.70)). Leave the car, walk down the road until you reach some holiday homes and beach bars overlooking a scrappy bit of coast. Turn left as you face the sea and follow the coast for a few metres and you'll come to Es Trenc proper. Access to the other end of the sands is via the Campos–Còlonia de Sant Jordi road. About 6 km from Campos turn right at the salt flats. The road again leads to a pay car park near the beach (€4 (£2.70)). This end of the beach has no development and fewer tourists.

There is a bar which sells drinks and snacks and has shaded tables. You can also rent sunbeds and parasols.

Note that this beach is popular with **nudists.** Public nudity is perfectly legal on Mallorca, so you are likely to see it on any beach. But there are some beaches which have become traditional spots; this is one of them.

Es Port & Es Dolç These beaches run south-west from Còlonia de Sant Jordi's port. Es Port, as the name suggests, is right by the harbour. Small and busy, it's bordered by a palm-tree promenade and backed by apartment buildings, shops and cafes. You can hire sun loungers, beach parasols and pedal boats, and there are life-guards in season. Follow the promenade to the end of the beach (away from town) and then take a path along the coast for 250m to Es Dolç, a quieter, wilder beach backed by pine-covered dunes and with a sandy sea bed, a beach bar, and of course sun loungers and parasols.

Cala Llombards ★★ In this idyllic spot, easily reached by car, small fishermen's boathouses, with whitewashed walls and green doors overlook a thumb-nail of sandy beach nestled among low, pine-covered rocks. The water is crystalline blue with a sandy-rocky floor and some curious fish to watch through snorkelling masks. The bar-cafe (☎ *649 416 349*; closed Nov–March) serves sparklingly fresh fish, simply grilled and served with lemon. It's pricey for a no-frills beach bar, but the food is great and the situation unbeatable. There are sunbeds and beach umbrellas for hire, as well as showers and toilets.

Cala Santanyí This small beach resort has two hotels, some apartments and three restaurants. The gently sloping, sandy beach leads down to clear blue water, surrounded by sandstone cliffs topped with pines. Though small, the beach is bigger than many of the surrounding coves and so gets very full. The facili-ties include parking, a Red Cross station, beach umbrellas and loungers and pedal boats for hire.

Cala Figuera The most developed spot in this corner of the island, 4 km north of Cala Santanyí, this cute fishing port sports traditional whitewashed and green-shuttered cottages, giving it an almost chocolate-box character. There's no beach, but people sunbathe and swim from the slipways and rocks: there are steps to make getting in and out easier. If you need to buy necessaries, there's a supermarket and a pharmacy, as well as cafes and restaurants.

Nature Reserves & Historic Buildings

Botanícactus ★ AGES 5 AND UP
Fat ones, thin ones, spiky ones, furry ones, round ones, tall ones: there's a cactus for every mood, and this is one of Europe's biggest collections. As a botanical garden it's not particularly structured, and its claim to being the largest botanical garden in Europe concerns land space rather than species numbers, but it is a pleasurable amble through 150,000 square metres of tropical and arid vegetation. While it may not seem an obvious attraction for the children, its chaotic plan makes it rather like romping through an out-of-control maze – and it would take a hard heart indeed not to be enamoured of the real-life renditions of the cartoon cacti of youth. There are 12,000 in all, along with vast tropical and endemic gardens, and a man-made lake. Invariably quiet, this is a much underrated showpiece, and a must for any garden enthusiast.

Ctra. Ses Salines – Santanyí km 1, Ses Salines ☎ 971 649 494. Mobile: 619 119 676. Fax: 971 649 479 www. botanicactus.com. €6.90 (£4.60) adults, €4.20 (£2.80) children. Open summer 9am–7pm daily, winter 9am–5pm daily.

Cabrera National Park ★★★
AGES 8 AND UP This archipelago, an hour by boat south of Còlonia de Sant Jordi, has been called "The Mediterranean of Ulysses" on account of its wild beauty

---

Salines de Salobrar

If you take the PM604 road from Campos to Còlonia de Sant Jordi, as you approach Còlonia you will see to your right an enormous stretch of what, you may be forgiven for thinking, are mini, snow-covered mountains rising from a post-apocalyptic wasteland. These are the salt flats of **Salines de Salobrar,** which range for 130 hectares behind the beach at Es Trenc. The grey flats and glistening mounds of salt make for a stark kind of beauty. The fact that these salt deposits have been exploited since ancient times just adds to their eeriness. They're also the perfect spot for spotting rare migratory birds such as **Temminck's Stint** and the **White-winged Black Tern.**

and untouched, frozen-in-time feel. A visit to the main island of Cabrera (the only one open to the public) is a treat for nature lovers, particularly bird watchers and anyone who likes scrabbling around in rock pools. The islands are a veritable Galapagos in the Med – it's a favourite research spot for biologists, who've found species that appear nowhere else: from cliff-clinging plants to 10 subspecies of Balearic lizard, and several unique crustaceans in just one very popular cave. Rare birds that can be spotted here include the Audouin's gull and Eleanor's falcon. There are 23 feathered species living on the islands, and thousands more stop by during the migratory season. There are lizards everywhere – every step will produce a darting blur of brown or green as another sun-bathing reptile is disturbed.

But it's the wild beaches that are the big draw. There are two you are allowed to visit – the sandy **Sa Platgeta** and just next to it the rocky **Platja de S'Espalmador,** teeming with marine life. You can swim and snorkel, so be sure to bring your gear. The path to the beaches starts to the left (facing the sea) of the harbour. Just follow it around the coast past some accommodation buildings (used by research scientists) and after about 2 km you reach Sa Platgeta. Here there's a picnic area and toilets. There's also a pier, from where the boat back to Mallorca leaves. Do make sure your children respect the wildlife, particularly the marine life at the beaches.

Although there's no permanent human life on the island any more, it does have a rich, *Boys' Own* history. In the Middle Ages the islands were used by pirates as a base to launch raids on Mallorca. So in the late 14th century, Cabrera castle, which still stands overlooking the harbour, was built to house soldiers and keep the pirates at bay. It was given a change of use 400 years later when French prisoners of war were held here during the Napoleonic Wars: read soldiers' graffiti still etched on the walls. You can walk to the beaches and castle on your own, but to visit the **El Celler ethonographic museum,** to learn how people on the islands used to live, and the lighthouse, you'll need to go on one of the free guided tours. When you land at the harbour, the Cabrera guides will be waiting to give you more information about tours and meeting times.

The only way to get to the archipelago is on a tour with one of the tourist boat services that leave from Còlonia de Sant Jordi (like Excursions a Cabrera; see p. 126). Tickets must be booked in advance. If you have your own boat, you need a permit to moor within the park's boundaries, available from the National Parks office in Palma (Plaza de Espana 8,1 ☎ *971 725 010;* Cabrera@mma.es).

The island has a small information centre, toilets and a very limited bar (bring your own food and drink – and take your

A Hike for Active Families

If you and the family are keen walkers, a lovely way to take in some of the south's remote and wild beaches is on foot from the **lighthouse at Cap de Ses Salines to Còlonia de Sant Jordi.** It's a long way (about 4–5 hours' walking), so it's best to start from Ses Salines and get a taxi back to your car from Còlonia de Sant Jordi (ask at the Hostal Colonial: see 'Family-friendly Accommodation', p. 127). From the lighthouse, take the path that leads from the right of the coastal research station. After about 2 km you'll reach the virgin beach of **Es Caragol.** This wilderness is usually disturbed by boats that anchor just off the beach, spoiling the view somewhat. The beach of **Entugores** is another couple of kilometres, followed by **Ses Roquetes** and **Es Carbó.** Throughout the walk you'll have a magnificent view of Cabrera to the south: clean white sand and clear blue water.

Note: this walk involves some scrambling over rocks, and you'll be quite exposed to the sun: take a high-factor sunscreen. You'll also need to carry food and water. As the path passes through protected natural areas, there is no development, so no facilities like toilets. I wouldn't recommend it for children younger than 10.

rubbish away with you!). It's all at the harbour.

On the return journey – which will be very wet if you sit on deck at the front – the boat stops at **Sa Cova Blava** (the blue cave) with its strikingly blue water, so you can have a dip from the boat. You should arrive back at about 5pm.

Cabrera Island

Excursions a Cabrera, C/Lonja, Còlonia de Sant Jordi ✆ *971 649 034* **www.excursionsacabrera.com**. *€31–35 (£20.80–23.50) adults, €15–17 (£10.05–11.40) children 3–10, children 0–2 free. Lunch (not recommended) €7 (£4.70).*

Capocorb Vell AGES 6 AND UP

This prehistoric village is one of the most important archaeological sites on Mallorca. There are remains of over 30 buildings, including dwellings and grave sites, from the Tailotic era (1300–800 BC). A leaflet in English helps you to follow the marked trail around the settlement, and there's a cafe for thirsty time-travellers.

Ctra Llucmajor-Cap Blanc km 23 ✆ *971 180 155. Open 10am–5pm; closed Thu. €2 (£1.35).*

FAMILY-FRIENDLY ACCOMMODATION

Hotel Villa Sirena Named for its clifftop position, where normally you would expect to see a lighthouse, the Hotel Sirena is all about location. Its stark terraces tumble down to open sea, the more handsome for a lack of accessories. Expect nothing more than a sun bed and a parasol for shade. This is where the Sirena's flirtation with designer minimalism ends: rooms are 1980s Spanish vintage, clean, comfortable, but lacking much by way of features. The apartments are similar. On the plus side, all have balconies, with those looking out to sea the ones to bag. There's a pool for anyone disinclined to leap from the rocks.

C/Virgen del Carmen 37, Cala Figuera 971 645 303. Fax: 971 645 106 *www.hotelvillasirena.com. 45 double rooms and 2 apartment blocks. Double April, May €57 (£38.20); June–Oct €63 (£42.20). €40 (£26.80) per additional person in room. Apartment for 2, Jan–March, Nov, Dec €57 (£38.20); April, May €63 (£42.20); June–Oct €68 (£45.55). Apartment for 4, €98 (£65.70), €107 (£71.70), €112 (£75) respectively. Buffet breakfast inc. in room rates. Amenities: cyber-cafe, restaurant (12–3pm), bar-cafe, fax, taxi, parking garage, swimming pool, laundry, cots, car hire. In room: balcony, TV, phone, hairdryer, safe. In apartment: cleaning service, telephone, TV, hairdryer, safe, coffee maker, cot, garage, laundry, swimming pool, car hire. Can also use hotel facilities.*

Hotel Cala Santanyí

Particularly family-friendly, this hotel runs a special children's programme from March to November. There are 30 hours of activities a week (painting, handicrafts, play) for children from three to 12. There's also six hours' free nursery care for one to two year olds, from Monday to Friday, plus a babysitting service (at extra charge). In the rooms they can supply baby beds, changing mats with bench and potties, as well as safety frames for beds and highchairs.

Sa Costa dets Etics s/n, Cala Santanyí 971 165 505 *www.hotelcala santanyi.com. From €160 (£107.20) for a junior suite, double occupancy; children from 2–6 years 50% reduction, 7–12-year-olds 30% reduction, under 2 years €10 (£6.70)/day. Self-catering apartments and studios from €57 (£38.20) per day, extra bed for child 2–12 years €18 (£12.10), cots free. Amenities: beauty centre, sauna, gym, children's activities, childcare, tennis, table tennis, pool table, swimming pool, car hire, bicycle hire. In room: A/C, heating, TV, telephone.*

Pinos Playa Hotel y Apartamentos

Though large, this apart-hotel offers very personal service. As well as 94 hotel rooms, there are 54 apartments and five studios, all within extensive gardens. The large rooms offer views over a ravine that runs down to the sea. Among the hotel's facilities are a diving centre, two pools (one heated), squash and tennis courts, a sauna, Jacuzzi, disco and three bars. The hotel staff organise activities for the whole family, from archery to water polo. There's free childcare with a children's playroom, and your little entertainers can even take part in a special show performed by and for children staying at the hotel. So pack the camcorder.

Costa d'en Nofre 15, Cala Santanyí ☎ 971 165 000 www.pinosplaya. com. Closed Nov–Apr/May. 59 apartments and studios, 94 doubles, 10 singles. Double from €33 (£22.10) per day, child bed from €7 (£4.70), cots free. Amenities: gardens, lounge, disco, swimming pool, restaurant, bar, entertainment, TV room, disco, childcare, currency exchange, internet access at reception, fax, laundry, taxi, car, moped and bike hire, doctor's surgery. In room/apartment: ceiling fan, phone, safe, satellite TV, fridge, balcony.

Can Canals This friendly farmhouse hotel, just 3 km from Es Trenc beach, has cows, chickens, donkeys and horses. You and the children can lend a hand looking after them, cycle the country lanes, or just play in the pool and run around the gardens and orange groves. The rooms all have fridges, so you can keep drinks handy for children waking up thirsty in the night. Families can book adjacent rooms with a communicating door. Breakfast is on a lovely covered terrace, and there's a restaurant in high season in a rustic dining room with a barbecue and old stone oven. The owners use their own produce to rustle up traditional Mallorcan cuisine like roast leg of lamb and courgettes stuffed with cod. Mains cost between €11 (£7.40) and €22 (£14.75).

Ctra Campos-Sa Rapita km 7, Campos ☎ 971 640 757. From €110 (£73.70) double, child under 12 €15 (£10.05), child under 3 free.

Amenities: conference room, Internet corner, left luggage, parking, restaurant, swimming pool, bikes available. In room: bathroom, central heating, A/C, telephone, fridge, hairdryer, Internet connection, safe, satellite TV, cot on request.*

Finca Sant Blai ★★ This converted farmhouse is surrounded by herb, flower and vegetable gardens, and has a small pool under the old mill. Studious children will enjoy rooting through Sant Blai's collection of *National Geographic* magazines (going back to 1922) or gazing at the stars through one of its two telescopes. Active children will love riding the finca's bikes, donkey and cart or motor dinghies, moored at Còlonia Sant Jordi. Parents might prefer the hammocks, self-service bar and general air of forget-it-all relaxation. Accommodation consists of two double rooms, a junior suite, a suite and an apartment. The last two both feature a large living room and small kitchen.

Ctra Campos-Còlonia Sant Jordi km 2 ☎ 971 650 567 www.santblai. com. Double €96 (£64.30) per person inc. breakfast; junior suite €115 (£77) per person inc. breakfast; suite €128 (£85.75) per person inc. breakfast; apartment €103 (£69), no breakfast. Extra bed €22 (£14.75); cots for up to 2-year-olds free. Amenities: swimming pool, lounge with satellite TV and hi-fi, astronomy telescopes, bikes, motor boats, donkey rides, self-service bar, buffet breakfast, lunch and dinner on request. In room: heating (junior suite), A/C (suite/apartment).

Hostal Colonial For no-frills, good-value accommodation and

Countryside around Campos

friendly, helpful service, try this good bet that's been in the same family for three generations. The rooms are simple but spotless, and all have a balcony or terrace, heating and air conditioning. Their home-made ice-cream is so good locals queue up for it. Còlonia de Sant Jordi's port is the main point of departure for the Cabrera marine park (see 'Nature Reserves & Historic Buildings', p. 124).

*C/Ingeniero Gabriel Roca 9, Còlonia de Sant Jordi ☎ 971 655 278 **www. hostal-colonial.com**. Doubles from €50 (£33.50); children up to 12 in triple room, 20% off adult rate; children 0–2 years €6 (£4). Apartments for 3–4 from €64 (£42.90). Closed Dec–Feb.*

FAMILY-FRIENDLY DINING

Hostal & Restaurante Playa

The little whitewashed terrace at the rear of this family-run eatery overlooks the *cala*, and has been serving fresh fish from small-scale fishermen for nearly 80 years. They also do takeway menus (such as *paella mixta* and *trampo* – tomato, pepper and onion salad – €18 (£12.10) per person) for owners with boats moored in the harbour, though it's unlikely you need to prove your sea legs to get one; but you do need to pre-order.

C/Major 25, Còlonia de Sant Jordi ☎ 971 655 256; closed Mon lunch. Mains €9–18 (£6–12.10). Reservations recommended.

Es Pinaret ★★ It's only been open a year, but already chef Peter Urbach, who previously had restaurants in Munich, is making waves with his fresh approach to island cuisine. This is a place where children get to play grown-ups in elegant surroundings, while still being made welcome by Urbach's charming wife. Much work has been done to create the enchanted garden with its covered porticoes strung with red wooden hearts, flagstone floors and candle-lit terraces. Dishes include carpaccio of Es Pla pears with baked goat's cheese; duck breast with saffron risotto and fig salsa; and roast tuna (done rare) with a sesame and ginger crust. Plans for summer barbecues are also under way, and children with less sophisticated palates are catered for with schnitzel and other basic fayre. Failing that, the pool should keep them amused.

Ctra. Ses Salines-Còlonia Sant Jordi km 2.5, Ses Salines ☎ *971 649 230.* **www.germanhost24.de/es-pinaret**. *Open Mon–Sat 5.30pm–11pm, Sun 1pm–11pm. Main dishes €18 (£12.10) and up. Reservations essential.*

L'Arcada VALUE Dining in Cala Figuera is disappointing. As locals will tell you, most of the places, especially those strung together like pearls along the clifftop, sell mediocre fayre. L'Arcada is a good bit better than the others; cheaper certainly and still with that view. It's good for a romantic dinner for two, or for an early supper with the children. The menu offers a good range of fish, including a mixed grill of whatever's in season. There are also stout, traditional Mallorcan dishes like *tumbet* (a basic salad of tomatoes, onions and peppers) and *lomo con col* (pork stuffed in cabbage leaves). Add to this affable, accommodating service, and suddenly eating out in Cala Figuera doesn't look quite so bleak. Wine is

served by 25cl, 50cl and 1 litre carafes, as well as by the bottle.

C/Virgen del Carmen 80, Cala Figuera ☎ *971 645 032. Mains €14.50–21.50 (£9.70–14.40). Reservations recommended.*

Restaurant Es Trenc ★
Tucked away in the sand dunes, this is a good option if you're looking for something a little more substantial, or special, than the usual beach-bar food. It has indoor and outdoor seating and specialises in Catalan dishes of *arroz negre* made with cuttlefish ink and *fideu* with clams and prawns. There's also good grilled fish sold by weight, and juicy steaks. While the rice dishes are reasonably priced, eating here can add up once you thrown in a few starters. *Pa amb oli*, for example, at €2.60 (£1.75) is about double the norm.

Platja des Trenc, Campos ☎ *971 181 089. Fax: 971 786 144. Rice dishes €13.60–14.40 (£9.10–9.65). Reservations recommended.*

Sa Terrassa Worth a stop in Cala Pi is this basic restaurant offering a superb value €7 (£4.70) lunchtime set menu, meat cooked on hot stones (*piedras*) accompanied by roast vegetables and potatoes. It's a fairly simple place, and if your tastes run to more exotic fayre it won't be for you. However, children get a buzz out of seeing their chops cooked caveman-style, and it's very family friendly.

Passeig Cala Pi 391, Cala Pi ☎ *971 123 165. Closed Sat. Reservations not required.*

8 Es Pla: The Central Plains

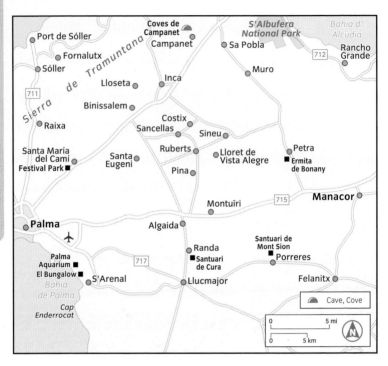

Although Es Pla takes up a huge chunk of Mallorca, it's actually the least known and least visited part of the island. 'The Plain' is a great swathe of agricultural land; vineyards, olive groves and orchards dotted with old windmills and villages that define the term 'sleepy', only interrupted by the occasional blotch of industry seeping from the area's few towns. This is where you come to escape the crowds, chill in luxurious converted manor houses, and seek peace in hilltop monasteries and sanctuaries. Here you'll still be stared at as a novelty, and will find people who can't (or won't) speak Spanish, never mind English.

If you start yearning for some bustle, head to **Sineu** on market day to see real Mallorcan life in all its colour. Apart from Sineu, the main draws are **Petra,** birthplace of missionary (and founder of what eventually became San Francisco) Junípero Serra, and the pretty village of **Randa,** a must-see for pilgrims and coach parties, boasting three monasteries on its neighbouring mountain.

As opposed to the tortuous roads of the west coast, Es Pla's relatively straight highways make it quick and easy to get about in a car if you want to escape to the seaside for a few hours. Just watch out for cyclists taking advantage of the flat, and lorries heading for the industrial centre of **Manacor.**

Visitor Information

Reflecting the draw of the beaches, pretty much all of Mallorca's tourist offices are on the coast. The nearest main one to Es Pla is in **Manacor** (Plaça Ramón Llull s/n ☎ *971 849 100. Fax: 971 849 105 www.manacor. org*). It may be the only reason you'd want to visit the town.

Orientation

Es Pla is Mallorca's central plain, bordered by the Tramuntana mountains to the west and the resort coasts on the other three sides. All roads in Mallorca lead to and from Palma, and Es Pla's are no exception. The PM27 motorway runs along the plain's western edge, linking Palma with **Santa Maria del Cami, Binissalem** and **Inca.** The C715 road heads east from Palma to the coast, bisecting the plain along the way, passing close to Algaida, Randa, Montuiri and Vilafranca de Bonany. **Sineu,** the main town in the north

of Es Pla, is also linked by a direct though minor road from Palma.

Getting Around

Car hire (see 'Fast Facts: Palma and the Rest of Mallorca', p. 49) is essential for anyone intent on exploring the interior of the island – which can be easily as rewarding as the obvious beaches and resorts. If you don't have a car, there is a **train** line linking Palma to Sa Pobla via Inca, along the western edge of Es Pla. It takes about 45 minutes and costs €4.50 (£3) for adults, €3 (£2) for children under 11, one-way. Contact **SFM** (☎ *971 752 245*) for up-to-the-minute information, as timetables and routes are prone to change. The train leaves from the station on Plaça Espanya in Palma. There are also local **bus** services. The **Autocares Mallorca** (☎ *971 545 696 www.autocaresmallorca.com*) lines beginning with 3 and 4 serve this area, three times a day (more in high season). See its website for timetable details:

TIP ≫ Plain Warning

Everything in Es Pla seems to change frequently, often apparently at a whim. It's not unusual to find a restaurant shut on a day it would normally be open because of a wedding, a birthday or something entirely random. Even a reservation is occasionally no guarantee. Public transport is the same: routes, timetables and prices are all subject to change. It's not to say this is *definitely* going to happen, but it is something to be aware of. All the specifics in this chapter are as accurate as possible – no more. The islands tend to be more laid-back about this kind of stuff than the mainland, but nowhere is the *no hay prisa* (there's no hurry) mentality more evident than in Mallorca's interior.

On Your Bike

One of the best ways to get around Es Pla is by bike. In fact, on some stretches of road bikes outnumber cars, and if you're driving you really need to watch for cyclists round tight corners. There are plenty of established routes to follow, with bike-friendly bars *en route* where you can swap tips with fellow cyclists. The local government website (***www.illes balears.es***) has details of routes and maps (click on 'Sport Tourism' then 'Cycling Tourism'). A good circular route in Es Pla starts and ends at **Algaida,** passing through Sencelles, Ruberts and Pina. It takes about two hours along 25 km of mainly flat rural back-roads. You'll pass springs, old village churches and the Mallorcan Observatory in Costitx. It's a good route to do on Wednesdays when the weekly market at Sencelles is on. Pick up provisions there for a picnic lunch.

You'll probably be able to hire bikes from where you're staying, whether it's a hotel, apartment or *casa rural*. Otherwise, **Velo Sport Mallorca** (Apt 82, Primera Vuelta 108, Son Prohens/Felanitx. ℂ *971 580 541 www.velosportmallorca.com*) will deliver a bike to you anywhere on the island. But note that only the basic model comes with pedals, and you are responsible for any damage or loss. The cost for the most basic bike is €10 (£6.70) for the first day, then €8 (£5.36) a day thereafter. **Palma on Bike** (Pl. Salvador Coll 8, Palma ℂ *971 718 062 www.palma onbike.com*) offers seven-day hire from its shop in Palma for €49 (£32.83) including insurance and a helmet.

these change frequently. Fares are €4.50 (£3) for adults, €3 (£2) children under 11, one-way.

Buy tickets at the bus station in Plaça Espanya in Palma, or at the bus station in Inca.

Cycling

Child-friendly Events

One of the main reasons to visit Es Pla is to see the 'real' Mallorca – and one of the best times to see this is fiesta time. There are plenty throughout the year, often with locals dressed in colourful costumes sure to grab any child's attention. In **Montuïri** on 24th August, locals dress as devils and dance through the streets as part of one of the island's oldest festivals, the **Feast of Sant Bartolomeu.**

Animal-loving children may enjoy the annual **Sa Fira** fair in Sineu. This market town celebrates the agricultural bounty of Es Pla on the first Sunday in May. Since at least 1318, locals have gathered in the town to eat, drink, be merry and show off their prize pigs. There are plenty of rustic fun and games, like sheepdog contests and pig auctions – just be careful you don't get persuaded to adopt a new and unusual pet.

There's more animal magic at the feast of **Sant Antoni Abat** in Sa Pobla on 16th and 17th January. Sant Antoni Abat is the patron saint of domestic animals, and every year on his feast

A Day's Shopping & Eating in the Shadow of the Tramuntana

Get an early start and head for Inca on a Thursday morning for the **weekly market** (the best is on Dijous Bo/Good Thursday, the first Thursday in November). For breakfast try one of the bars on Calle Major, such as **Café Español.** Take a terrace table and watch the world go by. Alternatively, to breakfast on the hoof, pick up pastries from **C'an Guixe** (C/L'Estrella 3–5) or **C'an del Ante** (C/Major 27). When you've bought all the wicker baskets, ceramic bowls and olive-wood salad servers you could ever want, head to the outskirts of town for bargains in the factory stores lining the main road – or to the **Festival Park** shopping mall (see p. 143). If your children are clamouring for pizza, hotdogs and burgers, this is the place for them. The **RECamper shop** in Inca is the stop of choice for fans of the kooky-cool Mallorcan shoe-maker. Mango, Nike and Quiksilver are just some of the other labels with factory shops. If the weather's good, drive out to **Celler Son Aloy** ☆ (Ctra Inca-Sencelles km 3 ☎ *971 502 302*. Open Wed–Sat 1.30pm–4pm, 8.30pm–11pm; eve only Tue & Sun. Mains €8.50–22 (£5.70–14.74), highchairs, V, MC), a vineyard restaurant that specialises in grilled meats cooked on an outdoor barbecue. Its grapes make the famous Santa Catarina wines, and clients can taste the range for free while waiting for their chops. After lunch, take in some nature: head north to the **Coves de Campanet,** or south to **Natura Parc** (see 'Natural Wonders', p. 140).

Saints' Days

Fiestas Patronales (local patron saint's days) are always colourful, with children dressed up and adults feasting on local food and wine. For full details, and a proper schedule of events, contact the **tourist office in Palma** (see p. 46) nearer the time, but the main ones to look out for are as follows:

Campos	9th Jan
Muro and Porreres	First Sunday after Easter
Campanet, Felanitx, Sencelles	2nd Sunday in May
Manacor	Last week in May and first week in June
Llucmajor, Muro, Sa Pobla, Santanyí	28th July
Inca	30th July
Campos	7th–15th August
Sineu	15th August
Porreres	Last Sunday in August
Santa Ponça	First 10 days in September
Porreres	Last Sunday in October
Muro	First Sunday in November
Inca	Third Thursday in November
Santanyí	30th November
Montuïri	First Sunday in December

day the inhabitants of local farmyards are paraded through town to receive his blessing. But the real action happens the night before, when the saint does battle with the devil and his demons. Hundreds of bonfires (*foguerons*) are lit to set the appropriate fire-and-brimstone scene. Bawdy songs are sung before a procession of fantastically costumed demons, devils and temptresses run riot around the town and try and throw St Anthony to the flames. Good triumphs over evil, of course... until next year. In Spain, everyone from babies to grandparents attends these things, but of

Sant Antoni's Devils

course you may be more wary with little ones. On the whole, though, just like Bonfire Night, this is good fun for all the family.

Plain Towns

Binissalem ★ is one of the most attractive towns in Es Pla (though strictly speaking it's not part of the plain, nestled on the eastern edge of the Tramuntana). Natural resources, wine and stone, have brought great wealth to the area and the town boasts some fine 17th and 18th century mansions. Two have been converted into centres for local culture, craft and history: **Can Gelabert de la Portella** (on C/Portella) and **Can Sabater** (at C/Bonaire 25). The local area is one of Mallorca's main wine-making regions, and there are plenty of *bodegas* (tavern-style restaurants) in town to taste and learn more about the local produce. The wines by **José Luis Ferrer** in Binissalem are widely considered the best in Mallorca. However, if you just want to relax with a glass of local plonk in the shade of a vine, head for **Celler Son Aloy** (see p. 146).

Inca is Mallorca's third-largest town (with a population of 25,000), a mainly dusty and dull industrial centre at the edge of Es Pla under the Tramuntana. Its main attractions are leather outlet shops, including the Camper shoes factory store, **RECamper** ★ (Autovia Palma-Inca km 7, Pol Industrial s/n, Inca ☎ 971 507 158), on the outskirts of town, as well as the American-style mall, **Festival Park** (see p. 143).

Sineu is the geographical centre of the island. Famous for its **Wednesday market** ★ (see 'Market Days', p. 142), its position made it a meeting and trading post for Mallorca's country folk. It's now a popular refreshment stop for hordes of cyclists criss-crossing the island's flat centre. Its well-preserved townhouses and cobbled streets are charming, though there's little to see besides the restored **16th century church** (Placa Major. Open 9am–1.30pm, 5pm–8pm) and an **art gallery** (Placa Major. Open 10am–1pm) inside a converted railway station. You can also sample the products of the surrounding fields and farms at the celler restaurant **Celler Es Grop** (C/Major 18 ☎ 971 520 187. No credit cards. No reservations. Open 1.30pm–4pm, 8.30pm–11pm), with its authentic decor of giant barrels and strings of peppers. Unfortunately, the proprietor doesn't speak English. **Petra,** just south-east of Sineu, is the home of one of Mallorca's most famous sons, Junípero Serra. Serra was a gifted young priest and academic who, along with his fellow Franciscans, established the first missions along the American Pacific coast, including one which eventually became San Francisco. Its narrow cobbled streets are lined with squat, honey-coloured cottages and bordered with pots full of blooms. The only tourist attraction is the modest **Serra Museum** (C/Barracar 6) and the nearby **Ermita de Bonany**

Walking the Three Peaks' Monasteries

Get on your bikes and put on your walking boots for a triangular trek of three of Es Pla's high points. Start with an easy climb up to the **Santuari de Mont-Sion** (246m. Signposted just outside **Porreres** ℂ *971 647 185*. No public transport). Take a picnic breakfast (buy it at the Porreres market on Tuesdays). For lunch head to **Randa** where you could eat in style at the **Es Reco de Randa** (C/Font 13 ℂ *971 660 997*), which has lovely terraces and top-notch rustic fayre. The simpler, livelier **Celler Bar Randa** (see 'Family-friendly Dining', below) offers child-friendly omelettes and chips (as well as snails!). Alternatively, build up an appetite by walking up to the **Santuari de Cura** (ℂ *971 120 260*. Basic rooms €12 (£8). No public transport) at the top of the **Puig de Randa** (540m) and lunching in the monastery café-bar, with sweeping views over the plain. Finish the trinity of holy places with a stroll up to the **Ermita de Bonany** (follow signs from Petra along the PM-322 or PM-331), 'The Hermitage of Good Harvest', to the south-west of Petra for more views. This is where local boy and missionary Junípero Serra preached his last sermon before heading to the New World in the 18th century. You can drive to all the monasteries, but allow at least an hour if you want to walk from the main villages. If you use the roads, these are easily doable with a pushchair. Just watch out for passing cars.

(see 'Walking the Three Peaks' Monasteries', above).

Muro sits on the northern edge of Es Pla below the Albufera marshes. If you want your children to get a deeper understanding of the region's traditional ways, this is the place to come: it's the home of Mallorca's ethnological museum (see 'Museums & Monuments', p. 140). Its other main attractions are the **Sant Joan Baptista Church** (Plaça Major. Open 9am–1.30pm, 4.30pm–8.30pm. Free entry but donation for upkeep appreciated) with its colourful rose window, and the town's bull-ring dug from a quarry. **Sa Pobla,** just north-west of Muro, hosts one of the island's main modern art

museums, the **Museu d'Art Contemporani de Sa Pobla** (C/Antoni Maura 6 ℂ *971 542 389*), open 10am–1.30pm and usually 4pm–8pm. €5 (£3.35) adults, €2.50 (£1.68) children under 11), with about 100 works by Mallorcan artists. The **Coves de Campanet** caves are also nearby (see 'Natural Wonders', p. 139).

Among other places worth a stop, **Randa** towards the south of Es Pla is a leafy little village with Moorish irrigation systems trickling down the streets. It's a traditional stop-off point for pilgrims visiting the **three sanctuaries** ★★ on the **Puig de Randa** peak (see 'Walking the Three Peaks' Monasteries', box above), and so serves coachloads of visitors in its restaurants.

Montuïri's main street runs along a ridge slap bang in the middle of Es Pla, offering views across the surrounding fields. It's an almost ghostly quiet place except during the annual Sant Bartolomeu festival on 24th August (see 'Child-friendly Events', p. 135).

Vilafranca de Bonany, on the road to Manacor, is famous for its produce, displayed in colourful arrangements outside the village's many greengrocers. It's also Mallorca's melon capital and hosts a festival celebrating the fruit every September.

Natural Wonders

Because the terrain is so flat, it's pretty easy to get **good views** in Es Pla. Just hike (or drive) up one of its few hills: at the top you're sure to find a sanctuary or monastery offering refreshment, whether water fresh from a well or a fully-stocked bar. The Ermita de Bonany (see 'Walking the Three Peaks' Monasteries', p. 138) just south-west of Petra is one of the easier climbs for children. The Santuari de Cura, another of those three peaks, is easily reached by car. This is the highest point on the plain and offers amazing views. The monastery's cafe-bar serves great *pa amb oli* (€5 (£3.35)). You can study either the Real Mallorca team memorabilia inside, or the 360-degree views outside, while you eat.

Meanwhile, below ground level, the **Coves de Campanet** ★ **AGES 7 AND UP** (Ctra Palma–Alcúdia km 39, Campanet ☎ *971 516 130.* Open Apr–Sep 10am–7pm, Oct–Mar 10am–6pm. €9 (£6), children €5 (£3.35)) are among the smallest and least known of Mallorca's cave complexes. Like the rest of Es Pla, part of the charm is their relative obscurity. The 3200 sq m of caves features

Coves de Campanet

Colourful Glass Animals

chambers as deep as 300 metres. The **Sala del Llac,** as the name suggests, has a crystalline lake that multiplies the spectacular forms in the rock around it.

After seeing the weekly markets, you could be forgiven for thinking rural Es Pla only thinks of animals in terms of the dinner table. But at **Natura Parc** ALL AGES (Ctra de Sineu 15, km 4, Santa Eugènia ☏ *971 144 078 www.mallorcaweb.net/ naturaparc*. Open 10am–7pm daily. €7 (£4.69), children up to 12 €4.50 (£3), children under 3 free) you'll see a kinder appreciation of our animal cousins. It's a centre for the recuperation and care of wild animals, as well as a tourist attraction. Although there are indigenous (wild and domestic) mammals on show, and a few oddities, like kangaroos and llamas, the focus is on birds, from ducks to vultures and flamingoes. The park isn't that big, certainly not enough for a whole day out, but your entry fee funds a good cause.

Museums & Monuments

Els Calderers ALL AGES While not as spectacular as La Granja (see p. 78), this typically grand Mallorcan manor house has been preserved in its living 19th century state, *Marie-Celeste*-style. The cellars still hold barrels and presses, and you can even help yourself from some of the jugs lying around. Upstairs in the kitchens, the knives are ready chopping and the pot is on the fire. In the dining room, the table is set for a fine dinner party. It's as if everyone has just popped out for a 100-year-long fire drill and you can snoop around their home at will. In the grounds there are even animals in the outhouses: the Mallorcan black pig in its pen, dogs in the kennels and chickens in the coop. *Ctra Palma-Manacor km 37 ☏ 971 526 069 www.todoesp.es/els-calderers. Open daily 10am–6pm. €8 (£5.35) adults, €5 (£3.35) children under 12.*

Museu Etnologic de Mallorca
AGES 7 AND UP This museum, in a

16th century manor house, tries to bring the past to life in a similar way to Els Calderers, with reconstructed scenes featuring historic artefacts from day-to-day life. A bedroom and kitchen are furnished in traditional style. An old pharmacy has a curious pair of scales, blacksmith's and cobbler's workshops have their tools laid out ready for work. Other exhibits include examples of pottery and traditional local clay whistles (*siurells*) in curious shapes.

C/Major 5, Muro ☎ 971 860 647. Open Tue–Sat 10am–3pm, Thur 5–8pm, Sun 10am–2pm. Closed Aug. €2.40 (£1.60), free entry Sat afternoon and Sun.

Vidrierias Gordiola ★ ★

AGES 5 AND UP You can't miss the fake castle on the Palma–Manacor road: Vidrierias Gordiola, a glass-making factory that's been in the same family since the 18th century. Watching craftsmen blow bubbles from molten glass is a jaw-dropping experience for little ones, especially when you tell them that the fires are volcano-hot (1300°C). The resulting pieces range from beautiful wine glasses and fruit bowls, to ornate hanging lanterns and perfume bottles. After watching the glass-blowing demo you can, of course, buy some of the results: the glass-ware of Gordiola is among the best around. There's also a small museum of glass artefacts that the family has collected over the years.

Ctra Palma-Manacor km 19 ☎ 971 665 046. Open May to Sep, 9am–8pm Mon–Sat, 9am–1pm Sun. Entrance free.

Child-friendly Trips Out

Embotits Artesanals Matas

AGES 7 AND UP If you like your children to know what they're eating, a visit to this artesan charcutier is a must. Embotits Artesanals Matas is one of the few old-school sausage makers left in Spain. Their workshop isn't pretty – just a basic warehouse – but you do get to

Market Day

Tuesday: Porreres

The general market held here from around 9am to 2pm on the main *Plaça* harks back to the days when vegetables came in weird and wonderful shapes and livestock was still live. While trucks and cars mean that the excellent produce of Es Pla gets shipped all over the island, this market is still a great place to stock up on locally grown fruit and veg, and locally reared meat and poultry. Ideal for self-catering holidaymakers.

Wednesday: Sineu ★

This is one of the oldest markets on the island, with a long tradition as a meeting point for the campesinos of Es Pla. Although today you're as likely to find cheap clothes from China as live chickens, Sineu's market is still a weekly high point in the locals' diaries; a chance to catch up on gossip as much as stock up on provisions. It's also become something of a tourist attraction; there are plenty of potential gifts and souvenirs on sale, from hand-made pottery to herb-infused olives, artesan cheeses to colourful strings of peppers. The stalls are set up in and around the Plaza de la Iglesia (church square) and the Plaza del Fossar.

Thursday: Inca OVERRATED

Because the market in Inca (open 9am–2pm) is so well known, the hordes of tourists that now pass through mean that much traditional produce has been replaced by the same kind of tat you see in markets all over the world. It continues to attract crowds, however, who snake through the narrow streets of the old quarter, mixing with wicker baskets, olive wood bowls, plastic toys and nylon underwear. Get there early for the best of it, and reward yourself with lunch in one of the bodegas if you manage to find a bargain.

Sunday: Santa Maria del Camí ★

This is one of the best markets on Mallorca, with a huge range of goods, from sausages to handbags to caged birds. Go early – certainly no later than 1pm. Hungry bellies can be satisfied with freshly made sobrasada sandwiches from one of the market stalls. For lunch, try one of the bars and restaurants on the Plaza dels Hostals, Cafe Hostals or Sa Sinia. You can't miss them. Coffee and a sandwich will set you back about €5 (£3.35), and neither take credit cards or has highchairs.

see the whole process of making products like their patented *sobrasada* covered in pepper. It will give your children some understanding of what good food should be.

Cami Vell d'Arta, Maria de la Salut ☏ *971 525 621 www.embotits-matas.com. Closed Sat and Sun. Entrance free. Usually 10am–1pm & 4.30–6pm, but call ahead as these are erratic.*

Festival Park ALL AGES

Claiming to be Mallorca's number-one leisure destination, Festival Park is a temple to the world's favourite activity – shopping. Inca already had fame as Mallorca's bargain capital, with warehouse-sized outlet stores, especially for leather goods, lining the roads in and out of town. Now Festival Park has consolidated that trend, combining cut-price stores with family-focused entertainment like carousels, bungy jumps, bowling alleys, amusement arcades, a cinema, pedal carts and a creche for the children if parents want time for some uninterrupted shopping. Just to remind you there's still a bit of real Mallorca out there (sort of), there's a 'rural museum' where animatronic puppets play out country scenes in miniature, grinding wheat for flour, bringing in the harvest and baking old-style *ensaimadas*.

Ctra. Palma–Inca km 7.1 📞 *971 140 925* **www.festivalparks.com**. *Bus Palma–Inca from Plaça Espanya in Palma. Take the PM-27 out of Palma; Inca is clearly signposted. Parking €2 (£1.34) per hour.*

FAMILY-FRIENDLY ACCOMMODATION

One of the best things about opting for the Es Pla rather than the beaches is the abundance of high-quality *agroturisme* (rural and farm accommodation). These are places where your children can roam free. Although many old farmhouses have been converted to chi-chi spa-hotels and minimalist *fashionista*-friendly guesthouses, some have taken the laid-back route, retaining a rustic roustabout feel that's child-safe and offers the chance for your children to experience real country life.

Son Xotano ★★ A rural hotel between Algaida and Sineu, it seems exactly the sort of place where children wouldn't be welcome. But though this stately home is a grand place, with fine antiques (furniture that's been here, like the family, for generations), it's actually a warm and welcoming spot with lots of nooks and crannies for children to play in, huge grounds for them to run around, plus bikes and horses to ride. There's further diversion in the form of swimming and paddling pools and a crazy-golf course. Owner Don Pedro cuts a daunting aristocratic figure on first meeting, but soon melts into the character of a cuddly grandpa.

Ctra Pina-Sencelles km 1.5, Pina 📞 *971 872 500. Double €120 (£80.40) exc 7% IVA. Extra bed 25% of full price. 16 rooms. V, MC. Breakfast included. Amenities: restaurant, bar, massage and reflexology, swimming pool, 100 hectares of grounds. In room: phone, TV, heating, A/C, fridge, mini-bar.*

Can Feliu ★★★ **FIND** Just outside the pretty village of Porreres, this old farmhouse has tasteful rooms on a working organic farm. As well as the usual cows and pigs, there are ostriches, fish and tortoises. You can pick fruit straight from the tree for your breakfast and enjoy the other farm produce during your stay. Children and adults have the opportunity to learn about the day-to-day tasks and even roll up their sleeves and help out. There are bikes for hire and a secret Wendy house hidden among the trees.

Finca Son Dagueta, Camí de Sa Serra s/n, Porreres ☎ *971 168 078 www.sondagueta.com. Double €100 (£67) and up. Child supplement €20 (£13.40), cot free. Breakfast included. 1 suite, 4 junior suites, 1 single, 2 double rooms. V, MC. Amenities: heating, pool, bar, half-board options, Jacuzzi, farmyard animals. In room: satellite TV, A/C.*

Finca Es Pla Nou Experience absolute tranquillity here: there are just two apartments, for two and four people, and two double bedrooms, all with their own terrace. There's plenty of space for children to let off steam in the grounds, and a pool to splash about in. The finca has a *nispero* (lomquat) plantation and grows its own seasonal veg, plus there are the usual farmyard beasts, from chickens to pigs and donkeys.

Ctra Felanitx-Petra km 8, Felanitx ☎ *971 183 212 www.finca-es-pla-nou.de. Double €73 (£48.91). Apartment for two €88 (£58.96). Apartment for four €94 (£62.98). Breakfast €7 (£4.69) adults, €3.50 (£2.35) children. No credit cards. Amenities: swimming pool. In room: bath and shower, kitchen, private terrace.*

Son Torrat ★★★ **FIND** An unusual development featuring six little *casitas* created out of one large, 15th century stone house. The apartments, though small, are pretty, cosy and big enough for parents and two small children; each has a private terrace. The grounds have orchards and

Porreres

mature pine woods, landscaped gardens and a pool with a view. It's near some lovely walks, and is just 200m from the Ermita de Bonany (see 'Walking the Three Peaks' Monasteries', p. 138).

Cami de Bonany km 2 , Petra ☎ 971 854 146. playamonte@lavila.org. 6 rooms. Low season €455 (£304.85)/week, high season €620 (£415.40)/week for apartment for 4. Cash only. Amenities: swimming pool, Jacuzzi, gardens, cafe-bar, barbecue area, washing machine. In room: heating, satellite TV, hi-fi, kitchen (fridge, microwave).

Sa Rota d'en Palerm ☆ For doing-nothing luxury, you won't do much better than the self-contained house/apartment at Sa Rota d'en Palerm. This *agroturismo* property has a few apartments and junior suites as well as the house, all tastefully and comfortably kitted out, with fabulous views and private terraces. There's a pool and hammocks slung between orange trees, all adding to the soporific air that should chill out even the most highly-strung child. Great home-cooked dinner is available if requested in advance. About €25 (£16.75) per person for three courses.

Ctra Lloret-Montuiri km 0.8, Lloret de Vistalegre ☎ 971 765 359. Double €124 (£83.08) and up. Apartment for 4 €198 (£132.66) low season, €232 (£155.44) high season per apartment. Extra bed €30 (£20.10). Cot €6 (£4). Breakfast €10 (£6.70). 50% discount for children under 12. 5 apartments, 3 double rooms. V, MC. Amenities: swimming pool, massage, walking & cycling, boat hire. In room: A/C, heating, mini-bar.

Moli d'en Pau

TRADITIONAL MALLORCAN A converted flour mill, now a cosy and friendly restaurant serving seasonal Mallorcan cuisine, from fresh fish and steaks to tongue and tripe. In good weather, get a table on the terrace where children can be distracted from tantrums by an aviary with songbirds, ducks and parrots.

Ctra Santa Margarita 25, Sineu ☎ 971 855 116. Open 1.30pm–3.30pm, 8.30pm–11pm; closed Mon. Main courses €7–15 (£4.69–10.05). V, MC. Reservations recommended. Highchairs.

Es Celler **GRILL** Es Pla's traditional cellar restaurants are echoing underground vaults, usually lined with huge wine barrels; they're bustling places filled with families taking their time over post-market lunches. The menu is usually devoted to fresh local meat grilled over wood fires. Petra's Es Celler, a fine example, serves scrumptious home-baked bread and herby olives to accompany its fine grilled meats.

C/Hospital s/n, Petra ☎ 971 561 056. Main courses €7–13.20 (£4.69–8.84). Open 1.30pm–4pm, 8.30pm–11pm. V, MC. Reservations recommended. Highchairs.

Son Bascos **FARM RESTAURANT**
Just outside Montuïri is this restaurant on a quail farm, so you know your main course is as fresh as it can get. Of course, quail is the star of the menu,

from quail eggs with garlic mayonnaise as a starter to grilled quail with salad for mains. Non-quail alternatives include partridge in vinaigrette and grilled pork loin. Prices are good and the atmosphere is lively.

Ctra Palma–Manacor km 29 ☎ *971 646 170. Open 1.30pm–4pm, 8.30pm–11pm. Two quails with salad €6.40 (£4.29), mains €7.50–18 (£5–12). No credit cards. Reservations recommended.*

Ca'n Mateu ☆

TRADITIONAL MALLORCAN A favourite with locals for Sunday lunch, this traditional hostalry has been serving travellers for hundreds of years. It's a real 'family' restaurant with a large playground and swimming pool in the gardens. Their specialities include traditional rice and pork stew, grilled vegetables, roast lamb and home-made tarts.

Ctra Vieja de Manacor km 21.7, Algaida ☎ *971 665 036 / 125 179. Fax: 971 125 267 www.can-mateu. com. Open 1.30pm–4pm, 8.30pm–11pm; closed Tue. Main courses €7.50–19 (£5–12.73). V, MC. Reservations recommended.*

Celler Bar Randa **PUB GRUB** This

old-fashioned, spit-and-sawdust bar in the centre of Randa is good to have up your sleeve for fussy eaters. While pizza, pasta and burgers remain elusive in this part of the world, you can at least get a plate of egg and chips or sausage and chips, along with a solid variety of tapas.

C/Eglesia 20, Randa ☎ *971 660 989. Open 11am–11pm; closed Wed. Main courses €7–15 (£4.69–10.05). No credit cards. No reservations.*

Celler Son Aloy ☆ **GRILL** See

'A Day's Shopping & Eating in the Shadow of the Tramuntana', p. 135.

9 Menorca

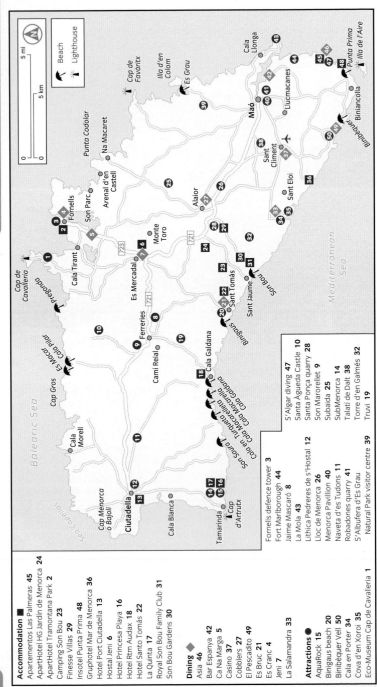

Accommodation ■
Apartementos Las Palmeras **45**
ApartHotel HG Jardin de Menorca **24**
ApartHotel Tramontana Park **2**
Camping Son Bou **23**
Finesse Villas **29**
Insotel Punta Prima **48**
Gruphotel Mar de Menorca **36**
Hotel Port Ciutadella **13**
Hostal Jeni **6**
Hotel Princesa Playa **16**
Hotel Rtm Audax **18**
Hotel Santo Tomás **22**
La Quinta **17**
Royal Son Bou Family Club **31**
Son Bou Gardens **30**

Dining ◆
Asia **46**
Bar Espanya **42**
Ca Na Marga **5**
Casino **37**
Cobblers **27**
El Pescadito **49**
Es Cranc **4**
Jeni **7**
La Salamandra **33**

Attractions ●
AquaRock **15**
Binigaus beach **20**
Binibèquer Vell **50**
Cala en Porter **34**
Cova d'en Xoroi **35**
Eco-Museum Cap de Cavalleria **1**
Fornells defence tower **3**
Fort Marlborough **44**
Jaime Mascaró **8**
La Mola **43**
Lithica Pedreres de s'Hostal **12**
Lloc de Menorca **26**
Menorca Pavillion **40**
Naveta d'es Tudons **11**
Robadones quarry **41**
S'Albufera d'Es Grau **35**
Natural Park visitor centre **39**
S'Algar diving **47**
Santa Águeda Castle **10**
Santa Ponça quarry **28**
Son Marorellet **9**
Subaida **25**
SubMenorca **14**
Talatí de Dalt **38**
Torre d'en Galmés **32**
Truvi **19**

The least-developed of the Balearic Islands, Menorca is the second-largest, with an area of 702 km^2. It measures just 47 km from east to west. It may have the same thriving tourist industry, but it's culturally very different to Mallorca, Ibiza and Formentera, and proud of the fact. Of course, the island has its fair share of typical Mediterranean resorts, but you won't find endless rows of hotels blocking your sea view. Instead, developments are subtle, split between the long beaches of the south coast, and the occasional sandy cove of the rockier north.

Menorca was declared a Biosphere Reserve by UNESCO in 1993, in recognition of the island's natural and cultural heritage – and the balance islanders have struck between this and economic development. As a result, a short distance from popular resorts are isolated beaches, remains of prehistoric settlements and footprints of military strongholds, turning the island into an open-air museum. Add unique flora and fauna, such as red cows and the cheeky black lizards on Illa de l'Aire, and you'll understand that there's more than English pubs for entertainment. Although Menorca may be small enough to drive across in around an hour, don't be fooled into thinking you can discover the island in a week.

In the summer, the sea and beach is an obvious family attraction. But if your youngsters are unlikely to want to stay still for the duration of their stay, Menorca is a safe spot to try out new watersports or improve existing skills; from sailing to diving, canoeing to windsurfing, there's plenty of opportunity to wear out children of all ages. When winter comes, the island's character changes: hotels and restaurants on the coast close, so tourism focuses on the towns. But on clear days, there's still nothing like walking a deserted beach for recharging the batteries.

From paddling in the gentle waves at Es Grau, to diving into the crystal clear water at Binisafúller; getting icing sugar on your nose when you bite into a crumbly *pastisset* to rolling up your sleeves to tackle a terracotta bowl of lobster stew; or simply relaxing in your villa while the children play in the gardens, Menorca has its own laid-back character that will inevitably rub off on you.

ESSENTIALS

Getting There

By Plane Just a few years ago, you could count on one hand the number of scheduled airlines that flew to Menorca direct from the UK. But for independent travellers, options in the summer months have increased, with the arrival of low-cost carriers like **easyJet** (☎ *0905 821 0905*

Sant Joan Festival

www.easyjet.com*) and **Jet2**
(📞 *0871 226 1737 www.jet2.com*)
connecting Maó (Mahon) with
London Gatwick, Bristol, Leeds
and Newcastle airports. **British
Airways** (📞 *0870 850 9850
www.ba.com*) and **Iberia** (📞 *902
400 500 www.iberia.com)* also fly
direct from London Gatwick –
it's just two hours – and
Monarch Airlines (📞 *0870 040
5040 www.flymonarch.com*) connects the island with
Birmingham, London Luton
and Manchester.

Package tour operators continue to dominate, however, and
if you're travelling to Menorca
from a regional airport not men-
tioned above, a charter flight is
your best bet. For flight-only
deals, try **Airflights** (📞 *0800 083
7007 www.airflights.co.uk*),
FlightLine (📞 *0800 541541; www.
flightline.co.uk*) or **XL** (📞 *0870 999
0069; www.xl.com*), though this is
far from definitive.

INSIDER TIP ≫

While last-minute breaks may be
ideal for many destinations, for
Menorca you're better off booking
in advance. During July and
August, hotels and apartments
are typically filled to bursting
point; few cheap deals are available. If you can visit the island
during May, June, September or
October, you're more likely to find
a bargain package, and will still
be guaranteed sunshine when
you arrive.

Menorca is well connected with
mainland Spain year-round,
with direct flights to Palma,
Valencia, Barcelona and Madrid
during the winter, as well as
additional destinations during
the summer months. Elsewhere
in Europe, charter flights connect Maó with several major
cities in Ireland, Germany and
Italy during the summer, as well
as other countries. France is one
important exception.

Between 31st October and
1st May, travel options are

limited. At the time of writing, the only direct flights between the UK and Menorca were on **Monarch** connecting Maó with Manchester and London Luton airports. This scheduled service is reasonably priced: you can pick up return fares for £100. The alternative is to fly via Palma Mallorca or Barcelona, and pick up a connecting flight. Barcelona in particular is an important base for low-cost carriers. Spanish carriers, Iberia, **Spanair** (✆ 902 131 415 www.spanair.com) and **Air Europa** (✆ 902 401 501 www.aireuropa.com) offer regular services between Maó and the mainland, as well as connecting flights from mainland Spain to the UK.

A public service is in operation between Maó and Palma Mallorca, meaning that islanders are guaranteed a minimum number of flights per day – there are usually at least eight

Ciutadella Postbox

connections with Iberia in each direction – at a fixed price (€167 (£111.89) in early 2007). This means that ticket changes can be made, subject to availability, without facing additional costs. Air Nostrum (part of Iberia) has launched twice-weekly direct services between Mahon and Ibiza.

By Boat There are regular ferry services connecting Maó's and Ciutadella's ports to Mallorca and mainland Spain, with increased journey frequency (a daily service) in the summer.

Trasmediterranea (✆ 902 454 645 www.trasmediterranea.com) connects Maó with Palma, Barcelona and Valencia on large ferries suitable for vehicles. The journey from Barcelona to Maó is overnight, takes nine hours and return ticket prices start at €78.20 (£52.39); Maó to Valencia includes a stop in Palma, with a journey time of 14 hours. **Balearia** (✆ 902 160 180 www.balearia.com) connects Maó with Barcelona (five hours) on a fast ferry service, as well as Ciutadella to Barcelona in the summer, and Ciutadella to Alcúdia, Mallorca, taking three-and-a-half hours. Finally, **Iscomar** (✆ 902 119 128 www.iscomar.com) joins Maó with Barcelona in the summer, a nine-hour trip, and Ciutadella with Alcúdia, by a service that takes two hours and 40 minutes. There are invariably a handful of days a year when bad weather prevents boats arriving or departing. If this occurs, companies do not usually offer compensation or accommodation. Children under two travel free on ferries, children aged two to 12 get a 50% discount on fares.

Bringing your car to the island by ferry is an expensive option. It is much cheaper to rent a vehicle here (see 'Getting Around', p. 155). If you do opt for the long drive south, a return journey for a family of four with a normal-sized car costs around €500 (£335) between Barcelona and Maó.

FAST FACTS: MENORCA

Baby Equipment Most hotels, apartments and villas can provide you with cots at a small extra charge, and *www.mental rentalsmenorca.com* rent cots from €22 (£14.74) per week, as well as sterilizers, bottle warmers, highchairs, car seats, stair gates and anything else you might need. Supermarkets and chemists sell nappies, formula milk and jarred food, but not nappy bags. For specialist baby clothing or equipment, try baby shops such as **Mares & Fills** (Avda de sa Pau 35-37, Sant Lluís) or **Es Guixonets** (Av. De la Indústria 90, Alaior).

Babysitters Most expensive and some moderate hotels arrange sitters for guests, and rates average €8–10/hr (£5.35–6.70).

Breastfeeding Breastfeeding in public is acceptable, but you may get stared at, especially if you're feeding an older infant. You may want to brazen it out, since breastfeeding is your natural right, or you might prefer to find an out-of-the-way spot.

Business Hours Shops Like the rest of the Balearics, shops and business generally open at 9 or 10am (6 or 7am for bakeries); closing again at 1–1.30pm and then reopening again between 5–6pm until 8.30pm. In Menorca, while some bakeries open on Sunday mornings, most shops remain closed. Supermarkets generally open from 9am until 9pm, with no break for lunch, with large stores opening on Sunday mornings during May and October, between 9am and 1pm. Banks open between 8am and 2pm, and are closed at weekends and bank holidays, although some banks open on Saturday mornings between October and May. Most have 24-hour ATMs. While bars and cafes open early, often from 6am, and stay open until past midnight, restaurants usually open from noon, and between May and October in resorts they will stay open all afternoon into the evening. Public museums usually close on Sundays, Mondays and public holidays, but most tourist sites open on public and school holidays. As an island heavily dependent on tourism, much of Menorca closes down between October and May – practically all bars and restaurants in resorts shut completely during this time, with just the odd restaurant opening at weekends. In towns and resorts with a year-round population, a handful of bars and restaurants stay open. Even in the towns, many businesses close down for a month after Christmas.

Car Hire See p. 155.

Chemists Staff at chemists (*farmacias*), recognisable by a green cross, can provide first aid in minor emergencies. Rotas of pharmacies operating out of normal hours (9am–1.30pm and 5–8.30pm) Monday–Friday; Saturday mornings only) are posted in every chemist window and in local papers. It's a good idea to take a first-aid course yourself; there's a CD-Rom version (about £30) developed in collaboration with St John's Ambulance: see www.firstaid forkids.com.

Consulates There are consulates for the UK (Hon. Vice Consul, Camí de Biniatap 30, Horizonte, Es Castell ☎ 971 367 818), Germany (Sant Andreu 32, Maó ☎ 971 361 668), France Deyà 30, Maó ☎ 971 354 387) and the Netherlands (Àngel 12, Maó ☎ 971 354 363) on the island.

Dentists For emergency dental treatment, go to your nearest hospital or health centre. Many dentists have English speaking staff, and in Maó, an English dentist operates the clinic at Carrer de l'Àngel 20, Maó (☎ 971 368 592) where an emergency service is available.

Doctors Some upmarket hotels have doctors on call, though they can be expensive private ones. Emergency services are available 24 hours at health centres across the island. If you're staying in one place for a while, it's a good idea to make a list of emergency contact details and pin them up by the front door (check first that your host hasn't already provided one in their welcoming pack).

Emergencies Staff in most hotels are trained to deal with emergencies, so call the front desk before you do anything else. Otherwise, for an ambulance call ☎ 112, for the police ☎ 062, for the fire service ☎ 112.

Ferries See 'Getting There', above.

Holidays Apart from public holidays common to the rest of the Balearic Islands, Menorca also celebrates its own island day (17th Jan).

Hospitals There are private medical centres with English-speaking staff at most resorts, but check first whether your holiday insurance will cover treatment beforehand. There are two private clinics on the island, Policlínica Virgin de Gracia (Vives Llull 6, Maó ☎ 971 054 507) and Clínica Menorca (Canonge Moll, Ciutadella ☎ 971 480 505). Both employ translators. In spring 2007, Menorca's new Mateu Orfila Hospital on Maó's ring road is scheduled to open. If a member of your family does end up there, take advantage of the ex-pat Red Cross volunteers who visit English-speaking patients in the hospital every morning from Monday to Saturday.

Internet Access The number of internet cafés is growing across the island, at **Alfa Scooter** (Centro Comercial Coves Noves, Local 17, Es Mercadal 📞 *971 358 126 www.alfascooter.com*) prices start from €5 (£3.35) an hour. Another central *cibercafé* is **Can Internet** (Av. Mestre Gari 48, Es Mercadal 📞 *971 375 359 www. caninternet.net*).

Language A bilingual region, in the Balearic Islands, both Spanish and Catalan (or Menorcan, in the case of Menorca) are official languages. English is widely spoken.

Lost Property Unless you know where you dropped an item and can ask there, go to the nearest police station. For important documents such as passports, contact your consulate. For lost credit cards, see p. 38. If you think your car may have been towed away for being illegally parked, ask at the local police station.

Mail Each town has its own post office, easily spotted by its yellow signs, Maó and Ciutadella's offices are open Mon–Fri 8.30am–8.30pm; Sat 9.30am–1pm while in smaller towns, the post office is open Mon–Fri 8.30am–2.30pm; Sat 9.30am–1pm.

Newspapers & Magazines
Local daily papers include *Diario Menorca* and *Ultima Hora Menorca*. On Tuesdays, *Diario Menorca* publishes a few pages of local news in English, with a list of events on the island for the week. The English language newspaper for the Balearics, *Majorca Daily Bulletin*, includes both local and international news. It also features a daily list of events on the islands. For general information on the island, as well as useful contact numbers and updates from ex-pat associations, the monthly magazine *Roqueta* is worth consulting, and is available from newsagents. Otherwise, English-language newspapers from the UK and USA are widely available at news stands and newsagents, without the supplements and at a premium price; the *Guardian* has an international edition sold in Europe.

Police In emergencies, call 📞 *092*. For theft, you have to file a report with either the National Police (Maó and Ciutadella) or the Civil Guard (Maó, Es Mercadal and Ciutadella). For straightforward reports, the police have recently introduced a new centralised number, 📞 *902 102 112*, which enables you to file a report in either English, German, French, Spanish, Arabic or Japanese. You will need a form of identity to hand (such as your passport), and the call centre will give you a reference number for your case, before it is passed on to the police in Maó and Ciutadella. See also p. 39.

Taxis There are taxi ranks in each town and many resorts, as well as at the airport and port. To order a taxi in Ciutadella call ☎ *971 482 222*; Ferreries ☎ *971 373 484*; and from anywhere else phone ☎ *971 367 111*. Journey rates are fixed. See p. 158.

Tipping Service is generally not included in restaurants, so if you are happy with the service given, leave a 10–15% tip.

Toilets & Baby Changing

There are few public toilets, so you are best making a small purchase at a bar or café before using their toilet. Public museums often have toilets, but few galleries do, and there are no department stores on the island with bathrooms for public use. Baby changing facilities are also few and far between – newer and larger bars are more likely to have a fold-down changing table – so it's wise to carry a changing mat with you.

Water See p. 40. In towns, tap water is safe to drink, but in resorts opt for bottled water. If you ask for *agua* in a restaurant, you will be given bottled water unless you demand *agua portable*. Still water is *agua sin gas*, while sparkling is *agua con gas*.

Weather See p. 22.

Visitor Information

The **Balearic Islands' Tourist Board** website, *www.illes balears.es,* has plenty of information about the characteristics of each of the islands in English. There is a section dedicated to Menorca. In addition *www.emenorca.org* is run by **Menorca's Island Council**, and apart from information about the island's attractions, it includes an events calendar in English. There is a tourist information office open all year round in the arrivals section of the airport. In addition, there are seasonal offices, open from May-Oct, in **Maó's port** (Moll de Llevant 2 ☎ *971 355 952*) and **bus station** (Av. J. Anselmo Clavé), **Ciutadella's town centre** (Plaça Catedral 5 ☎ *971 382 693*), and in **Fornells** (C/Major 57 ☎ *971 376 412*). In smaller towns, tourist information can be obtained directly from the town hall.

Getting Around

By Car Menorca may be a Biosphere Reserve, but limited public transport options mean that if you want to explore the island, a car really is your only transport option.

The island's capital is **Maó** in the east, and the main road, Me-1, or *carretera general* as it is known by locals, connects Maó with the towns of **Alaior, Es Mercadal, Ferreries** and finally, **Ciutadella** in the west. There are very few roads that run along the coast, so travel between resorts inevitably means rejoining Me-1 before heading out towards the sea again. A rented car is the best way to see the island: while public transport works well between towns, there are no services to virgin beaches or some smaller resorts.

There are numerous car rental companies on the island, from big names such as **Avis** (*www. avis.com*) and **Hertz** (*www.hertz. com*) to smaller local companies (see below). If you plan to hire a car, booking in advance is advisable, especially during July and August, when you may have trouble renting the vehicle you want if you leave it until the last minute. If you choose to book through a local company, most will meet you at the airport and take you to the vehicle personally. All will rent child seats, but do order them in advance. Staff at the majority speak English, and several are run by Brits. **Meno-cars** (Av. Vives Llull 128, Maó ☎ *971 368 762 www.meno cars.com*); **Doncars** (Son Cremat 8, POIMA, Maó ☎ *971 360 467 www.doncars.com*); **Sol Car Hire** (Camí 'Es Castell 235, Maó ☎ *971 364 552*) and **Villacars** (Crta Alaior-Cala en Porter

km 1, Alaior ☎ *971 371 575 www. villacars.es*) are just some of the independent companies that operate on the island. An Internet search quickly expands the list. Costs for renting a basic model vary from just over €100 (£67) in low season to €220 (£147.40) per week during July or August.

By law, hire companies cannot rent vehicles to drivers under 21. When collecting your car, you will need you driver's licence, and additional photo ID, such as a passport or national identity card, and a credit card. If you have trouble obtaining a car or booster seat from the hire car company, **Mental Rentals Menorca** (☎ *639 182 278 www.mentalrentals menorca.com*) can rent you one for the duration of your stay. A booster seat costs €15 (£10.05) for a week's rental and a car seat, €20 (£13.40).

The downside of driving here is parking. While resorts usually

Driving Times

Yes, Menorca is a small island, but that doesn't mean you can drive everywhere you want in a matter of minutes – distances can deceive. Take the beaches of Son Bou and Sant Tomàs: they may be side be side on the south coast, but it's 30 minutes' drive from one to the other. The villas in Cala Llonga are another example. From Maó's port, they look very close to the city, but you face a good 15 minutes of winding road to get there. The isolated beaches near Ciutadella are also further than they look on the map. As the only access is along narrow country lanes, you are forced to drive slowly. In general terms, the main towns along Me-1 are 15 minutes apart, so it takes up to an hour to drive from Maó to Ciutadella. Then add 15 minutes minimum to travel north or south to resorts and beaches.

Countryside around Monte Toro

offer ample space close to your accommodation, towns are a different matter altogether. Streets are often narrow, empty parking spaces are difficult to find, and locals can be very laid-back: you can easily get stuck behind a driver while he chats to a friend on the pavement, oblivious to the fact that you exist, let alone want to continue your journey.

In town centres, look out for the zona azul, blue-painted parking spaces where you are obliged to pay. Have coins handy as the machines do not give change; expect to pay around €0.60 (£0.40) an hour. Payment times vary from town to town, but typically, a ticket is required between 9am and 1.30pm, then 5pm until 8.30pm, while the shops are open. You cannot park in a zona verde: these green-painted parking spaces are for residents only.

By Bus Although travelling by bus isn't the best way to see Menorca, public transport has improved in recent years, and connections between major towns are much easier.

A **service connecting Maó with Alaior, Es Mercadal, Ferreries and Ciutadella** runs hourly all year. Buses depart from both Maó and Ciutadella at 6.45am, with the last bus departing at 11.40pm from Ciutadella and 12.15am from Maó. A single ticket between Maó and Ciutadella costs €4.15 (£2.78); buy tickets on board. In addition, check the local press – both *Diario Menorca* and *Ultima Hora* publish bus timetables every day. **Es Castell** and **Sant Lluís** are connected to Maó by regular shuttle services, approximately every half-hour; change in Maó if you want to head west.

Es Castell

Between May and October, major resorts are connected to towns by bus. Check the times at the bus stop or in the local press. Services tend to concentrate in the morning and afternoon, leaving a long gap for lunch. If you want to travel between resorts, a change in the nearest town is almost inevitable.

A **shuttle service operates in Maó,** connecting the port with the town and the airport. This service operates every half-hour and costs €1.10 (£0.74) for the town circuit, and €1.50 (£1) for journeys to the airport. It can save a tiring walk up the port steps.

On special occasions, like town fiestas, extra services are laid on. Details are published in the local press.

Menorca's buses are gradually being modernised, but even so, they currently all have steps, so are impractical with pushchairs. Drivers will usually open the trunk for you to store one during the journey: just ask them as you get on board.

Each town has one bus stop, in the case of Maó and Ciutadella the bus station. These are usually on the edge of town, so you will face a 5–10 minute walk into the centre.

By Taxi Taxis are an alternative if you plan to spend the majority of your stay in one place. There are taxi ranks at the airport and in towns, and they can be booked through Radio Taxis (☎ *971 367 111*). The journey from the airport to Maó costs around €12 (£8.04) and takes 10 minutes, while a taxi from the airport to Ciutadella costs around €43 (£28.81) and takes 40 minutes. There are set prices for journeys, so your driver can tell you what it will cost before you depart – although at the time of writing, drivers were debating whether to install meters.

There is a charge of 60¢ per suitcase, and night fares apply between 9pm and 6am.

By Bike Cycling is a popular sport on the island, especially around Ciutadella where the flat terrain makes ideal pedalling territory. There are still relatively few dedicated cycling lanes and tracks, so much of the time you're forced to share the road with drivers. Helmets are not obligatory, but are strongly advised. Bikes can be rented, or repaired if you bring your own,

at **Bike Menorca** on Maó's ring road (☎ *971 353 798 www.bike menorca.com*). Prices start from €12 (£8) per day for a basic mountain bike. In the west, **Velos Joan** (St. Isidre 32–34, Ciutadella ☎ *971 381 576*) also has a wide selection of bikes available for hire from €33 (£22.11) a week. Bike Menorca is run by avid cyclists, so if you visit the shop with a map in hand, they can recommend routes.

Child-friendly Events & Entertainment

Menorca's summer is one long celebration. Each town holds its own fiesta, with horses, fireworks, concerts, open-air markets and entertainment, all in the name of their patron saint. The fun begins in Ciutadella on 23rd June, then practically every weekend in July and August is

What's in a Name?

It's likely that you'll hear Menorcan places referred to by more than one name. During the Franco dictatorship, street and town names were switched from the island dialect of Catalan to Spanish, but nowadays the Catalan versions prevail. In many cases, there is little difference between one and the other – Alaior in Catalan and Alayor in Spanish. But in others, they are completely different: Es Castell (Catalan) and Villa Carlos (Spanish) are the same place; so are Es Migjorn Gran (Catalan) and San Cristóbal (Spanish). One of the biggest points of conflict is the name of Menorca's capital – Maó. Some locals have become passionate about the absence of an 'h' in its spelling, claiming that the loss of the letter ignores its Roman roots. So heated is the debate, a political party has been formed with a manifesto promise of restoring the letter should they get into power. For simplicity's sake, Catalan spellings have been used throughout this guidebook, as these are found on road signs.

Children's Top 10 Menorca Attractions

- Seeing red cows close up at **Lloc de Menorca**, see p. 167.
- Peering inside the prehistoric burial chamber at **Naveta d'es Tudons**, see p. 182.
- The spooky underground tunnels at **La Mola**, see p. 168.
- Bowling to disco music at **Son Bou**, see p. 171.
- Discovering the immense **Coloms Caves** hidden between Es Migjorn Gran and Binigaus beach, see p. 181.
- Braving the Kamikaze waterslide at **AquaRock**, see p. 186.
- Renting canoes from **Es Grau beach**, to head out to Colom Island, see p. 166.
- Underwater fireworks at midnight to end **Maó's fiestas**, see p. 161.
- Descending into the depths of the open quarry at **Lithica**, see p. 180.
- Finding out about the ancient Roman port and lost city at Sanitja, at the **Eco-Museum in Cap de Cavalleria**, see p. 183.

marked by a fiesta somewhere, until Maó's fiestas close the season, in early September (see p. 161). The fiestas are a family affair, and local children play an important part. You'll often see them participating in floats, playing instruments in street parades and pretending to be riders with toy horses of their own; or just taking their turn on the rides at the fairground that moves from town to town all summer. If you steer clear of the packed main square, even your little ones can take part safely. Riders usually let you stroke the horses, and may even let small children climb up alongside them for a photo.

Contact the Tourist office (see 'Visitor Information', p. 155) for fiesta dates. You can pick up fiesta programmes from individual town halls, with information on concerts, markets, fairground locations and firework times as well as any other events. Most town halls produce a programme with listings in English.

Family Concerts AGES 5 AND UP

La Caixa bank regularly organises a series of family concerts that aim to introduce young children to classical music, through adapted versions of classical pieces and explanations about different instruments.

Maó's Teatre Principal (Plaça de la Porta de Mallorca 3, Maó ☎ 971 355 776 www.teatremao.org. €3 (£2)) regularly hosts these through the year (usually on Sundays at midday). Check their programme to see if one coincides with your visit.

Basketball Matches ★ FIND

AGES 5 AND UP Menorca's basketball team was promoted to

Spain's top division, the ACB, in 2005. This giant step up led to the construction of Menorca Pavilion on the outskirts of Maó, with space for 5000 spectators. During the season (October to May), fortnightly home matches are packed – and the atmosphere is infectious, even if you don't understand a thing about the sport. Islanders of all ages flock to the stadium for matches, especially when Menorca plays against star-studded teams like Real Madrid or Barcelona. Locals bring their youngsters, whatever their age, but given the incredible amount of noise generated, it might be sensible to give it a miss if you have toddlers in tow. Older children and teenagers will undoubtedly be swept away, however.

Pabellón Menorca, Camí de Trepucó s/n, Maó ☎ 971 369 299 www.menorcabasquet.com. From €15 (£10.05). Children under 2 free. A special bus service connects every town on the island with the stadium on match-days; check local press for times.

MAÓ & THE EAST

The British are to blame for Menorca's capital city being transferred from Ciutadella to **Maó.** Under British occupation during the 1800s, it was decided that given Maó's strategic importance – its natural harbour is the second largest in the world after Pearl Harbor – the town should become the capital. The port itself makes for an excellent stroll along 3 km of waterfront, with enormous ferries, old Menorcan fishing vessels, spectacular sailing boats and flash motorboats to admire. If little legs are likely to complain at such a trek, then the **Maó town shuttle bus service** (see 'Getting Around', p. 155) drives the full length of the port. Near the ferry terminal, there are steps that connect the port with the centre of town, but if you have a pushchair, you'll need to opt for the winding road upwards instead. During the first weekend in September, Maó hosts a **classic boat regatta,** and the carefully restored craft together with information panels about their age and characteristics are worth a look. Should you be in Maó on New Year's Day or around the fiestas in September, a handful of brave (or crazy) individuals swim across the port. Save energy for the last day of Maó's **Gracia fiestas,** when the port is closed to traffic, and there is entertainment at several points along the waterfront, including folk dancing and live music, with food and drinks stalls set up along the way. At around 11pm, find a space to watch fireworks that leap out from under the water.

There are several companies offering **boat trips** around the port (see 'Child-friendly Attractions', p. 171), but the most interesting sights are above water, so glass-bottomed vessels can be a disappointment.

MAÓ

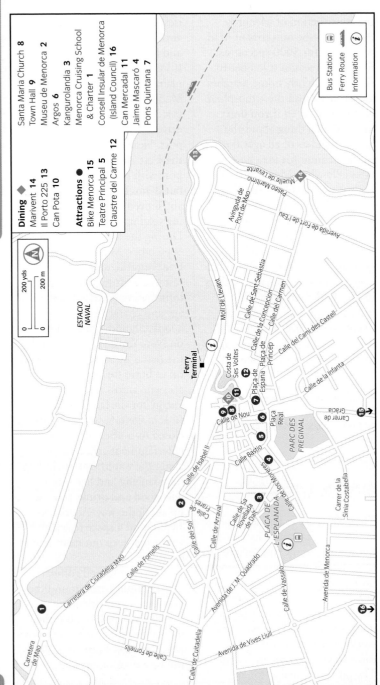

Santa Maria Church **8**
Town Hall **9**
Museu de Menorca **2**
Argos **6**
Kangurolandia **3**
Menorca Cruising School & Charter **1**
Consell Insular de Menorca (Island Council) **16**
Can Mercadal **11**
Jaime Mascaró **4**
Pons Quintana **7**

Dining ◆
Marivent **14**
Il Porto 225 **13**
Can Pota **10**

Attractions ●
Bike Menorca **15**
Teatre Principal **5**
Claustre del Carme **12**

Bus Station
Ferry Route
Information

ESTACIO NAVAL

Ferry Terminal

200 yds
200 m

Moll de Llevant

Costa de Ses Voltes

Plaça de Espanya

Plaça de Princep

Calle de Sant Sebastia
Calle de la Concepcion
Calle del Carmen
Calle del Carni des Castell

Calle de la Infanta

Carrer de Gracia

Calle de Nou

Plaça Real

PARC DES FREGINAL

Calle Bastio

Calle de Sa Moreria

Calle de Sa Rovellada de Dalt

PLAÇA DE L'ESPLANADA

Carrer de la Sinia Costabella

Calle de Isabell II

Calle de Ses Voltes

Calle de Frares

Calle de Arraval

Calle del Sol

Calle de Fornells

Carretera de Cutadella-Mao

Carretera de Mao

Calle de Cutadella

Avinguda de J. M. Quadrado

Avinguda de Menorca

Calle de Vassalo

Avenida de Vives Lluil

Paseo Maritimo
Muelle de Levante
Avinguda de Port de Mao
Avenida de Fort de l'Eau

During the summer, the **Plaça del Carme** hosts an **artesan market** every Friday, while at the market on Saturdays and Tuesdays at the **Plaça de l'Esplanada,** you can find clothes, accessories and souvenirs. Here you'll also find swings for the children. The square is just a minute away from the bus station. The indoor market at **Claustre del Carme** (see 'Buying Arts & Crafts', p. 170) is also worth a look. At several stalls, you can sample cheese or sausages before you buy. If shopping wears you out, then take a break in the cool of **Santa Maria Church**, where there are daily organ concerts at 11am between May and October.

There is a **tourist information office** in the port (Moll de Llevant, 2 ☎ *971 355 952*), and at the bus station (Av. J. Anselmo Clavé *www.ajmao.org*), and the town hall (Plaça de la Constitució 1, Maó ☎ *971 369 800*) has leaflets with suggested walking routes around town. Alternatively, between June and September, there are free guided walks, departing from the town hall at 7.30pm and lasting approximately two hours. In addition, Maó's **Teatre Principal,** in **Plaça de la Porta de Mallorca,** is open to the public on Tuesday mornings at 10.30 for guided tours behind the scenes.

A short drive south of Maó, along Me-8, is **Sant Lluís.** Founded by the French, the grid-layout makes it difficult to get lost. Two key landmarks

stand out above the town: **Es Molí de Dalt** and **Es Molí de Baix.** Of the two windmills, the former, at the entrance to the town, is home to a small **ethnological museum** AGES 8 AND UP (Carrer de Sant Lluís 4 ☎ *971 151 084.* Oct–May Mon–Fri 10–2; Sat 10–1; Jun–Sep Mon–Fri 10–2, 5–8; Sat 10–1; Sun 11–1 €1.20 (£0.80); children 12-18 years €0.60 (£0.40); under 12s free; free on Sundays) featuring old farming tools. It is also the bus stop. Opposite Es Molí de Dalt, there is a children's playground and small park area, and there's another park behind the church in town.

For live music, the town hosts a series of open-air classical concerts during the summer at several locations, including the **Pla de sa Creu,** where the Town Hall (☎ *971 150 950 www. ajsantlluis.org*) is located, Pick up a summer event leaflet (in Spanish, Catalan and English) from the town hall for details of open-air events in July, August and September. During Sant Lluís' fiestas, on the last weekend in August, Pla de sa Creu is a good place to watch the Sunday evening floats go by.

Es Castell is effectively a dormitory town, just a couple of miles from Maó. It is walkable, but if you prefer, the bus takes you to the entrance of the town, with half-hourly connections to/from Maó. The most easterly town in Spain, it was British soldiers and sailors that founded it when the British dominated Menorca, during the

18th century. Originally named Georgetown, Es Castell's military roots have marked the town, starting with the cannons outside the **Military Museum, AGES 8 AND UP** (Plaça de Esplanada. ℂ *971 362 100* Mon & Thurs 11–1, first Sun of the month 11–1. €2.70 (£1.81); children under 12s free) continuing, to **Fort Marlborough** in Sant Esteve and the remains of **St Philip's Castle** at the mouth of the port (see 'Museums & Monuments', p. 168). You'll find tourist information at the **Town Hall** (Plaça de l'Esplanada, 5 ℂ *971 365 193* **www.aj-escastell.org**).

A 15-minute drive west of Maó is **Alaior,** perched on a hill, with Santa **Eulàlia Church** in pole position. The steep streets can be hard work with a pushchair, especially if you arrive by bus. The stop is at the bottom of the town, on Carrer Sant Joan Baptista de la Salle. An industrial town, Alaior is home to many of the island's best cheese producers – visit Dalrit (Rvdo. Huguet 55, Alaior ℂ *971 371 155*) or COINGA (Crta Nova s/n Alaior ℂ *971 371 227*) in the industrial estate, or La Payesa (Carrer des Banyer 64, Alaior ℂ *971 371 072*) to buy direct. In fact, so important is the dairy industry to the town, it hosts an annual Countryside Fair – featuring cows and several stalls – on the third weekend in March. It attracts visitors from across the island.

Alaior is also home to the designer shoe company, Pons Quintana (see p. 187

During July and August, there is an evening **artesan market** on Carrer Major from 7 until 11, selling pottery, jewellery, trinkets and home-made toys. In the neighbouring square, there's often live music and entertainment.

On the Sunday night of Alaior's August fiestas, there are folk dancing displays around town, followed by an elaborate array of floats and midnight fireworks. The evening is a family affair, with even very young children on the streets until late, with plenty to keep them entertained. On Shrove Tuesday, the scene is repeated, with a parade of dressed-up locals marching through the streets. Tourist information is in the Town Hall (Carrer Major ℂ *971 371 002* **www.aj-alaior.org**).

Beaches & Resorts

With over 200 km of coastline, a book the size of this one could be dedicated to Menorca's beaches alone. In an attempt to do the island justice, I've listed the major resorts and most accessible virgin beaches (there are numerous coves that can only be reached by boat). As a general rule of thumb, the majority of sandy beaches are located on the southern side of the island, while the north coast tends to be rockier and more barren, with tiny patches of sand breaking up sheer cliff faces. The north coast also suffers the full force of the *tramuntana* wind, so if you come in early or late season, or during the winter, note that waves can be whipped up for days on end when the north wind blows.

Punta Prima A popular family resort with a good-sized, clean, sandy beach with views of the lighthouse on Illa de l'Aire (Air Island), opposite. When arriving by car, you can park on the short street opposite the beach, but if this is full, follow the street round the corner, by Insotel hotel, where there are usually spaces. This is also where the bus will drop you off. Along the seafront, there are several restaurants, souvenir shops and two supermarkets for snacks and ice-creams. On the beach itself, there are pedalos (though you can't venture far), sun beds and parasols for hire. There are also showers for rinsing the sand off your feet. Little children will love exploring the rock pools to the east of the beach. For older children, walk from Punta Prima along the ancient Camí de Cavalls perimeter path up to a defence tower, then across the rocks to Cala d'Alcalfar until you reach S'Algar. Alternatively, there is a small stretch of coastal road, connecting Punta Prima with Binibèquer that is ideal for cycling.

Binibèquer New (Nou) and Old (Vell) Binibèquer are popular self-catering destinations. The small, sandy cove makes for safe swimming, even with little ones, and the beach bar with straw parasols perched on the rocks above the sand is good for snacks. There are pedalos, sun beds and parasols for hire, and the beach is suitable for disabled

Cala en Porter

users. In the old part of the resort, coach-loads of tourists are bussed in to explore the narrow labyrinthine whitewashed houses and brown shutters of Binibequèr Vell. The village may be a 'fake' – it was built in 1968 – but it is still well worth exploring, a perfect spot for hide-and-seek.

Cala en Porter One of the first resorts on the island, very popular with the first batch of British tourists, some of the self-catering accommodation in Cala en Porter is starting to show its age. That said, its well-protected sandy beach makes it perfect for children; the steep cliffs either side of the cove ensure that the waters stay calm, whatever the weather. It is safe to take even little children out on pedalos, as you are unlikely to be surprised by big waves and few motor boats enter the bay. Sun beds and parasols can be rented, and there are a handful of bars on the waterfront for drinks and snacks. Access to the beach is via a winding road (the bus drops you at the top), to a small car park, or via steps. Easily the most famous local attraction is the **Cova d'en Xoroi** (see 'Natural Wonders', p. 167). The fact that it doubles as a night-club shouldn't put you off.

Son Bou ★★★ Two high-rise hotels block your view at first, but Son Bou is the longest beach on the island and a family favourite. The beach gradually becomes less crowded the further west you walk, but if you do decide to search out an isolated patch of sand, bear in mind that there are only three bars on the entire stretch, so it's a long walk back for an ice-cream. In fact, you're better off bringing a pic-nic, as it's a long walk back to the resort, and the beach bars are pricey. There is plenty to keep children entertained: rent canoes and pedalos; ride on the back of a sausage pulled by a motor boat; or search for life in rock pools. There are also sun beds and parasols for hire. If arriving by public transport, the bus covers a circuit through the resort before leaving you at the two tower

block hotels, the best stop for visiting the beach. There is a large car park, but at weekends this is often full by lunchtime. In the resort itself, the hill overlooking the beach provides accommodation for every budget (see 'Family-friendly Accommodation', p. 188). The resort also has waterslides at **Club San Jaime** **ALL AGES** (Urb. Sant Jaume, Alaior ☏ 971 372 787. May–Oct pool and waterslides open 11am–7pm. Free entry. Bar/restaurant 10am–midnight), bouncy castles in the commercial area and fam-ily-friendly bars and restaurants.

Es Grau ★ The heart of S'Albufera Natural Park (see 'Natural Wonders', p. 167), Es Grau is a tiny fishing village with a curved, sandy beach in a shal-low bay, making it ideal for even tiny children. You can swim out far and still touch the bottom, but be careful of the fishing boats. Renting canoes is safe even with younger children; you can opt for doubles or singles.

Exploring the dunes at Son Bou

With older children, paddle across to **Colom Island** to its deserted beaches (exploring inland is forbidden). S'Albufera is ideal for walking and bird watching, and if you head west along Es Grau beach, you can enter it by a footpath through the sand dunes.

The small car park right by the beach fills up quickly, so opt for the first car park you see on your right hand side as you enter the resort. The beach is just five minutes' walk away. The bus stop is right next to the entrance to the beach.

Natural Wonders

Cova d'en Xoroi ★★

AGES 5 AND UP Better known as a nightclub, a visit to Cova d'en Xoroi by day is not to be missed. Steep steps lead down to a series of terraces and bars (a drink is included in your entry price), and teenagers will enjoy the sundown session, with its backdrop of chillout music. From the many lookout points, you can peer down at the waves crashing below.

Unless you are staying in Cala en Porter, it is wiser to drive to the caves; the bus stop is a good half-hour's walk away. With younger children, leave the pushchair in the car: it's impractical carrying it up and down the steps, and you'll miss the view, which is the main reason for visiting.

Cala en Porter ✆ *971 377 236* **www. covadenxoroi.com**. *€8.30 (£5.55). May-Oct Mon-Sun 10.30-sundown. Oct-May Sun 10.30-sundown.*

Lloc de Menorca ★ ALL AGES

Recreating the elements of a typical Menorcan farm, and adding a few exotic species, Lloc de Menorca makes a good day-trip for children. As well as several species unique to the Balearics, such as Mallorcan goats and Menorcan red cows, there's also kangaroos and ostriches. Following the circuit around the farm takes about an hour, and apart from animals, there is also an organic vegetable patch, play area, cafe and shop. The clear pathways are pushchair-friendly, and children are safe to run on ahead. If you're not squeamish, and don't have young ones with you, the farm organises typical *porquetjades*: you can watch a butcher kill a pig, before a class where you learn to make your own Menorcan spicy sausages (€900 (£603) for a group of up to 30). You of course take home the finished result.

There is a car park on site; the nearest bus stop is in Alaior; from there take a taxi to the farm.

Me-1 km 7, between Alaior and Maó ✆ *971 372 403* **www.llocdemenorca. com**. *€6 (£4.02) adults; €4 (£2.68) children. Children under 3 free. Oct-May 10am-6pm; May-Oct 10am-9pm; closed Dec-mid-Jan.*

S'Albufera d'Es Grau ★★

ALL AGES When Menorca was declared a Biosphere Reserve in 1993, the 2000 hectares of marsh, dunes and headland here was designated the core. Over 100 bird species can be found in the park, as well as many other flora and fauna; You can easily spot fish in the network of lagoons. The visitor centre can recommend walks within the park, but with younger children the best option follows the wooden pontoons in the northern part, accessed by a bridge near kilometre 6 on Me-5 between Maó and Es Grau. Roped walkways steer you along the path – which is suitable for pushchairs – and lead you behind the dunes to the western end of Es Grau beach. If you want to find out more, join one of the guided walks, held every Saturday during the winter and on Tuesdays, Wednesdays and Thursdays between May and October. They are free, but places must be booked at the visitor centre.

Visitor centre: Es Grau Me-5 km 3.5 ☏ *971 356 302. Admission free. Open Oct–May 9am-2pm, May–Oct Wed–Fri 9am–7pm; Sat, Sun, Tue 9am–2pm; closed Mon. Park open sunrise to sunset.*

Monuments & Museums

La Mola ★ ★ ★ AGES 5 AND UP

Worried that Menorca wasn't adequately protected from the French and British navies, the Spanish government decided to built a fortress to defend Maó's harbour in 1848. Isabel II Fortress was the result of 25 years of work, and although it never had its defences put to the test, soldiers were present here until the 1990s. Allow plenty of time to explore the fortress: the guided tour takes two hours and 30 minutes, as there is plenty to see both above and below ground. Tunnels, moats, British-built cannons, prisons and artillery stores; you get a really close look at how the fortress was designed. Children are welcome, and the guide may even invite them to run ahead in the underground tunnels. Although there are no age limits, given the fortress is spread out over a considerable area, young ones

La Mola Fort

Prehistoric Menorca

The word 'archaeology' may not provoke much interest in children, but Menorca is filled with the remains of prehistoric settlements dating back to the 4th century BC. At the most interesting ones children can get close up to the stones, step inside the remains of old houses (the roofs have long disappeared) and invent their own theories as to how ancient populations managed to create giant 't' structures with slabs of stone, and no machinery to give them a hand.

If you're travelling on a budget, visit prehistoric sights and military buildings on Sundays, as many are free. You can find out more about the prehistoric sites on the island at **www.menorcamonumental.org**.

are likely to tire with so much walking, and a pushchair isn't always practical. The summer guided tours at 5.30pm are recommended: the shafts of setting sunlight that penetrate the underground tunnels are an impressive sight. There is no public transport to the fortress, but free buses from Maó's bus station are available on Sundays, departing at 11am and leaving La Mola at 2pm.

Follow Me-3 from Maó's port towards Cala Llonga until it ends ☎ 971 411 066 www.fortalesalamola.com. €5 (£3.35); children under 12 free. 10% discount with Green Card (see p. 17 for details). Nov–Apr 10am–2pm; May and Oct 10am–6pm; July–Sept 10am–8pm. Closed Mon.

Fort Marlborough AGES 5 AND UP

On the south side of Maó's port stands one of Menorca's most important British legacies: Fort Marlborough, named after Sir John Churchill, Duke of Marlborough at the time it was built (between 1710 and 1726). The site also includes the remains of **St Philip's Castle**

(never completed) and **Stuart Tower**, where executions were carried out. Fort Marlborough's construction was no easy task; it is built on solid rock and underground are hundreds of metres of tunnels dug by British sailors and coerced Menorcans. The guided tour lasts 45 minutes.

Parking is at the top of Sant Esteve cove, and the entrance to the Fort is a good 15-minute walk downhill. There is no public transport available. Pushchairs are impractical here.

Follow Me-4 from Es Castell, past Sol de l'Est ☎ 971 360 462. €3 (£2); OAPs and 8–16-year-olds €1.80 (£1.21); under 8s free. Green Card 20% discount. Free Sun. Apr Tues–Sun 10am–2.30pm; May–Sept Mon and Wed 10am–2.30pm; Tues, Thurs, Sat, Sun 10am–8pm; Oct–Dec Tues– Sun 10am–2.30pm. Closed Jan–Mar.

Torre d'en Galmés ALL AGES An

ancient town situated high up to gain maximum control of the surrounding countryside, this is the largest prehistoric settlement on the island. Excavation work continues on the south side of the site, and every year a group of archaeology students from Boston University works on the dig. A guided walk leads you between ancient houses, *taules* and temples. It is easy to negotiate with a pushchair, although it is wise to visit early in the morning or late in the day; there is no shade and in mid-summer the heat is unbearable.

Between May and September a guided tour is included in the ticket price.

There is no public transport, although it is possible to cycle from Son Bou or Alaior. There is a small car park.

Head south towards Son Bou from Alaior; it is signposted from the road. €2.40 (£1.61); OAPs and children aged 8–16 €1.20 (£0.80); under 8s free. Free Nov–Mar and on Sun. Green Card 20% discount. Apr and Oct Tue–Sun 10am–2.30pm; May–Sept Tues–Sat 10am–8pm; Sun–Mon 10am–2.30pm.

Talatí de Dalt AGES 5 AND UP

In archeological terms, the highlight of this settlement is the unusual addition of a slab of stone, leaning at an angle at the 't' shaped *taula*. One of the quieter settlements in terms of visitors, the remains at Talatí de Dalt are spread out across the countryside, making for a good walk. It is not so practical for pushchairs. There is a small car park, but no access by public transport.

Me-1 Kilometre 4; signposted from the main road. €3 (£2); OAPs and students €1.50 (£1); children under 8 free. Daily 10am–sunset.

Museu de Menorca

AGES 5 AND UP As its name implies, this place charts the island's history, and the cultures that have dominated here. Children will probably be most interested in the rooms with tools and displays about traditional

Buying Arts & Crafts

For Menorcan pottery, works of art and hand-made trinkets and toys, the **artesan markets** held across the island are best for browsing. Summer markets are held in **Maó,** outside Claustre del Carme, every Friday, and in **Alaior** on Carrer Major on Wednesday evenings during July and August. Ask at tourist offices for more information on occasional markets and fairs.

Argos An art-lover's haven, Argos stocks numerous prints and paintings, art, craft and painting materials and greeting cards – including old maps and enlarged photographs of Menorca. If your budget can't stretch to that, the postcards, bookmarks and calendars by island photographer, Lluís Real, are far more original than your traditional picture-postcard images.

Deià 4, Maó ☎ 971 362 652.

Menorcan trades. Entry to the museum is worthwhile for the building alone. The elegant cloisters often host open-air concerts during the summer (such as Menorca's International Jazz Festival; ask at the tourist office for more details, or see *www. jazzobert.com*) . The ground floor is easily negotiated with a pushchair. What isn't such a breeze is parking: there is no car park for museum visitors, so you have to search Maó's narrow streets. Maó's bus station is a 15-minute walk away.

Plaça de Sant Francesc, s/n, Maó 971 350 955. *€2.40 (£1.61); Green Card 50% discount. Sat pm and Sun free entry. Nov–Mar Tue–Fri 9.30am–2pm; Sat–Sun 10am–2pm; Apr–Oct Tue–Sat 10am–2pm and 6pm–8.30pm; Sun 10am–2pm.*

Child-friendly Attractions

Boat Trips ALL AGES Several companies offer boat trips around Maó's port. They are, inevitably, aimed at tourists, but are still a good way to see the port's highlights close up: the old British Naval hospital on King's Island (or Bloody Island, as the British called it), the military forts of La Mola and Fort Marlborough (see p. 168 and 169) from the sea. Boats have a cafe and toilets on board, and although it is a bit tricky boarding with a pushchair, staff are used to entertaining youngsters, and they'll genuinely enjoy the hour-long ride. As Maó's port is well protected from stormy

weather, a boat trip is an option even on a rainy day.

There's plenty of parking in the port (don't forget to buy a ticket), and if you arrive by bus, the Maó shuttle service stops right next to the boat's departure point.

The Yellow Catamaran, Moll de Llevant 12 639 676 351 *www. yellowcatamarans.com. €8.50 (£5.70); children 5–12 €4.50 (£3); under 5s free. April 1–2 departures; May and Oct Mon-Sat departures every 45 min 10.30am–3.30pm, Sun 10.45am, 12.15pm, 1.45pm; Jun–Sep Mon–Sat departures every 45 min 10.30am–4.30pm; Sun 10.45am, 12.15pm, 1.45pm.*

Son Bou Bowling ★
AGES 5 AND UP Ideal on a rainy day, the newly opened bowling alley in Son Bou has 16 lanes as well as a bar, video game machines and a children's play area for the little ones aged two upwards. Popular with locals, at night there are strobe lights and disco music. There is plenty of parking nearby, and the bus stop is just five minutes' walk away – although there are no buses between Alaior and Son Bou in the winter. In Maó, there is a smaller bowling alley underneath the OciMax cinema on Carrer Ramon y Cajal 15 (971 364 771).

Son Bou Bowling, Son Bou. Games €5 (£3.35), shoe hire €1 (£0.67). Mon–Sun 5pm–2am.

Kangurolandia AGES 12 AND UNDER
If you're stuck for ideas on a rainy day, pack the children off

to Kangurolandia to let off steam. This indoor adventure playground has a café for parents to relax while the little ones run riot. The only problem is its location, right in the heart of Maó. Parking outside is impossible, although there is an underground car park at Plaça de l'Esplanada, five minutes away. The bus station is a five-minute walk.

Carrer d'es Forn 42, Maó ☎ 971 368 238. Mon–Fri 5pm–8.30pm; Sat 11am-1pm, 5.30pm–8pm. Closed Sun.

For Active Families

Canoe Hire ★ ★ AGES 5 AND UP

You can rent canoes from several beaches, but with young children **Es Grau** (see 'Beaches & Resorts', p. 164) is one of the safest venues to go paddling; the water is shallow a long way out. With older children, you can head across to Colom Island, but take care for motor boats cutting across the strip of water that separates the island from the shore. Paddle Indian-style in single canoes, or if your child gets easily tired, opt for a double canoe so they don't have to do too much work. There are life jackets available, even in small sizes: make sure you ask for one. As soon as you arrive, you'll see the canoes lined up on the beach. Another good beach for hiring a canoe is **S'Arenal d'en Castell** (see p. 178).

Es Grau beach. An hour's rental costs €10–15 (£6.70–10.05). May–Oct 10am–6pm approx.

Sailing ★ ★ AGES 8 AND UP

Maó's protected port is an ideal enclave for teaching youngsters how to sail. For complete beginners, Maó-based **Menorca Cruising School & Charter** (☎ *971 389 003 www.menorcasailing.co.uk*) offers a two-day introductory course, with prices from €290 (£195). The company is happy to host families, and since RYA-recognised courses and qualifications are held in small groups, you can always arrange a boat to yourselves. Accommodation is on-board for advanced courses, and in nearby hotels for day courses. The boat is moored at the west end of Maó's port, within walking distance of the recommended hotel, so a car isn't essential.

Cycling AGES 2 AND UP

This is one of the best ways to see the island, but unfortunately there are only limited cycle paths on Menorca's roads. For longer rides, you are forced to use the main road between Maó and Ciutadella, distinctly not ideal for children given the traffic. With younger children, short rides around Cala en Porter, Cala en Bosc and Fornells are usually stretching enough. One slightly more taxing route starts from Sant Lluís and heads towards s'Ullastrar, past the prehistoric ruins at Binissafullet, and either loops round towards Llucmaçames, or continues westwards, passing around the bottom of the runway before connecting with a road that either leads north to

Sant Climent or south to Binidalí, from where you can head back to Sant Lluís along the coast.

Bikes can be hired from most resorts, but in Maó, **Bike Menorca** (Francesc Femenies 44 ☏ *971 365 726 www.bike menorca.com*. From €12 (£8) a day) easily has the widest selection on offer, and they also do on-the-spot repairs. They rent seats and helmets for toddlers, and for €20 (£13.40) offer a pick up / drop off service.

Don't forget to take water, snacks, a mobile phone and a puncture kit on longer rides. A good map, marking country lanes, is also essential. Bike shops can usually recommend routes, and if you ask at a tourist office, they will give you a detailed map for free (ask for the one published by IBATUR). **Menorca's Island Council** (in Plaça de la Biosfera, Maó) also has maps and leaflets available at its information desk.

Walking AGES 12 AND UP There are endless walks around Menorca's coastline and countryside. So many, in fact, that it's difficult to know where to begin, as many of the best routes are not published in guidebooks, or involve passing through private property – something I would not recommend.

Menorca's premier footpath, the **Camí de Cavalls,** is an ancient path that follows Menorca's perimeter. Today some of the footpath is on private property, but the Menorcan Island Council is in midst of expropriating the land. Parts are already open to the public, and clearly signposted so – such as between Punta Prima and S'Algar – and gradually more sections will be opened up. Easier walks for children include the three miles of coastline following Son Bou (see 'Beaches & Resorts', p. 164) west, following the headland upwards, before descending to Sant Tomàs; or

A Walking Holiday?

For keen walkers, and families with older children, guided walking holidays are an excellent way to find hidden parts of the island. **Menorca Walking Holidays** (☏ *0800 072 4832* from the UK; *www.menorca walkingholidays.com*), run by a friendly British couple, organises weekly holidays for groups as small as two. In a typical week, you spend five out of seven days walking. Their minibus picks you up and drops you off, as well as meets you mid-way for biscuits. The walks are never longer than eight miles. A week's walking, with accommodation and lunches, costs from £429 per person. The holidays run all year, apart from July and August. If an entire week seems too much, they occasionally let people on holiday join them for the day.

along the waterfront at Cala Galdana, climbing up the steps at the eastern end to the lookout point above the bay.

The usual rules apply when out walking. Wear sturdy footwear: on even the hottest days, you may come across slippery rocks or puddles; carry a map and mobile phone; take a supply of water and snacks; and close any gates you come across – they may enclose fields where sheep or cattle are grazing.

Shopping

With no department stores, and only a handful of well known high-street names, shopping certainly isn't Menorca's main attraction. That said, the island has an important shoe and leather industry, as well as costume jewellery, pottery, wines and cheeses made on the island: these are Menorca's famous exports. For artesan goods, **summer markets** are the best place to shop, as potters and jewellers often have workshops in their own homes. See 'Buying Arts & Crafts', p. 170.

Cas Sabater Pagès There are numerous shops selling traditional Menorcan sandals, *albarcas*, but the authentic ones, with recycled car tyres for soles, are not easy to find. Cas Sabater Pagès stocks the original, with greased beige leather and soles that have done several thousand miles already. They even do baby sizes. In addition, you can find modern variations on the sandal in various colours, leathers, designs and styles, with several Menorcan versions for children, tiny buckle sandals with lady-birds or lizards on them. Prices start from around €20 (£13.40) a pair.
Plaça Nova 4, Alaior 📞 *971 378 694.*

Box Of the many shops selling children's clothes, Box has a reasonably-priced range from three upwards, including bold body-warmers and embroidered cardigans.
Bonaire 12, Maó.

Petit Món This place in Sant Lluís also has a good selection of baby and toddler clothes. For a Menorcan touch, look out for Ecològic Line: great T-shirt designs with island features, such as boats, lizards and lighthouses printed on cotton. Pou Nou has a range of simple T-shirts for children as young as six months.
Carrer de Sant Lluís 101, Sant Lluís 📞 *971 151 775.*

Can Mercadal This tiny shop is an Aladdin's Cave for fishermen and divers. If you can't see what you want, don't be afraid to ask – the owner may not speak any English but he will endeavour to find what you're looking for. A laid-back shop, you'll notice that the wooden stools aren't just for customers trying on shoes. They are also used by Menorcan passers-by who have just stopped for a chat.
Portal de Mar 6, Maó.

CIUTADELLA & THE WEST

Steeped in tradition, Ciutadella ★★ somehow manages to conserve the air of a small village even though it's Menorca's second-largest town. From narrow cobbled streets (walk along the aptly-named *Carrer Qui No Passa*, where you can almost touch houses on both sides with outstretched arms) to the grand Born Square, picture-postcard scenes are around every corner. You can appreciate Ciutadella's grandeur by visiting a handful of its stately homes: there are guided tours in English every Friday, departing from Plaça des Pins at midday. Just turn up to join in the walks, pre-booking isn't required Unfortunately, two of Ciutadella's main attractions, Es Born Theatre and the town's gothic Cathedral, are in the midst of a lengthy restoration process, and so closed to the public. As a result, morning organ recitals, at 10.30 every day apart from Sunday in the summer, are held in Socors Church (Carrer del Bisbe Vila ☎ 971 481 297. Tue–Sat 10.30am–1.30pm).

Ciutadella lives and breathes its annual June fiestas, and as they draw near, locals hang out flags bearing St John's cross. The town is extremely busy at fiesta time, and as horses parade down the narrowest of streets – they even enter a handful of houses – be careful with younger children. A horse can surprise you with a kick or jump.

The tourist office is at Plaça de la Catedral 5 (☎ 971 382 693 www.ciutadella.org), the same square that hosts a farmers' market on Saturday mornings, and open-air concerts during the summer. Ask at the tourist information office for a programme, or visit www.jjmmciutadella.com. During Ciutadella's Summer Music Festival, classical music fills the peaceful setting of Claustre del Seminari, where you can relax among landscaped gardens.

A few minutes from the centre of town, you can visit the ambitiously named Platja Gran, a small beach, popular with locals, where you can stretch out on smooth rocks leading up to the sand. There are steps into the sea for swimming. In addition, a new public pool was opened in late 2006.

Nearby, in Ferreries, the marquee in Plaça d'Espanya is the location for frequent fairs, including artesan markets on Saturday mornings, Christmas fairs and other events. For information, contact the Town Hall at

Ciutadella

CIUTADELLA

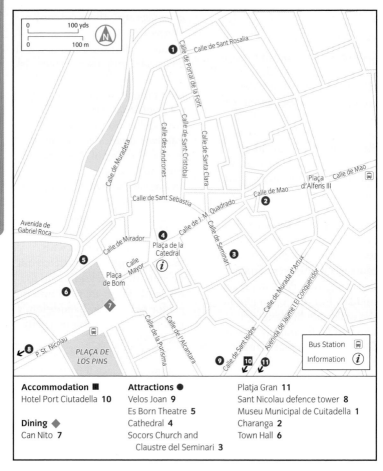

0 100 yds
0 100 m

Calle de Sant Rosalia

Calle de Portal de la Font

Calle de Muradeta

Calle des Andrones

Calle de Sant Cristobal

Calle de Santa Clara

Plaça d'Alfens III · Calle de Mao

Calle de Sant Sebastia

Calle de Mao

Calle de J. M. Quadrado

Avenida de Gabriel Roca

Calle de Mirador

Calle de Seminari

Plaça de la Catedral

Calle Mayor

Plaça de Bom

Calle de Murada d'Artux

Calle de Jaume I El Conquerdor

Avenida de Jaume I El Conquerdor

P. St. Nicolau

PLAÇA DE LOS PINS

Calle de la Purisima

Calle de l'Alcantara

Calle de Sant Isidre

Bus Station 🚌

Information ⓘ

Accommodation ■
Hotel Port Ciutadella **10**

Dining ◆
Can Nito **7**

Attractions ●
Velos Joan **9**
Es Born Theatre **5**
Cathedral **4**
Socors Church and
Claustre del Seminari **3**

Platja Gran **11**
Sant Nicolau defence tower **8**
Museu Municipal de Cuitadella **1**
Charanga **2**
Town Hall **6**

Sant Bartolomeu 55 (℡ *971 373 003 www.ajferreries.org*).

Ferreries is a good starting point for walks along the ancient **Camí Reial** towards the **Algendar Gorge** (see 'Natural Wonders & Spectacular Views', p. 179), as well as up to the ruins of **Santa Agueda** castle (see p. 180).

From Ferreries, head south to **Es Migjorn Gran,** the smallest (with just over 1000 inhabitants)

and the youngest of Menorca's towns: it gained independence from Es Mercadal in 1989. Es Migjorn still has plenty of character of its own – it was also the home of Joan Riudavets, at a sprightly 114 the oldest man in the world when he died in March 2004. Es Migjorn is a good starting point for walks, such as the route to **Cova des Coloms** – an impressive natural cave known by locals as 'the cathedral' (see 'Natural Wonders & Spectacular Views', p. 179); walks through pine trees down to Binigaus beach; and along Pou Nou path, past the well where local women used to do their washing. Information is available from the **Town Hall** (Plaça de l'Església 3 ☎ *971 370 110*).

Back on the main road, the cosy town of **Es Mercadal** sits at the foot of **Monte Toro,** Menorca's highest point at 357 metres above sea level, with impressive views of the island from the top. Try the melt-in-your-mouth *pastissets* ★ ★ in Sa Posada del Toro bar and restaurant at the summit (☎ *971 375 174*. Bar open 9am-7pm; restaurant May-Oct 1pm-4pm. Highchairs. MC, V. Main courses €8–16 (£5.36–10.72). Es Mercadal is also home to some of the best bakeries on the island. **Tourist information** is available from the Town Hall (C/Major 16 ☎ *971 375 002 www. aj-esmercadal.org*).

The fishing village of **Fornells** falls under Es Mercadal's control, and is home to some of the best restaurants on the island. Places such as **Es Cranc** (see 'Family-friendly Dining', p. 193) and **Es Pla** (Passatge d'Es Pla, Fornells ☎ *971 376 655*), where the King of Spain dines when he moors in Fornells' port. Popular for watersports, the protected bay is home to a sailing school, the Fornells' waterfront is perfect cycling territory, and if you head out to the mouth of the bay, you can visit Fornells' distinctive defence town.

Beaches & Resorts

Sant Tomàs ★ With three beaches to choose between, Sant Tomàs, Sant Adeodat and Binigaus, there is plenty of space to enjoy this resort's clean water and sugary sand. There are parasols and sun beds available for hire at the stretch nearest the hotels (if you choose to walk west to Binigaus you will not find any such services). There are also pedalos. There are several car parks right next to the beach, so younger children won't be tired out walking to the sand, and the bus stop is on the main road running through the resort, just a couple of minutes from the water. In the evening, you can walk the length of the resort just above the beach, and the beach bar, **Es Bruc** (see 'Family-friendly Dining', p. 193), is a perfect location for quick snacks and ice-creams.

Cala Galdana Protected by cliffs, the beach at Cala Galdana makes for safe swimming and pedalo hire, even for little ones. There are several beach bars on the adjacent walkway, and if you get there early, opt for the shade of the pine trees rather than rent a parasol. The car park and bus stop are a five-minute walk away, by a line of shops and restaurants next to a stream. Here several boats are moored, and if you linger too long, hungry ducks often make an appearance. It is also a good location to look out for fish. From Cala Galdana, over the bridge at the mouth of the stream, you can climb wooden steps that head along the cliffs through pine trees to the virgin sands of **Cala Macarella** and **Cala Macarelleta,** and even on to **Cala en Turqueta** if you have the energy (the return can be tiring: the steps back up from Macarella to Cala Galdana are never-ending).

Cala en Bosch Compared to other resorts, Cala en Bosch is highly developed, particularly around the small port area, affectionately called a *lago* (lake), and small beach. Of course, this means it is also one of the busiest beaches during the high season, and there are several beach bars for snacks as well as pedalos and sun beds for hire. Close to the sand are the waterslides, wave pools, karting and Jacuzzis of AquaRock (see 'Taking the Plunge', p. 186). There is plenty of parking around the resort, although in high season you may not be able to park right by the beach. The bus drops you just a couple of minutes from the sand.

Son Parc ★ ★ A perfect family resort, this well-protected beach has shallow waters and wide sand backed by huge dunes and protected by pine trees. Son Parc is ideal for swimming with little children, and is safe for taking them out on the bay in pedalos. There are also sun beds and parasols for hire, and a handful of beach bars for snacks. The car park is at the west of the beach, and the bus stop is about 10 minutes' walk from the sand. Son Parc is also the location of Menorca's only **golf course** (Golf Son Parc ℭ *971 188 875 www.golfsonparc.com*. Open 9am-dusk. Single green fee €55 (£36.85); juniors 50% discount).

Arenal d'en Castell Another of Menorca's long-established family resorts, Arenal d'en Castell is

Cala Pregonda

Hidden Beaches

The west of the island boasts some of Menorca's finest undeveloped beaches and coves, with not a hotel in sight. These are not ideal for visiting with very young children, however. There are no beach bars or shops, so you have to bring all your food and drink with you; there are no toilets; and they are usually a fair walk from the nearest car park. Some of the best include **Cala Pilar,** accessed via a farm track at Kilometre 34 on Me-1. It's a 4 km drive along narrow roads, and a 60-minute walk through the pine forest before you reach the sand. Behind the headland to the west is another cove, **Es Macar** `FIND`, with enormous smooth stones. **Algairarens** (or La Vall) is a fabulous beach set against the backdrop of pine trees (there are even picnic benches under the trees for when the sun gets too hot). Investigate the lookout post left over from Spain's Civil War, with little square windows where soldiers would rest their weapons. **Cala Pregonda** ★★ is signposted from the Me-15, heading north from Es Mercadal to Fornells, and is a 45-minute walk west when you reach the end of the farm track. Pregonda is the last beach you'll see, protected by a small islet. When visiting the virgin beaches around Ciutadella, like **Son Saura, Cala en Turqueta** and **Macarella,** in July and August, go midweek. They are packed at weekends, and once the small car parks are full, police will turn you away.

built around a curved, sandy beach, and is ideal for renting canoes or pedalos. If you are with younger children, ask for life jackets as the water gets deep quickly. Sun beds and parasols are available for hire and there are several beach bars for snacks. Parking is available at almost every point along the bay. If you drive west, you'll have to walk down steps to reach the sand, however, so if you have a pushchair, the eastern end is an easier option – the car park is just a few minutes' walk away. Similarly, the bus stops at several points along the road overlooking the bay; the beach is just a short walk down the steps.

Natural Wonders & Spectacular Views

Monte Toro ★ `ALL AGES`. While the title 'mountain' is probably a bit generous, this is the closest Menorca gets to one. It's a steep drive uphill, so it's good manners

Statue, Monte Toro

to cheer on any cyclists attempting the climb. In fact, in October as many as 400 race to the top as part of Menorca's annual three-day 'tour', and a handful of professionals are always invited to participate. In 2005, former Tour de France winner Miquel Indurain joined in. See *www.ciclomenorca.com* for dates and further information.

You can spot several Menorcan towns from the top, and the bay off Fornells is a fantastic sight. The collection of aerials isn't so attractive, but alas is essential for island communication. Popular legend claims that an image of a Virgin was discovered by a group of monks in the 13th century, who climbed to the top of the mountain with a bull that helped clear a pathway. Inside the simple church here, you can see the patch of earth that bull supposedly cleared. Today the white-washed monastery is used as a retreat; there are a few nuns who live on El Toro permanently. The patio outside the church leads to a souvenir shop, bar and restaurant, Sa Posada del Toro. The bar's terrace has impressive views over the island, and the restaurant has a good set menu, but it gets very busy at weekends. There is no public transport up to the church.

Monte Toro, Es Mercadal.

Santa Agueda Castle

AGES 8 AND UP Today there's not much left of this castle. Records indicate that it was built before 1232, but by 1351 it was already in ruins, although attempts were made to rebuild it in the 16th century. The castle is a key monument from the Islamic occupation of the island. A walk up to Santa Agueda's ruins is worthwhile just for the views. To find it, from Ferreries, drive west towards Ciutadella, turning right down Camí dels Alocs at kilometre 31. Follow the road for 3 km until you see a pathway signposted to the castle (it isn't clearly marked), and there is a small parking area next to a building. An uphill walk follows, so it isn't ideal with very young children. unless they are small enough to sit in a baby carrier. A Roman footpath leads up to the ruins (using a pushchair is unthinkable), and perhaps the most incoherent feature of all is a rusty car abandoned at the top. Guessing how it made it up such a narrow path is a good game. There is no public transport to the castle.

Santa Agueda Castle, Ferreries. Free admission.

Pedreres de s'Hostal, Lithica ★ ALL AGES

Not exactly a *natural* wonder, but Lithica certainly qualifies for its presence in the 'spectacular views' category. These sandstone quarries, abandoned in 1994, impress by their size – standing at the bottom you're dwarfed by the sheer walls. Accessed from Ciutadella's southern ring road, Lithica is divided into two parts: the older quarries (dating back 200 years) that were mined manually, now turned into botanical gardens

Lithica

it is within cycling distance of Ciutadella. There is ample parking.

Camí Vell km 1, Ciutadella ☎ *971 481 578* **www.lithica.com**. *€3 (£2) adults; €1.50 (£1) OAPs; children under 10 free. Oct–Apr free entry. Mon–Sun 9.30am-sunset.*

Cova des Coloms ★ ALL AGES

Hidden between pine trees on the slopes that lead from Es Migjorn Gran to Binigaus beach, Cova des Coloms is nicknamed 'the cathedral' because of its size: it is 24 metres high, 11 metres long and 15 metres wide. At the far end of the cave, you can climb up on to a platform and fully appreciate its size. From Es Migjorn Gran, ask for directions to Camí de sa Mala Garba, where the primary school is situated. Park here, walk along the path to the cemetery, and continue along the track past farms. The footpath to the caves is signposted on your left-hand side; the terrain is uneven, so wear suitable shoes (smaller children could be taken in baby carriers: a pushchair isn't an option). From the caves, you can continue along the path down to **Binigaus** beach, which should

(there are guided tours on Sundays); and the enormous quarries that were mined mechanically. Mining may have had a drastic impact on the landscape, but the mines still have a certain beauty. They say that if you hear whispers, they're the goblins that protect Lithica.

The quarry is the venue for numerous events in the summer, including children's parties, and at night, live music under the full moon. There is no public transport to Lithica, although

Menorca Undug

In addition to Lithica (see above), other quarries include **Santa Ponça** in Alaior (turn right at Kilometre 14 on Me-1, when heading eastwards, the quarry is on the left, hidden from the road) and **Camí d'en Robadones** in Es Castell (on the right hand side, just after leaving Maó on the road to Es Castell), which has been turned into a museum for fishing boats.

take about an hour in total. There is no public transport available.

Cova des Coloms, Es Migjorn Gran. Free admission. Mon–Sun dawn–dusk.

Algendar Gorge AGES 8 AND UP

Walking through this oasis, home to 220 species of flora and fauna, 26 of which are endemic, makes you feel light years away from the island's touristy zones. The gorge was cut by a stream that runs down to Cala Galdana, and while the footpath is good, patches lower down may be flooded. You can reach the gorge from Camí Reial: park at Ferreries cemetery, cross the road and follow Me-22 to Cala Galdana for 30 metres until you see a signpost on your right. This path runs through pine trees, farmland, and gradually descends into the gorge. Alternatively, for a shorter walk, head west out of Ferreries, and turn left at kilometre 29 down a country lane. Park near the bottom, and pick up the footpath. It is impossible to reach the coast, however, as the gorge cuts through private property. Given the uneven terrain, these walks suit older children or babies in carriers. There is no access by public transport.

Algendar Gorge, Ferreries. Free admission. Mon-Sun dawn-dusk.

Sant Nicolau Defence Tower

ALL AGES Just one of the many defence towers strategically placed on Menorca's coastline, Sant Nicolau was built at the end of the 18th century. Entry is via a bridge, and inside you'll find vaulted ceilings, impressive lookout points and a spiral staircase up to a terrace. Just a 10-minute walk from Es Born Square in Ciutadella, there is ample parking nearby, and the bus stop is within walking distance. Elsewhere, the defence tower in Fornells AGES 5 AND UP (*www.menorcamonumental.org*. Apr and Oct Tue-Sun 10am–2.30pm; May-Sep Tue–Sat 10am–8pm Sun–Mon 10am–2.30; Nov–Mar closed. €2.40 (£1.61); OAPs and children 8–16 €1.20 (£0.80); children under 8 free. Free admission Sun) has also been restored, and is open to the public.

Plaça de l'Almirall Ferragut, Ciutadella ☎ 971 381 050 www.menorcamonumental.org. Tue–Sat 11am–1pm and 6pm–8pm. Free admission.

Monuments & Museums

Naveta d'es Tudons ★

AGES 2 AND UP A funeral chamber dating back to the Bronze Age, when excavated in the 1950s bodies were found here with personal belongings like bronze and china figures. You can peer inside the narrow stone entrance and guess how many bodies fit on the two floors. (Historians believe the correct answer is 'as many as 100 at any one time'.).

From the main road, the burial chamber is a short walk across fields, so close the gates behind you. It's a bumpy ride to the

Naveta d'es Tudons

museum often holds special exhibitions, so check with the tourist office or posters around town to see what's on. The museum is easily explored with a pushchair.

Plaça de sa Font s/n, Ciutadella ☎ *971 380 297 www.ciutadella.org/museu. €2.13 (£1.43); OAPs €1.03 (£0.69), children under 12 free. Tue–Sat 10am–2pm. Free admission Wed.*

monument on a pushchair, so if you can persuade your little ones to walk, they will be more comfortable. There is no public transport to the site, but ample parking off the main road.

Me-1 Kilometre 40 www.menorcamonumental.org. May–Sep Tue–Sun 10am–8pm; Oct–Apr Tue–Sun 10am–2.30pm. €2.40 (£1.61); OAPs and children 8–16 €1.20) (£0.80); children under 8 free. Nov–Apr and Sun free admission.

Museu Municipal de Ciutadella ALL AGES

While the exhibits charting the history of Ciutadella may not capture your child's attention, the building itself is certainly worth a visit, with long galleries built from blocks of sandstone. The

Ecomuseu de Cap de Cavalleria ★ AGES 5 AND UP

With exhibits indoors and out, the Ecomuseu links the information on display with real monuments surrounding the building: the lighthouse, the defence tower, the Roman port of Sanitja and the abandoned city of Sanisera. The museum even organises underwater archaeological explorations, as well as digs on land. If you visit in the morning, you can see the excavation site. The mix of exhibits, and the seven different routes recommended by the museum, should keep children interested. Given the walking involved, the museum is better suited to older children. There is no public transport to the museum.

Craft Markets in the West of Menorca

Summer markets are held in **Es Mercadal** at Plaça del Pere Camps on Thursday evenings; and **Ciutadella** at Carrer del Seminari on Monday evenings during July and August. **Es Migjorn Gran** hosted fortnightly artesan markets on Tuesdays in the summer of 2006; ask at the town hall if these will be repeated. In April, **Es Mercadal** hosts an artesan fair at its exhibition site. Ask at tourist offices (see p. 155) for more information on occasional markets and fairs.

From Es Mercadal, follow Me-15 to Fornells, turning left at kilometre 5. Continue along the lane, and follow signs at the first right-hand turn to Cap de Cavalleria and the museum. ☎ *971 359 999* **www.ecomuseo decavalleria.com**. *€3 (£2); children under 8 free. Green Card 20% discount. Apr, May, Jun, Oct 10am–7pm; Jul–Sep 10am–8.30pm.*

Child-friendly Attractions

Subaida ALL AGES Younger children will enjoy the chance to see cows close up at this dairy farm. Set in the heart of Menorca's countryside, you can visit the animals, see cheese being made, and there's a shop and café. Children will love being close to the animals, and the farm is very family-friendly, with plenty of space for pushchairs. There are no connections with public transport.

Camí de Binifabini s/n ☎ *971 368 809* **www.subaida.com**. *Free admission. Mon-Sat 9am-2pm. Clearly signposted from the road heading north from Alaior, connecting the town with the Me-7, between Maó and Fornells.*

Dressage Shows ALL AGES

Horses have long formed an integral part of Menorcan life, and at **Son Martorellet Stables** (Km 1.5 Me-22, between Ferreries and Cala Galdana ☎ *609 049 943* **www.sonmartorellet. com**. May-Oct Tue and Thu 8.30pm. €12.50 (£8.40); children free), children will adore the dressage show. Horses dance to the music, and at the end, you can meet the animals up-close for photographs. If the

Menorcan Cheese

evening show is a little too late, then visit the stables during the day – it's free.

For Active Families

Horse Riding AGES 8 AND UP

Several stables offer experienced riders the chance to take guided rides in the countryside. At **Santa Rita farm** in Ferreries (Me-1 kilometre 24, between Es Mercadal and Ferreries ☎ *630 212 228*. Around €20 (£13.40) an hour), those not so keen on mounting a horse themselves can opt for an hour's tour in a carriage instead; either way, your ride ends with a Menorca tea. Santa Rita runs regular hacks during the summer, as many as five a day, with routes through the pine forests.

Riding for Tots

Very small children can try a short pony ride, in Son Bou, near the car park at the entrance. In **Maó's** Esplanada square on Saturdays, children can trot on ponies – they are very placid, and steered by a guide – for five minutes at a time.

Sailing AGES 5 AND UP The tranquil bay of Fornells is a safe location for potential sailors of all ages to try their hand at the sport. **Minorca Sailing Holidays** (☎ *020 8948 2106* in the UK; *www.sailingminorca.com*) will take babies as young as four months in its crèche, run by British nannies, and children as young as five can practice on the water, and study towards RYA qualifications. The school offers courses for sailors of all abilities, as well as low-key programmes for those not keen on sailing every day. Prices, including flights from London airports

Parading Horse

and tuition, start from €1045 (£700) for a week. Qualifications, with accommodation, are also included.

Diving AGES 8 AND UP Several dive schools provide tuition for all levels, including experienced divers. **SubMenorca** (C/ Rosa des Vents, Cala en Bosc ☎ *609 656 916 www.submenorca.de*) runs a junior course to get children interested. The day includes theory and practice diving in a swimming pool, and costs €80 (£53.60). At the other end of the island, as well as numerous internationally recognised courses, **S'Algar Diving** (☎ *971 150 601 www. salgardiving.com*) also runs scuba trips off the coast, aimed at all the family.

Cycling AGES 2 AND UP The flat terrain around Ciutadella on the west of the island is ideal for cyclists, and there are many family-friendly routes to choose between. In Ciutadella itself, you'll see many locals on bikes, although do be careful as a car or motorbike may surprise you on even the quietest of streets. Resorts may rent bikes, but you'll have more choice from a specialist like **Velos Joan** (St Isidre 32–34, Ciutadella

Cycling around Ciutadella

☏ *971 381 576*. From €33 (£22.11) a week).

When out with older children, longer bike rides include following **Camí Vell** south out of Ciutadella to several isolated beaches, such as **Son Saura** or **Cala en Turqueta** (see 'Hidden Beaches', p. 179), as well as the prehistoric site **Son Catlar** (Son Saura beach road, km 8 *www.menorcamonumental.org*.

Admission free. Open dawn–dusk) and the whitewashed church of Sant Joan de Missa (Road to Cala Macarella, 5 km south of Ciutadella).

Shopping

Shoes An internationally renowned designer, **Jaime Mascaró** ★★ (branches at Ferreries Industrial Estate; Dr Orfila 29, Maó; Maó Airport *www.jaimemascaro.com*) is famed for elegance and style. His daughter, Ursula, opts for more modern designs, and the company's **Bini Bini** range of colourful, casual footwear also includes a line of children's shoes. At the factory shop in Ferreries' industrial estate, there is a selection of leftover stock, where you can pick up a bargain. Next door, tired parents can stop for a drink at **JM Café (Ferreries Industrial Estate)**, leaving children in the playground while one of you shops in peace. There is parking

Taking the Plunge: An Active Day In & Out of the Water

AquaRock ★ **ALL AGES** (Urb. Cala en Bosc ☏ *971 387 822 www. aquarockmenorca.com*. Adults €17.20 (£11.52); children €11 (£7.40). May–Oct, Mon–Sun 10.30–6.00pm) in Cala en Bosc has enough to keep children of all ages entertained. Between intertwined waterslides (gradually work up to the Kamikaze), several pools and a wave machine, Jacuzzis, trampolines and, at an additional cost, go-karting, even the most energetic of children will end up exhausted by the end of the day. There's also a restaurant on site (with fast food to keep youngsters happy), so it really makes for a full day out.

Countryside Walks

outside the store, and while in theory you could walk from Ferreries' bus stop, it means a dangerous crossing over the Me-1: not recommended with children.

Another leading shoe designer is **Pons Quintana** ★, with a factory shop in Alaior (Baixamar 120 ℂ *971 371 050*); a shop in Maó (S'Arravaleta 21 ℂ *971 355 851*); and one in Ciutadella's industrial estate.

Children's Clothes Of the many shops selling children's clothes, try **Charanga** (Carrer de Maó 4, Ciutadella ℂ *971 380 585*) for a blast of colour. The clothes have plenty of character, with bright designs, bold prints and a grown-up feel. Some items can be pricey, but during the summer and at sale time, you can pick up excellent bargains. The shop itself is a little narrow, however, so quickly fills when pushchairs are inside. The store is in the centre of Ciutadella's old town, so you will face a short walk to parking spaces or the bus stop.

Gardens A garden centre may not sound like a good choice with children, but **Truvi** (Ctra Cala Galdana km 2, Ferreries ℂ *971 373 874*) is designed to keep your little ones entertained while you browse. Apart from a dedicated play area, with tubes, tunnels and balls, children will also love chatting to the parrot, and checking out the fish, birds and other pets on sale. Apart from plants, trees and garden ornaments, Truvi sells smaller gifts and decorative items that are more practical for taking home. There are no public transport links to the centre, but ample parking is provided.

FAMILY-FRIENDLY ACCOMMODATION

Of the four Balearic Islands, Menorca is traditionally a popular destination for families. Every hotel below will welcome you with open arms, many offering children's clubs, entertainment and sports activities. I've also listed apartment complexes set in gardens with plenty of space for children to play. If travelling with a tour operator, you'll usually find kids' clubs.

In order to make comparison easier, prices are given for a week's stay in low season (typically May or October), as few self-catering properties are available to rent for a single night, and in high season most hotels enforce a minimum stay of at least three nights. Unless otherwise stated, hotels and apartment blocks listed here are open between May and October inclusive.

VERY EXPENSIVE

Insotel Punta Prima Prestige and Insotel Club Punta Prima ★★ This five-star accommodation, choose from apartments or hotel rooms, is in a privileged location right on the water's edge at Punta Prima. With the beach just a few metres away and a large pool and sun terrace area, if you're only planning on swimming and sunbathing, there's no need to go any further. Children have their own park and swimming pool; there are babysitters, tennis and squash

courts and bicycles for hire. Kids' clubs are divided into four age groups, starting with the BabyClub for two to three year olds, and for rainy days, there are even televisions in the rooms and apartments. Children are put up on sofa beds, but the rooms are so spacious you won't feel on top of each other. The only downside is that the restaurants within walking distance all serve similar food, piling chips on almost everything. If you want to dine like Menorcans, drive into Sant Lluís.

De sa Migjera s/n, Punta Prima, Sant Lluís ☎ 971 159 200 www.insotel. com. 52 suites, 479 rooms. €875 (£586) double with breakfast; Prestige double €2268 (£1520) with breakfast. V, MC, AE, DC. Amenities: A/C, central heating, gym, supermarket, nursery, swimming pool, garden, sauna, hairdressers, restaurant, café, squash courts, tennis courts, beauty salon, playground, laundry service, bike hire. In Room: A/C, central heating, safe, iron, hairdryer, satellite TV, minibar, telephone.

La Quinta One of the many hotels in the Cala en Bosc and Son Xoriguer area, the rooms at this five-star hotel form a 'u' shape around a central square with a large swimming pool. In ground-floor rooms, you can walk directly from your terrace on to the pool and garden area, so you'll need to keep an eye on younger children if they tend to go walkabout.

With a spa, gym and indoor pool on-site, the hotel also has tennis courts, and can organise bicycle hire – the resort is ideal for cycling because it's so flat. For rainy days, each room has a television, and if you opt for a Senior Suite, there is plenty of room for two adults and two children. There are no clubs for children.

The hotel is close to Cala en Bosc, and its small harbour, is filled with restaurants and boats, as well as AquaRock (see p. 186).

Av. Son Xoriguer s/n, Son Xoriguer, Ciutadella ☎ 971 055 000 www. laquintamenorca.com. 80 rooms. €2121 (£1421) double room. V, MC, AE, DC. Amenities: A/C, central heating, laundry service, hairdresser, sauna, bar, garden, swimming pool, beauty salon, bike hire, gym, indoor pool, tennis courts, restaurant. In Room: A/C, iron, hairdryer, satellite TV, mini bar, safe, telephone.

Finesse Villas This newly-built complex of 14 chalets adds a touch of luxury to the self-catering holiday. Each villa has three bedrooms and three bathrooms, its own private pool and garden, sea views, and includes a welcome pack, a daily cleaning service and 24-hour emergency contact. Because of their location (the villas are a couple of miles uphill from Son Bou beach) a hire car is included in the price. If you prefer to eat in, the kitchen is well equipped (including a dishwasher) and they will lend portable barbecues on request. As the villas are self-contained, they are safe for children, although the swimming pool isn't covered.

Torresoli, Alaior ☎ 971 371 575 www. menorcarentals.com. 14 villas.

€2520 (£1668). V, MC. Amenities: heated swimming pool, garden. In room: A/C, central heating, fridge, radio, satellite television, iron, hairdryer.

EXPENSIVE

Hotel Port Ciutadella ★

Newly built, this hotel is close enough to Ciutadella to go into town on foot. But with sea views and proximity to the small beach, Platja Gran, it feels like a seaside holiday. For swimming, you can choose between the hotel pool, or pop down to the rock platforms and swim in the sea a few metres away. There's also a gym and spa. There's no specific kids' clubs on-site, but Ciutadella's shops, markets and entertainments are to hand. The other major advantage is this place is open all year round, when most others close during winter. The rooms have broadband internet access and TVs for rainy days.

Passeig Marítim 36, Ciutadella ☎ 971 482 520 www.sethotels.es. 94 rooms. Double, two adults one child, €1155 (£774), breakfast included. V, MC, AE, DC. Amenities: A/C, central heating, laundry, Internet, pool, indoor pool, beauty salon, gym, garden, restaurant, sauna, bar. In room: A/C, central heating, hairdryer, telephone, minibar, satellite television, Internet.

Grupotel Mar de Menorca

In the secluded resort of Es Canutells, this really is a self-contained holiday centre, with everything included in the price. It's a series of apartments built around gardens and two swimming pools; children are well entertained with kids' clubs, mini-golf and playgrounds. For family activities, there are tennis courts, and bicycle hire is available, with the beach just a short walk away. A nursery and babysitting service is available, too. With a buffet for meal-times, there's plenty of choice for even the fussiest of eaters. Of course, the downside of an all-inclusive holiday is it discourages trying restaurants elsewhere, and the novelty of the buffet wears off after a few days.

Urb, Canutells s/n, Maó ☎ 971 153 100 www.grupotel.com. 278 rooms. Apartment/room €1288 (£863) all inclusive, two adults, two children. V, MC. Amenities: bike hire, laundry, playground, tennis courts, gym, mini-golf, supermarket, swimming pool, bar, A/C, nursery, restaurant. In room: satellite television, fridge, telephone, safe.

Hotel Santo Tomàs Just metres from the beach, this is one of several hotels that line the water-front at Sant Tomàs. In the hotel itself there is an indoor and out-door pool, as well as ample garden space. The hotel makes a good base for walking: you can head over the cliffs to Son Bou, or walk along to Binigaus beach and Cova des Coloms. Sant Tomàs is a quiet resort, so unless you plan to stay by the pool for the week, a car is essential; there is little entertainment nearby, and for restaurants, you're better off driving into Es Migjorn or Es Mercadal.

Sant Tomàs, Es Migjorn Gran ☎ 971 370 025. 85 rooms. Double room,

two adults one child, €1155 (£774) half-board. V, MC, AE, DC. Amenities: A/C, pool, indoor pool, gym, beauty salon, sauna, laundry service, bar, restaurant. In room: hairdryer, satellite TV, radio, mini-bar, telephone, A/C, central heating.

MODERATE

Royal Son Bou Family Club ★★

With endless activities and entertainment on offer, there'll be no fear of children getting bored here. Choose from volleyball, water polo, tennis and basketball, just for starters, then there are two large pools – the infants' pool is completely separate – as well as an adventure playground and numerous kids' club activities. Entertainment is staged every evening. It's also just a few metres from the eastern end of Son Bou beach, when it all gets too much. Perhaps the only downside is that the resort has only recently been promoted to British tourists, so the majority of families there are German, Dutch or Italian – so your children may struggle to make friends. In addition, being a family resort, you could well have young babies or noisy toddlers as neighbours, so bring ear plugs just in case. Like everything else, the food is also well tuned-in to children's tastes, but with relatively few British tourists at the resort up to now, your children may turn their noses up at it.

Son Bou, Alaior ☎ 971 372 358 www. royalsonbou.com. 252 apartments. Apartment €976.50 (£654) for half-board. V, MC, AE. Amenities: laundry service, pool, gym, tennis courts, bar, nursery, playground. In room: fridge, safe, hairdryer, satellite television, iron, telephone, A/C.

Hotel Rtm Audax Relaunched as a spa and wellness centre in 2004, this hotel now caters for both parents and children. Set amongst the pine trees of Cala Galdana, there are plenty of activities to keep you all busy, including table tennis, bicycle hire and a split-level swimming pool. Just minutes from Cala Galdana beach, it is also close to the waterslides, several shops and restaurants. The hotel has its own Sports & Nature Activities Centre, which organises hikes, canoeing, fishing and diving excursions.

Urb. Serpentona s/n, Cala Galdana, Ferreries ☎ 971 154 646 www.rtm hotels.com. 280 rooms. Double room, two adults one child, €830 (£556) including breakfast. AE, V, MC. Amenities: A/C, bike hire, central heating, laundry service, pool, bar, gym, indoor pool, tennis courts, hairdresser, restaurant, sauna. In room: hairdryer, A/C, radio, satellite TV, mini-bar, telephone.

Princesa Playa A popular family hotel, Princesa Playa offers numerous activities at its kids' clubs to keep little ones entertained all day, while in the evening, they even get their own mini-disco. In addition, there are playgrounds and a large pool. But if you want to venture elsewhere, the hotel can recommend activities like horse riding or sailing. They also organise bicycle hire, and have a creche. The small beach at Son Xoriguer is a short walk away, but for eating out, you're probably better off going into Ciutadella. You can choose from hotel rooms or apartments; if you prefer to do some cooking, the latter is the best choice with small children. All accommodation has satellite television.

Gran Via Son Xoriguer, Ciutadella ☎ 971 387 271 www.princesaplaya. net. 170 double rooms. 64 apartments. Apartment €815 (£546) including breakfast. AE, MC, V, DC. Amenities: A/C, bar, garden, restaurant, bike hire, playground, nursery, pool, supermarket, tennis court. In room: A/C, central heating, telephone, hairdryer, fridge, safe, radio, satellite TV.

ApartHotel HG Jardín de Menorca ★★ As its name suggests, these apartments are set in large gardens, with three swimming pools on different levels. Although the hotel is a long way from the beach, there is a free bus service, as well as plenty to do on-site, including mini-golf, squash, table tennis, a playground and a programme of children's activities. A babysitting service is also available. The rooms are airy, with large terraces, but only have basic kitchenettes. Many visitors opt for half board.

Torresolí, Alaior ☎ 971 378 040. 110 rooms. €595 (£399) including breakfast. V, MC, AE. Amenities: A/C, playground, laundry service, restaurant, sauna, squash courts, bike hire, gym, mini-golf, pool, indoor pool, supermarket, bar, central heating, nursery. In room: A/C, central heating, fridge, telephone, satellite TV, hairdryer, safe.

Hostal Jeni FIND In the centre of Es Mercadal, Jeni is a clean, simple hostel open year-round. The place itself has a swimming pool, garden and small terrace, as well as an excellent restaurant (see p. 196) downstairs, which is usually filled with islanders for Sunday lunch. Es Mercadal is just a few minutes' walk away, and the bus stop is close for visits to other towns. Monte Toro is within walking distance, too, but it's a long two miles uphill to the top. The rooms are large enough for extra beds or cots, and each has a television.

Mirada del Toro, Es Mercadal ☎ *971 375 059 www.hostaljeni.com. 36 rooms. Family room €392 (£263) including breakfast. V, MC. Amenities: laundry service, A/C, bike hire, pool, bar, restaurant, central heating. In room: fridge, A/C, satellite TV, central heating, iron, hairdryer.*

Apartamentos Las Palmeras

A low-rise built around a large swimming pool and landscaped gardens (with a tropical theme), these bright, clean apartments make excellent family accommodation. With a second swimming pool for children, a playground and babysitting service, younger ones will be well entertained. There are two kids' clubs, for children aged 4–10 and 11–15, with activities every morning and afternoon. As S'Algar is a key centre for watersports, there's plenty for bigger children to do as well. The downside is that S'Algar has no beach of its own: you have to walk to Alcufar or Punta Prima for a patch of sand. The resort has several restaurants and bars, if you don't feel like cooking.

S'Algar, Sant Lluís ☎ *971 055 400 www.salgarhotels.com. 72 apartments. From €266 (£178). V, MC, DC, AE. Amenities: bike hire, garden, playground, supermarket, restaurant, nursery, pool, laundrette, bar. In room: fridge, safe, satellite TV.*

Son Bou Gardens ★ ★ ★ VALUE

My personal favourite, these good-sized whitewashed apartments are set in large gardens. There are three zones in total, and while they are just metres apart, each has its own restaurant, swimming pool and reception area. There is also a tennis court, water slides and a giant maze, and the restaurants have evening entertainment like mini-discos and live music. The ground-floor apartments are particularly good for young children to play on the grass outside under your watchful eye. The apartments themselves have two or three bedrooms, back and front terraces and an open plan kitchen and living room. The beach, bars, restaurants, and a mini-fairground are all within walking distance.

Son Bou Gardens, Alaior ☎ *971 371 802 www.menorcarentals.com. 120 apartments. €265 (£178). MC, V. Amenities: gardens, supermarket, restaurants, pools, laundrette, tennis courts, playgrounds. In room: fridge, iron.*

Aparthotel Tramontana Park

Overlooking the beach at Fornells, this apartment complex

includes a large swimming pool and infant pool with ample terrace space, and a children's playground. At reception, you can arrange to rent bikes, and the two-mile cycle to Fornells town is flat and safe for children. Both Platges de Fornells and Fornells have several bars and restaurants, and there is also a restaurant in the apartment complex if cooking in the basic kitchenette seems too much like hard work. The rooms have satellite TV.

Platges de Fornells www.menorca hotelsguide.com. 172 apartments. €224 (£150). MC, V. Amenities: gardens, restaurant, pool, A/C. In room: telephone, safe, fridge, satellite TV.

Camping Son Bou. Slightly more up-market than Menorca's other campsite, Camping Son Bou offers cabins in addition to tents, although there are no private hot showers. You can play football, tennis, basketball or volleyball, and there is also a large swimming pool. Surrounded by pine trees, the campsite also has a large children's playground, a restaurant and bar, Internet access and barbecue area. Bikes can be rented from reception, but though the beach is a short downhill ride (just over two miles), the journey back is tortuous, and definitely not recommended under the midday sun. There are no bus services connecting the site with shops, bars and restaurants in Son Bou, so a car is recommended. Again, while the walk to the centre of the resort is possible, the return journey involves lots of steps, and then a long stretch along a road with no street lighting.

Carretera de Sant Jaume km 3.5, Torresolí, Alaior ☎ 971 372 727 www. campingsonbou.com. In low season, adults pay €5.60 (£3.75), children €4.15 (£2.78) and renting a large tent costs €10.15 (£6.80) a night; a bungalow costs €48 (£32.16) per night. 7% tax is added. Open 1st Apr until 30th Sept. V, MC. Amenities: supermarket, pool, playground, hairdryers, laundrette, bike hire, bar, restaurant, showers and bathrooms, Internet.

FAMILY-FRIENDLY DINING

Menorcan restaurants are used to hosting children. Even late at night, you'll see young ones sitting at tables, or toddlers asleep in their pushchairs – even at the smartest restaurants. Spaniards are not afraid to bring theirs with them, so follow their lead. If a special children's menu isn't listed, ask the waiter (most speak English, especially in resorts) what they can recommend: it's usually a child-size version of a main course.

In the island's resorts, restaurants often offer variations on a similar theme, usually including burgers and chips. While I've listed a handful of restaurants in resorts, these usually close during the winter, I've concentrated on restaurants in Menorca's towns, where the food is generally better. Given the differences in British and Spanish dining habits, most restaurants open around midday with the kitchen closing at midnight-ish.

EXPENSIVE

Marivent Sporting spectacular views over Maó's port from its second-floor dining room and first-floor terrace, Marivent is run by a couple from Ferreries who strive to create a mix of modern and Mediterranean cooking. During the day, children are welcome for lunch, and the menu offers a reasonably-priced selection of dishes. There's no children's menu as such, but waiters are happy for children to share a fixed menu between them (one eating the starter, the other the main course, then sharing pudding). In the evenings, you're better off leaving the children with a babysitter. Vegetarian dishes are limited, but those that are on the menu, such as asparagus wrapped in batter with garlic mayonnaise, are fabulous. Leave room for puddings, too: the chocolate brownie is worth every calorie. **Ses Salines Restaurant** in Fornells is run by the same couple, and has a similar menu.

Moll de Llevant 31, Maó ☎ 971 369 801. Open 1pm–6.30pm; 8pm–11pm. Closed Tue and 23rd-25th Aug. MC, V, AE, DC. Highchairs. Reservations recommended. Main course €18–28 (£12.06–18.76).

Cobblers Don't let the description 'English restaurant' put you off. This garden restaurant, in a restored town house on one of Alaior's steep streets, mixes English traditions with

Ice-cream in Maó

Mediterranean ingredients – and the staff are incredibly friendly, taking time to explain the contents of every dish if asked. The English aspect is also reflected in eating times: you can't reserve a table later than 9.30pm, incredibly early by Menorcan standards. In the summer, book a table to eat out among the plants and lemon tree on the patio. Children are welcome, even in the evening, and as the menu is geared towards English tastes (this is probably the only place on the island where you'll find sticky toffee pudding!), there will almost certainly be something to their liking. The portions are large, so arrive with an empty stomach.

Costa d'en Macari 6, Alaior ☎ 971 371 000. MC, V, AE. Reservations recommended. Main courses €15–25 (£10.05–16.75).

El Pescadito As its name implies, this restaurant specialises in fish, and being set in an old fishing village, you wouldn't expect anything less. Right at the entrance of Binibèquer Vell, the maze of whitewashed houses is just a few metres away, and there are almost always children playing in the pedestrian-only street. From the restaurant's terrace, you can sit back and watch while you wait for your meal to be served.

Binibèquer Vell, Sant Lluís ☎ 971 150 970. Closed Oct–May. MC, V. Main courses €15–25 (£10.05–16.75).

Es Cranc For the very best lobster stew on the island, reserve a table here for lunch. It feels more like you're eating in someone's home than in a restaurant, with checked table cloths and lace curtains, and as such, children are just a natural addition to the scene; expect to see entire families eating here at weekends. On your placemat, you'll find a bib to protect your clothes from lobster juice and out-of-control pieces of shellfish. Once you've eaten several portions, you can even go and see the lobsters on death row. Lobster stew is one of Menorca's most famous dishes, but also among the most expensive. Restaurants usually charge the market rate for a kilo of lobster per head for each ration of stew, so expect to pay around €60 (£40.20) a portion.

Ses Escoles 31, Fornells ☎ 971 376 442. Reservations recommended. MC, V. Main courses €15–60 (£10.05–40.20).

Bar Espanya It you want to eat where locals do, try Bar Espanya. A converted terraced house in the heart of Es Castell, it may be off the tourist track, but that's part of the charm. Specialising in fish and shellfish, the lunch menu is good value, but you'll have to get there early to grab a table. The chef makes a fabulous soufflé for pudding: it is wise to order this at the start of the meal, to avoid a long wait. Children are welcome; in fact, on Sunday lunchtimes there will be plenty of them eating here with their parents.

Victori 50, Es Castell ☎ 971 363 299. Open 1pm–3.30pm; 7.30pm–midnight. No reservations. MC, V, AE, DC. Highchairs. Main courses €6.75–18.50 (£4.52–12.40).

Il Porto 225 Among the endless choice lining Maó's port, Il Porto is a safe bet for families. Large enough to ensure you'll get a table (although it does get busy from 9pm), the menu varies from Italian home-cooked favourites, pastas and excellent pizza, to meat and fish dishes, and even a few vegetarian options. Although there is no children's menu, you can order a pizza for them to share. When it's busy, you may have to wait for your food. When I was there, a magician was making his way from table to table to entertain young diners with empty stomachs.

Moll de Llevant 225, Maó ☎ 971 354 426. Open 1pm–3.45pm; 7pm–midnight. Highchairs. Closed Wed; closed Jan–Easter. V, MC, AE. Main courses €7–19.50 (£4.69–13).

Ca Na Marga Invariably filled with sailors staying in Ses Salines, Ca Na Marga is a lively restaurant where everyone seems to know each other. The house speciality is barbecued meat, and you can keep a close eye on your steak's progress on the grill by the front door. Try the Mahón-Menorca cheese sauce on your meat. For vegetarians, there is a wide range of pizzas. Portions are large, so you'll have to ask for child-size versions, or split a meal between two children. And do make sure you leave space for pudding: the caramelised pineapple and tiramisu are both recommended.

Ses Salines, Fornells ☎ 971 376 410 www.canamarga.com. Highchairs. Open Mon–Sun 7pm–1.30am; closed Nov–Easter. Reservations recommended. MC, V. Main courses €7–22 (£4.69–14.74).

Casino Sant Climent's premier restaurant, the Casino, was relaunched in 2005, but fortunately no changes were made to the excellent food. In the bar, there are endless tapas, ideal for coping with smaller appetites, or if you just fancy a quick snack. In the main restaurant, Mediterranean cooking prevails – the lunchtime fixed menu is well priced. During the summer, there are jazz sessions on Tuesday evenings, and spectators are welcome to bring their own instruments and join in.

Sant Jaume 4, Sant Climent, Maó ☎ 971 153 418. Highchairs. Open 8am–midnight. Closed Wed. MC, V, AE, DC. Main courses €8–20 (£5.36–13.40).

Jeni Extremely popular with locals – entire families dine here at the weekends, and there is often live music and dancing on Saturday nights – Jeni has a laid-back feel, and the menu is filled with island specialities. While there are no specific children's meals, smaller stomachs will certainly be satisfied with dishes like stuffed aubergines Menorcan style, tomato soup or plates of bread with tomato. Sunday lunchtimes can be particularly busy, so turn up early or book beforehand. Afterwards, sit on the comfy armchairs in the reception area over a coffee.

Mirada del Toro 81, Es Mercadal ☎ 971 375 059. Highchairs. Open 1pm–4pm, 7pm–11pm. Reservations recommended. MC, V. Main courses €10–22 (£6.70–14.74).

Asia You'll need to book a table here, as this quirky restaurant fills up quickly. A non-smoking eatery, it is ideal for bringing older children; younger ones will feel far too low-down on the wicker armchairs. The portions are just right, and if you've room after a bowl of noodles, the puddings are equally original (try the lychee sorbet). If you see no vegetarian dishes on the menu, just ask them to prepare a meat-free version of whatever you fancy.

S'Algar ☎ 687 886 587. Open Tue-Sun 7pm–11pm. Reservations recommended. MC, V. Main courses €12–25 (£8.04–16.75).

INEXPENSIVE

Can Pota ★ More of a bar than a restaurant, Can Pota is ideal for a quick snack in Maó. The menu consists of delicatessen specialities and home-made quiches and rolls. Opt for a generous plate of bread with tomato, and add slices of ham, sausage or cheese. A spacious cafe, there is plenty of room for pushchairs.

Portal de Mar 11, Maó ☎ 971 362 363. No credit cards. Open 8am–midnight. Tapas from €4 (£2.68).

Es Bruc One of Menorca's original beach bars, Es Bruc not only boasts an unbeatable location, but is also a perfect escape from the midday sunshine for a hearty meal and an ice-cream. Es Bruc's menu has the tourist-standard burgers and chips to keep the children happy; but in addition, there are salads and fresh fish dishes. The owners make their own cheese (Hijo de F. Quintana), so look out for that. This is an ideal eatery for children; they can play on the sand until the meal is served. There are no reservations, so if you don't spot an empty table, just wait.

Urb. Sant Tomàs, Es Migjorn ☎ 971 370 488. MC, V. Open May–Oct 10am–10pm. Main courses €5–17 (£3.35–11.39).

Can Nito Centrally located in the middle of the emblematic Es Born Square in Ciutadella, Can Nito is a perfect stop-off point for snacks, tapas and rolls, whatever the time of day. When five minutes seems like an eternity to your child's stomach, the quick

Snacking in Ciutadella

service is definitely appreciated. There's a restaurant at the back if you want a more substantial meal.

Plaça des Born 11, Ciutadella ☎ 971 480 768. Highchairs. No credit cards. Open 6.30am–1am. Tapas from €3 (£2).

La Salamandra ★ ★ ★ VALUE

A no-nonsense eatery, La Salamandra has a straightforward menu, good, fast service, and is perfect for families. Every time I've passed it has been packed, no matter what time of day, so be prepared to wait if necessary. It's certainly worth it. The restaurant has a set menu system, but there is plenty of choice and vegetarians are well catered for. For children, there is a playground next door, as well as several tortoises roaming the flower beds.

Passeig Marítim 4, Cala en Porter ☎ 971 377 453. Set menus €9–18 (£6.03–12.06). Highchairs. MC, V.

10 Ibiza

IBIZA

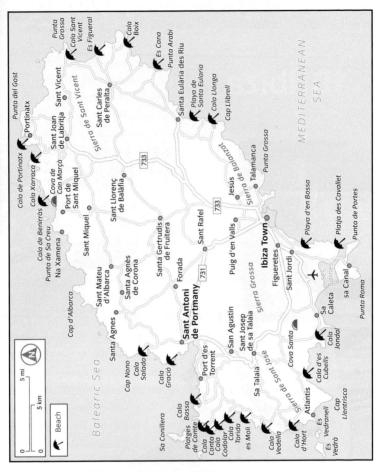

If Mallorca is the mainland in miniature, Ibiza (or Eivissa in Catalan) is a proper island, laid-back and beautiful, with a real-life hippy history. Although its story dates from 650 BC, it first hit the headlines in the 1960s as an idyllic haven for children of the revolution, floating like a raft in the jewel-blue waters of the Mediterranean Sea. While the capital of Ibiza (often referred to as 'Ibiza Ciudad' or Ibiza Town to avoid confusion) is better known these days as a clubbers' paradise, and parts of the island have been adopted as the playground of the rich and famous, those early hippy vibes of flower-power, peace and love live on. Mortals of lesser sorts, namely northern

Europeans, come to live here for the near-perfect weather and lifestyle. A 2005 census showed that immigrants now outnumber the natives: only 44.7% of the island's present population was born here.

Along with its smaller cousin **Formentera** (see Chapter 11), Ibiza was named one of the **Pine Islands** (for the abundance of Mediterranean pine forests) by the Phoenicians. They sailed here in 654 BC, and over the next 600 years Ibiza was occupied by Carthaginian, Roman and then

Regional Dance

Byzantine empires, before falling to the Moors in the 9th century. They were overthrown by Jaume 1 of Aragon in 1235. Today Ibiza is, in a symbolic sense, very much part of the *Països Catalans* (or 'Catalan Countries'). **Catalan**, along with Castilian Spanish, is an official language, which is why you will find places with two names (in what follows, I've used the Catalan ones).

At mere 25 km wide and 45 km long, Ibiza is split into five main sections, each their own micro-region. The capital is party-central, with all the big name clubs and a slew of hot beach bars that open and close by season. It's probably the least child-friendly part in terms of stuff to do, though its beautiful old town is a great place to pass a morning.

Sant Antoni de Portmany is the second-largest resort. While it still has its fair share of über-clubs, and English pubs, it is nevertheless popular with young families and couples. It has a more chilled-out atmosphere than the capital, and safe, clean beaches. An early evening stroll along the Passeig Maritim, winding up at the **Café del Mar** for sunset, is an essential part of getting to know Sant Antoni.

Santa Eulària des Riu is quieter still, with a much more family-focused vibe. If you still want the facilities of a relatively big town, minus the partying masses, this is the place for you. It's also the gastronomic heartland of the island, with some wonderful restaurants in its interior. The main town has a smart, palm-lined boulevard and up-market marina packed with leisure activities and great beaches.

The region around **Sant Joan de Labritja** is all tiny, whitewashed villages against a back-drop of moss-green hills, steep cliffs and hidden beaches. It's a haven for hippies, with a couple of markets and a New-Age vibe. It's here that you'll find yoga retreats, belly dancing and the hidden homes of the rich and famous.

Finally, **Sant Josep de sa Talaia** is the largest of the municipalities, though the main town is tiny. It boasts some of the island's most spectacular beaches backed by soaring cliffs and accessed by hairpin bends. Be aware that in high season you are likely to find these populated by clubbers rather than families.

FAST FACTS: IBIZA

Airport San Jordi Airport (☎ *971 809 900*) is just 7½ km from Ibiza Town. From the UK several airlines fly direct, including easyJet, bmiBaby, Virgin, and Air Berlin. Iberia (*www.iberia.com* ☎ *902 400 500*) offers services to Ibiza from most major Spanish cities. The low-cost carrier Vueling (☎ *902 333 933 www.vueling.com*) flies direct from Barcelona, Madrid and Valencia.

Babysitting Try the Canguro Agency (☎ *971 318 188*), a team of professional, multilingual sitters.

Boat Charter Captain Dan from DanyBoats (☎ *600 413 069 www.danyboats.com*) has a fleet of four speedboats at your disposal. He can show you some of the island's 'secret' spots, with masks and snorkels thrown in. From €100 (£67) per person, per day.

Bus Information The island's bus service is good, but timetables and routes change frequently. Always check *www.ibizabus.com* before you go.

Car Hire Rental agencies tend to be local affairs, rather than the big beasts. Try Betacar Car Rental (Ground Floor, Ibiza Airport ☎ *971 396 744 www.betacar.es*), Centauro Car Hire (Ground Floor, Ibiza Airport ☎ *971 394 917 www.centauro.net*) or Hertz (Ground Floor, Ibiza Airport ☎ *971 809 178 www.hertz.com*). Roads are generally in good condition, and these days all are tarmac. However, at the time of writing the controversial new Sant Antoni–Ibiza Town route across the heart of the island looks set to continue. Expect hold-ups and road works. Be aware that nearly everybody hires a car to get around the island: in peak season the going is slow.

Consulates The British Consulate is at Isidoro Macabich 45, in Ibiza Town (☎ *971 301 188*).

Chemists There's a pharmacy in Ibiza Town, J. A. Maritur, at C/Anibal 11 (☎ *971 310 371*).

Emergencies The emergency number is ☎ *112*.

Ferries Ibiza Town is the main point of entry from the mainland, with regular services for car and foot passengers from Barcelona, Valencia and Denia. Operators include Trasmediterranea (*www.trasmediterranea.es* ☎ *902 454 645*) and Balearia (*www.balearia.com*

902 160 180 or *966 428 700* from outside Spain). Iscomar has services to Ibiza from Mallorca and Menorca (*www.iscomar.com* *902 119 128* or *971 437 500* from outside Spain). To get to Formentera you also need to catch a ferry: see Chapter 11.

Internet There are Internet cafes in all the main towns. Try Chill Bar (Via Punica 49, Ibiza Town *971 399 736*), E-station (Avda Dr Fleming 1 – above Cafe Vertmell by the Egg – Sant Antoni *971 348 712*), or Mark & Dani (Calle del Mar 12, Sant Eulària *971 338 079. Fax: 971 336 077*). For reliable online information about Ibiza itself, *www.illesbalears.es* and *www. ibiza-tourism.net* both have plenty in English.

Post Office There's a post office at Isidoro Macabich 76, Ibiza Town.

Quad Bikes La Salamandra (*669 886 611 www.ibiza-spot light.com/salamandra*) organises excursions by quad bike all over the island, as well as speedboat tours and paintball events.

Safety Generally Ibiza is a safe island, but you need to watch out for your belongings in the capital's old town and in Sant Antoni. Bag-snatchers operate in both areas, especially if you're looking lost. Late at night you are also likely to come across people who are drunk or on drugs, and while usually harmless, it isn't the greatest thing for young eyes to see. Away from the main towns, Ibiza is still the kind of place where people leave their doors unlocked and their windows open.

Taxis Taxis are usually available outside the airport terminal. Prices and journey times include: Ibiza Town 15 mins, €10 (£6.70) approx; Sant Antoni 25 mins, €25 (£16.75) approx.; Santa Eulària 25 mins, €25 (£16.75) approx. Otherwise call Radiotaxi (*971 800 080*).

Telephone As in the rest of Spain, prefix 0034 from outside the country. Ibiza numbers start 971.

Time Zone GMT + 1.

Ibiza's Family Highlights

- Roaming the ramparts of Ibiza's **Vila Dalt,** see p. 205.
- Hanging loose in the **hippy markets,** see p. 217.
- Riding through the Ibizan countryside on **horseback,** see p. 219.
- Dining at **Daffers,** see p. 222.
- Birdwatching on the salt flats at **Ses Salines,** see p. 213.
- Exploring the **Cova de Can Marçà,** see p. 225.

IBIZA TOWN

Often referred to as Ibiza Town or simply 'la Vila', the capital of Ibiza is a formidable presence overlooking the Mediterranean. Divided into two quarters, the **Vila Dalt** (high town) is its monumental heart, protected by surprisingly intact ramparts that served as a model for guarding colonised cites in the New World. Other highlights include the 13th century **Catedral de Santa María,** built on the remains of a Mosque, and the **Museu Arqueológico de Ibiza y Formentera.** Like the cathedral, this museum bears testament to an unstable past, with relics from Phoenician, Roman and Arab cultures on display.

Narrow whitewashed streets form the lower part of Ibiza town, known as **Sa Penya,** the old *marineros* quarter. In summer it serves as a stage for the thousands of clubbers that invade; dance music screams from every bar. Off-season, its whitewashed streets are great for a stroll, to discover myriad funky, hippie-inspired shops and cafes.

Essentials

Ibiza Town is the main point of entry by **ferry** from the mainland, with regular services running from Barcelona, Valencia and Denia. It's also linked by ferry with the other three Balearic islands. See 'Fast Facts: Ibiza', p. 202, for contact details.

San Jordi Airport, is just 7½ km away. Taxis are generally available outside the terminal, or call **Radiotaxi** (☎ *971 800 080*); it costs roughly €10 (£6.70) to the centre of town, a 15-minute ride. An hourly **bus service** (☎ *971 340 412*) also runs between the airport and the **Estación**

Ibiza Coastline

Ibiza from the Air

Flights over Ibiza and Formentera give an incredible perspective on the islands, but remember the environmental impact of this form of tourism. You can **charter tiny planes** from the General Aviation Building at Ibiza Airport (☎ *676 500 200*). They take a maximum of three people and cost €250 (£167.50) per flight.

Marítima (the port) with several stops along the way. It runs daily, from outside the airport, 7.20am to 11.20pm. It costs €1.30 (£0.87) and takes about 20 minutes.

There is a **Tourist Information Office** in the arrivals hall of Ibiza Airport (☎ *971 301 900*). In Ibiza Town, you'll find one at C/Antoni Riquer 2 (☎ *971 301 900 www.visitbalears.com*), and in front of the harbour station.

Child-friendly Events

The Balearic Islands in general go mad for the saint's day of **San Juan de Bautista** (23rd June). Expect to see loads of fireworks and bonfires along the beach.

During the second week of May, Ibiza Town celebrates a **Medieval Festival** with magicians, witches, jugglers and clowns performing in the streets. Children will love the fake swordfights and battles, including a mock assault on the old fortress.

During the first week of August the **Festa de la Tierra** takes over the whole city, with street performances, gastronomic displays and music. The grand finale, on 8th August, celebrates the conquest of Ibiza by Catalan/Spanish troops with a flag-waving procession through the streets of the old town.

WHAT TO SEE & DO

Walking the Vila Dalt ★★

Ibiza's old walled city is living testament to battles, defeats and conquests of its 1000-year history. Declared a UNESCO World Heritage site in 1999, entry to the Vila Dalt is via a drawbridge and through the imposing **Portal de ses Taules** (Gate of Inscriptions).

Look out for the **Església de Sant Domeneç** (C/General Balanzat s/n), a beautiful three-domed Baroque church with frescoed walls. The **Catedral de Santa María** (Plaça de la Catedral s/n) is an imposing Catalan Gothic structure with later Baroque additions in the interior. Its small **museum** houses some impressive religious works. **Carrer Major,** the Vila Dalt's 'main street', is the highest point of the city, with some impressive 16th and 17th century mansions that can be viewed from the outside only. Continuing south along the street (which becomes Calle Ciriac), number 10 is a small **chapel.** It marks the Christian

View from Vila Dalt

A day's charter to Formentera leaves at 11am and returns at 7pm. The price includes gasoline and crew, but no food or drinks. If you can get a gang together, it's a memorable day out.

Eivissa Port s/n ☎ 649 051 324 www. pirate-living.com. €1,650 (£1105.50) for up to 19 passengers.

Aguamar AGES 3 AND UP Your children will love this fun water-park near the airport and **Playa d'en Bossa.** Waterslides, wiggly-bouncy-watery attractions, picnic areas and fast food outlets will keep the little ones entertained for hours. Playa d'en Bossa itself is one of the island's largest beaches, but has the reputation of a 'party beach'. It's best for families in the early morning.

Playa d'en Bossa s/n ☎ 971 396 790. Open 14 Jun–11 Oct.

soldiers' point of entry in 1235. The cafe/restaurant hub of the Vila Dalt is the pretty **Plaça de la Vila,** a good place to rest after you have explored the area's cobblestoned streets and admired the views from the watchtowers.

The tourist office (C/Antoni Riquer 2 ☎ 971 301 900) organises **guided walking tours** of the Vila Dalt in English, suitable for all ages.

The Top Family Attractions

Willem Charter Formentera ★★ Just what

your children always wanted: a real-life pirate galleon to terrorise the high seas. Oo-aargh, me hearties! This majestic ship evokes the days when the Balearics were plagued by pirates, and of course it was better to be for them than against. This unique charter allows you to live out *Pirates of the Mediterranean* fantasies complete with black flags, skull-and-crossbones and plenty of cheer.

Museu d'Art Contemporani d'Eivissa AGES 5 AND UP Perched

on top of the old town, this smart, new art gallery extends over two floors of barn-like interior. The building dates from the 1920s and originally belonged to the military. Its incarnation as a museum of modern art hosts international and local artists exhibiting, with some interesting installations, such as Martí Anson's minimal apartment block, *El apartamento 2002.* Exhibitions change regularly, but if you're passing it's worth popping in to see what's going on.

Ronda de Narcís Puget s/n ☎ 971 302 723. €1.20 (£0.80). Open 10am-1.30pm, 5pm-8pm. Closed Sun afternoon, all day Mon.

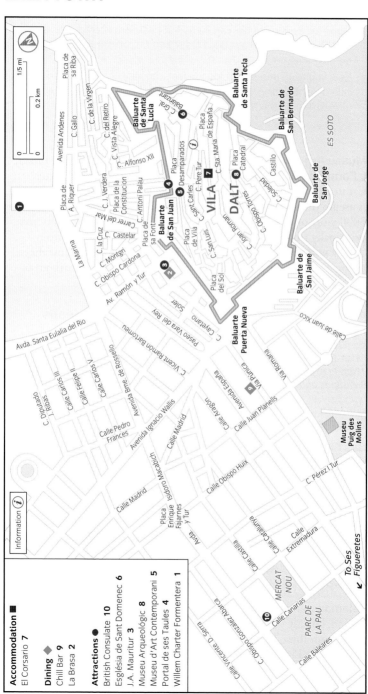

Information (i)

Accommodation ■
El Corsario **7**

Dining ◆
Chill Bar **9**
La Brasa **2**

Attractions ●
British Consulate **10**
Església de Sant Domenec **6**
J.A. Mauritur **3**
Museu Arqueològic **8**
Museu d'Art Contemporani **5**
Portal de ses Taules **4**
Willem Charter Formentera **1**

0   1/5 mi
0   0.2 km

Avinguda Andenes
Plaça de sa Riba
C. Gallo
C. de la Virgen
C. del Retiro
C. Vista Alegre
C. Alfonso XII
Plaça de A. Riquer
C. J. Verdera
Plaça de la Constitucion
Carrer del Mar
C. Antoni Palau
Plaça Gran sa Font
C. la Cruz
C. Castelar
C. Montgri
C. Obispo Cardona
La Marina
Av. Ramón y Tur
Soler
C. Cayetano
Paseo Vara del Rey
C. Vicent Ramón Bartomeu
Avda. Santa Eulalia del Rio
C. Diputado J. Ribas
Calle Carlos III
Calle Felipe II
Calle Carlos V
Avenida Bme. de Rossello
Calle Pedro Frances
Avenida Isidoro Wallis
Calle Madrid
Plaça Enrique Fajarnes y Tur
Avda
Calle Madrid
Calle Obispo Huix
C. Pérez I Tur
Calle Obispo González Abarca
Calle Vicente D. Serra
Calle Canarias
PARC DE LA PAU
MERCAT NOU
Calle Castilla
Calle Cataluña
Calle Extremadura
Calle Baleares
To Ses Figueretes
Museu Puig des Molins
Calle Aragón
Calle Juan Planells
Avenid España
Via Punica
Via Romana
Calle de Juan Xico
Baluarte Puerta Nueva
Baluarte de San Jaime
Plaça del Sol
C. San Luis
C. Joan Roman
C. San Carles
Plaça de Vila
VILA
DALT
C. Obispo Torres
C. Soledad
C. Sta. Maria
Castillo
Catedral
Plaça Catedral
C. Pere Tur
Plaça Desamparados
Plaça de España
ES SOTO
Baluarte de San Jorge
Baluarte de San Bernardo
Baluarte de Santa Tecla
Baluarte de Santa Lucia
Baluarte de San Juan
Gran C. Balanzat

1
2
3
4
5
6
7
8
9
10

Fun for Active Families

Good old-fashioned fun can be had at La Bolera (Centro Comercial, C/Murtra 2-4, Playa d'en Bossa ☎ 971 300 356), an indoor bowling centre near Playa d'en Bossa. There are four alleys, as well as billiards, 'elastic chairs' and lots of touchy-feely, bouncy contraptions for your little ones. Budding cowboys might like to try the monitored 'electric toro' while you relax in the restaurant/bar.

Museu Arqueológic d' Eivissa y Formentera ★ AGES 7 AND UP

Created in 1907, this interesting museum displays pieces from 3000 years of the island's history, principally from the Phoenician colony in Sa Nostra. Entrance to the museum allows access to the bastion of Santa Tecla, with its spectacular views over the Bay of Ibiza.

Plaza de la Catedral 3 ☎971 301 231. €5 (£3.35), €3 (£2) children under 11. Open 16th Mar–15th Oct, Tue-Sat 10am-2pm and 4pm-8pm. Otherwise 9am-3pm, and 10am-2pm Sun.

Beaches

Ses Figueretes is one of the most family-oriented of Ibiza Town's beaches. There is no nudity (though topless sunbathing, like everywhere in Spain, is the norm), just over a kilometre-and-a-half of white sand, kiosks and a promenade from which to view the clear, still water.

Talamanca is another good option, an easy 15-minute stroll from Ibiza Town's marina or connected by a regular boat service. The bay offers a broad, sandy beach, shallow water and hammocks and pedalos for hire. Shady areas are scarce, so don't forget hats and sunscreen. Directions are posted from downtown Ibiza. Follow the signposts from the harbour or the Marina Botafoc.

A Side-trip to Jesús

Once an outlying village, Jesús has now been annexed by Ibiza Town proper, but still has pretty cobblestone streets and rustic housing. The highlight is the Parròquia de Nostra Senyora de Jesús AGES 5 AND UP (☎ 971 315 452. Free entry. Open daily 9.30am-12.30pm and 4pm-6pm), a 15th century monastery with a gothic table by Rodrigo de Osona, one of the masters of medieval Catalan painting.

Jésus also has it own **pony park** (Ponylandia, Ctra Eivissa–Jesús ☎ 630 204 272) which on Sunday mornings turns into a **flea market,** where everything from second-hand fishing rods to local arts and crafts can be had for a song.

Shopping

Divina ★ The children's and babies' clothes here are so beautiful that even if you don't have children, you might still be tempted. Made from 100% natural cotton in pure Ibiza style, and available only in white (to represent purity), and black, these clothes are a lifelong addition to any wardrobe.

C/Santa Cruz 7, Vila Dalt ☎ *971 301 157.*

Only T-Shirts More natural cotton baby-grows and children's tees here, this time in soft, vegetable-dyed colours with retro motifs: lizards, bicycles and smiling faces. They make great gifts.

C/Mayor 29 (also C/del Mar 25 and C/Cautelar 13).

José Pascual Lovely handmade straw baskets and hats, plus a selection of *espadenyes*, the comfy canvas shoes favoured by the locals.

C/ de Sa Creu 30 ☎ *971 310 874.*

Family-friendly Accommodation

Hotel Mare Nostrum ★ One of the few family-friendly options in or near Ibiza Town, this 500-room hotel is located right on the palm-lined, golden-sanded Playa d'en Bossa. Rooms lean towards the functional/practical side, but the big plus is that families with children outnumber clubbers amongst the clientele. Facilities for children include their own indoor and outdoor playroom, swimming pool and a team of animators whose sole job it is to keep them entertained morning to night.

Avenida Pedro Matutes Noguera s/n, Playa d'en Bossa ☎ *971 332 551. 500 rooms. Double €32.30–117 (£21.64–78.39), 50% discount for children under 11. Children under 2 free. Amenities: two swimming pools, play areas, sun terraces, buffet restaurant. In room: A/C, satellite TV, telephone, baths, terraces.*

El Corsario Families looking for an authentic Ibizan experience away from the resort-hotels

Only T-Shirts

might like to try this boho guesthouse perched high in the Vila Dalt. The 15 rooms are eclectically fitted out with second-hand furniture and curios, and most have privileged views. There is no air conditioning, but a constant sea breeze cools the place. Breakfast can be taken on the tree-lined terrace, but if you're allergic to cats, stay away: the neighbourhood's strays tend to gather in the hotel garden. El Corsario also has its own restaurant for lunch and dinner. Overall, then, great if you want a night out on the town in old Ibiza, but move on if you're looking for easier family comforts.

C/Ponent 5 ✆ *971 301 172/393 212. Fax: 971 391 953. 15 rooms. Double €118–188 (£79–126). Extra bed €35 (£23.45), cot free. Amenities: restaurant, bar, garden, babysitting service. In room: TV, mini-bar.*

Family-friendly Dining

Plaza del Sol This is a smart, Mediterranean joint overlooking the new town, with the ruins of the cathedral to the rear. Dishes here are fresh and original, ranging from pizza and pasta to more adventurous food. Seated beneath a terrace shaded by vine leaves, it makes a romantic spot for soaking up the atmosphere of the old town.

Plaza del Sol 7 ✆ *971 390 773. Mains €15–22 (£10–14.75). V, MC. Open 1.30pm–4pm, 8.30pm–11pm. Reservations recommended.*

La Brasa Set in a lovely bougainvillea-filled garden at the base of the old walls, La Brasa serves up fine Mediterranean food at good prices for both lunch and dinner. Specialities include fish and seafood of all sorts, plus a substantial selection of desserts like blueberry cheesecake and fruit pudding. In cooler temperatures, you can step into the cosy indoor dining room.

C/ de Pere Sala 3 ✆ *971 301 202. Mains €11–22 (£7.37–14.74). V, MC. Open 1.30pm–4pm, 8.30pm–11pm. Reservations recommended.*

Cafe Sidney Near the Playa Talamanca, this is one of the few eateries in town that offers a substantial breakfast, from the full eggs, bacon and sausages fry-up to cornflakes and chocolate milk for the children. Mains are equally child-pleasing, with

TIP ❯❯ Advice on Accommodation ❮

The bottom line is this: not everywhere on Ibiza is family-friendly. Most hotels and restaurants make their policies clear. Ibiza Town, for example, is largely oriented to the party-going scene, and as such isn't a good base for families with young children. Your older teens may certainly get a kick from it, though. If you don't intend to allow your teenagers into the fray, it may be wise to remove them from temptation. Ibiza Town is a hedonist's paradise.

Tex Mex chicken wings, nacho chips and guacamole, as well as more risqué herring and German potato salad for grown-ups. It is located right on the marina, so the little ones can be entertained by boats coming and going. On Sundays they serve a substantial buffet brunch. A children's menu is also available.

Marina Botafoch s/n ☎ 971 192 243. Highchairs. Mains €7–15 (£4.69–10). No credit cards. No reservations.

El Sitio Tapas is a great way for children to eat: portions are small and they get to see it before they order. This bright, new, two-storey tapas bar has over 79 varieties with an outdoor terrace on a pedestrianised street for them to run off the carbs later.

Boulevard Abel Matutes 2 ☎ 971 312 266. €2–2.50 (£1.34–1.68) per tapa. Open 10am–11pm. No credit cards. No reservations.

Sant Josep de sa Talaia

Sant Josep de sa Talaia, the island's largest municipality (and the one closest to the airport), is more family-oriented than neighbouring Ibiza Town. Surrounded by pine trees, Sant Josep's main attraction is the whitewashed 18th century church, one of the loveliest on the island. The town makes a handy lunch stop if you're making your way to the coves of the south-west, and will be considerably cheaper than anything you'll find near the beach. Otherwise, there's little in the town itself. But it does make a good base: this part of the island has more coves and *calas* to discover than anywhere else, plus the incredible natural reserve at Ses Salines.

Essentials

To get here by car from Ibiza Town, head north-east along the C731 then turn left on to the PM803 at Ses Paisses petrol station. Bus 8 or 42 from Ibiza Town and bus 8 from Sant Antoni de Portmany will also take you to Sant Josep. Check *www.ibizabus.com* for details on timetables. There is no tourist office as such; glean the basics before setting off, from *www. sanjose-ibiza.net*. You can call a local taxi on ☎ *971 398 340.*

Beaches & Resorts

Cala Jondal beach is great for children with plenty of facilities, pedalos and restaurants. The beach has its glamour element, but on the whole children are welcome and it's one of the loveliest spots on the island. Follow the signs at the road to Sant Josep de Sa Talaia at km 7.

Cala Vedella ★ is a tiny village-turned-resort tucked into the back of a cove, quite lively despite its diminutive size. Families flock here to take advantage of the clean, sandy beach, calm water within the enclosed bay and an abundance of eating options. There's also a dive school (see p. 213) for active types. It makes a good base if all you want is a bucket-and-spade holiday, with a couple of

Cala Jondal

aparthotels as well as plenty of houses to rent (see 'Family-friendly Accommodation', p. 209). It's lovely and unspoilt – even the road that runs through it has yet to be paved. Located 9 km from Sant Josep de sa Talaia, take the Ibiza Town road to km 13 and follow the signs.

At **Platjes de Comte,** you'll find two great sandpits divided by a spit of land marked by the café-bar Sunset Ashram. The south-facing beach is more for grown-ups, while the north spit offers child-pleasing facilities like Lego-brick coloured pedalos complete with slides. Bring a picnic as the Indian nibbles, gloopy pastas and greasy fried fish at **Sunset Ashram** OVERRATED leave much to be desired, or head back around the headland to Amarant at **Cala Codolar** (see 'Family-friendly Dining', below). Take the Sant Antoni de Portmany Road to Port d'es Torrent and follow the signs.

Cala d'Hort is a pebble beach with two *chiringuitos* (beach bars). Lined by red cliffs bitten out by angry Mediterranean storms and lined by grey, weather-beaten boathouses, there is something very dramatic and old-fashioned about the place. It's worth the drive just to take a look. It's also the best place on the island to view the imposing rock of **Es Vedra,** Ibiza's very own Gibraltar. You can't get on to it, but there are plenty of boat trips from Ibiza Town and Sant Antoni. To find Cala d'Hort, take the road from Sant Josep de sa Talaia to Es Cubells, making a left towards the beach at km 5.

Elsewhere on this coast, try **Atlantis.** This rocky *cala* has been a hippie destination since the 1960s and is legendary in the island's counter-culture. A giant figure of a Hindu deity has been painted into the rock and the coastal caves are decorated with more New Age imagery and wind chimes. It's accessible via boat from Cala d'Hort. Alternatively, you can get there on foot from the **Torre de Pirata** ★, an old defence tower located 20 metres above the coast between Cala d'Hort and Atlantis. It was built in 1763 and offers great views of **Es Vedrà** and **Es Vedranell,** both considered 'mystical' by the Ibizans. Note, though, this option isn't recommended with small children: the hike is too tricky.

The famed **Cova Santa,** off the Sant Josep–Ibiza Town road near the Sa Caleta turn-off, has stalactites over 1000 years old. **Sa Talaia,** meanwhile, is the highest point on the island (475 metres above sea level). Just 30 minutes by car from Sant Josep, on a clear day you can see the mainland.

The Top Family Attractions

Ses Salines Nature Reserve ★ ★ ★ ALL AGES In days
of yore, Ibiza was known as the 'Island of Salt'. Extracting has been going on in these marshes since the 5th century, and still is. (Look out for the pretty blue 'Ibiza Salt' pots sold all over the

island). The white salt hills and pink pools make for an incredible landscape. Migrating flamingos and herons rest here from July to October (the best months to visit), and February to May; endemic vegetation includes juniper and rosemary bushes, pine forests and of course reeds. The park has its own information service (☎ 971 302 561). Ask them about the horse and cart tour of the marshes (summer only). Or for a panorama, drive to **Puig d'es Corb Marí**. If you've rented bikes, cycling the flat marshes is also a good option. Ses Salines is about 10 km south-west of Ibiza Town, close to the airport.

Big Blue Dive Resort The advantage of diving here is the close proximity of Es Vedrà and Es Vedranell – the two monolithic rocks that loom off Cala d'Hort. However, you'll need to be a fairly experienced diver for that. Otherwise, the chaps here are fun and friendly, offering a range of beach and boat dives to suit everybody.

Cala Vedella s/n ☎ 650 769 296 www.bigbluedive.net. One dive with all equipment €45 (£30.15). Insurance €4 (£2.68).

It's a Fact!

From the 18th century onwards, pirate attacks on Ibiza were a regular event, hence the *torres* (watchtowers) dotted around the coast. When the culprits were caught they were hanged on a small island between Ibiza and Formentera called Los Ahorcados, which means 'the hanged ones'.

Island Flowers

La Casita Verde ALL AGES

Teaching the children about sustainability and ecology can be fun at the Casita Verde, a model ecological centre located in a valley near Sant Josep. Every Sunday the community has an open house, where you can participate in vegetarian cooking classes, help with the gardening, try natural skin care or just hang about in the children's playground.

Coll de Rossellons (follow the green heart signs from Benimussa) ℂ *971 187 353 www.greenheart.info. Open day Sun 2pm-6pm; Thu volunteer days.*

Shopping

Every day, from 9am-11pm between Easter and the end of October, the island's artists exhibit their work in the main square **of Sant Agust d'es Vedrà.**

Pomelo A step up from the usual tourist tat, Pomelo stocks rich brocade fabrics in tight rolls; brightly woven cushions; chintzy bed spreads; glass beads; candlesticks and candles; and interesting trinkets like gaily painted miniature dogs and cats.

C/Sa Talaia 9, Sant Josep de sa Talaia ℂ *971 801 586. Fax: 971 801 587.*

Es Trenent & Cia This place is worth a stop for its wide range of hand-made wooden toys.

C/Pere Escanelles 24, Sant Josep de Sa Talaia ℂ *971 800 381.*

Flea Market ★ Every Saturday, the residents of the island empty out their closets for Ibiza's very

---

 Get Insured

In Spain, dive insurance is compulsory. If you don't have your own, all dive shops will provide it for an additional cost of around €5 (£3.35).

own car boot sale. From old books to new hooks, it's all here for a song.

Hippodrome de Sant Jordi de Ses Salines 📞 *971 396 669. Sat only 11am-7pm.*

Family-Friendly Accommodation

Villas & Visages ★★ A good option for cosmopolitan families looking for tasteful, high-end self-catering accommodation on the island, Villas & Visages has an impressive selection. Properties on their books range from luxury, clifftop apartments with sea views, infinity pools and Moroccan-style outdoor lounges, to rustic country accommodation. Styles range from traditional to modern, beachside to *campo*. Take your pick.

Cala Vedella s/n 📞 *971 808 122. Fax: 971 808 262 www.ibizahouse renting.com.*

Los Jardines de Palerm Hotel

Owned and run by a charming French woman, Los Jardines as the name suggests is a bit of an oasis perched above the village. While it's not specifically family-oriented, children are welcome: there are even two swimming pools so children can let off steam in one while adults snooze by the other. They are also happy to help with babysitting services and advise on local child-friendly activities. The beautiful gardens recall the Alhambra in Granada in miniature, while the interior is also in Moroccan style with low-slung couches and polished cement floors. Rooms are cool and airy, with interesting furniture, animal print rugs and knotted grass chairs. A secret pathway connects the hotel with the village, and there's also a walk behind that takes visitors up to **Sa Talaia,** the highest point on the island at 475 metres (it takes about 30 minutes).

Sant Josep de sa Talaia s/n 📞 *971 800 318. Fax: 971 800 453 www. jardinsdepalerm.com. 10 rooms. Double €150–203 (£100.50–136); double with terrace €166–216 (£111.22–144.72); mini-suite €189–259 (£126.63–173.53); Junior suite €246–304 (£164.82–203.68); Suite €265–336 (£177.55–225.12). Extra bed €40 (£26.80). IVA not included. V, MC. Amenities: 2 swimming pools, breakfast, gardens. In room: TV, a/c, heating.*

Apartamentos Cala Vedella

VALUE One of the best family-oriented options in the area if you want somewhere with lots of other children around. These modern apartment blocks aren't exactly oozing character, but they are clean, newly kitted-out and good value. Situated right on the seafront, they also have two swimming pools (one for children, the other for adults); a satellite TV room; a mini-club children's nursery; and a nightly mini-disco. Boredom shouldn't be a problem. The apartments themselves are spacious, open-plan affairs. The best have balconies overlooking the beach.

Apdo de Correos 134, San Josep 📞 *971 808 013. Fax: 971 808 125 www.aptospuertovadella.com. V, MC. Apt for 1–2 €45–137 (£30.15– 91.79); for 3, €50–145 (£33.50–97.15);*

for 4, €55–153 (£36.85–102.51); 5+, €75–170 (£50.25–113.90). Breakfast €5 (£3.35); dinner €10 (£6.70); half-board €12.50 (£8.38). 50% discount for children under 12; children under 2 free. Amenities: restaurant; cafeteria; satellite TV; 2 swimming pools; bus service to Ibiza and Sant Antoni.

Family-friendly Dining

Destino ★ Situated at the heart of Sant Josep, Destino serves excellent Moroccan-style tapas: you choose from refrigerated bars from a selection of meat, fish and vegetarian dishes. Children love being able to see the bright, colourful, freshly-made food before committing to anything, and friendly and willing staff are happy to guide them. Child-size portions include lentils and spinach, and more exotic egg-plant salads, *salpicón* (mixed seafood in vinaigrette), chicken *tagline* and pasta with grapes. Grab a selection and dig in.

C/Atalaya 15, Sant Josep de sa Talaia ☏ 971 800 341. Open Mon-Sat 1pm–1am. Closed Sun. Tapas from €2–4.50 (£1.34–3) per portion. V, MC.

Restaurant El Carmen The slightly scruffy looking El Carmen is the better of the two restaurants on Cala d'Hort, though prices can be eyewater-ing (€82 (£54.94) for lobster paella for two). A less luxuriant Spanish paella (meat, usually chicken, pork or rabbit and some seafood, usually mussels and cuttlefish) is a more afford-able €28 (£18.76) for two. The big draw is the view and the superb quality of the food:

it says something that the clientele is mainly Spanish and so generally pickier about the quality of the fish and shellfish. Much of the fresh catch, includ-ing crab and lobster, is sold by weight and prices can escalate, so be sure to check before you order.

Platja Cala d'Hort s/n ☏ 971 187 449. Main courses €12–50 (£8–33.50). Open 1.30–4pm, 8.30–11pm. Reservations recommended.

Amarant Beach Restaurant ★

The reputation of Amarant goes before it, especially among hungry divers and surfers – always a good sign. Wedged up in the hillside above the pebble beach at Cala Codolar, the price–quality equa-tion here is generally very good. Arrive in time to see the sunset: this is one of the very best spots on the island to gawp.

Cala Codolar s/n ☏ 971 806 449/ 435 www.amarantrestaurantibiza. com. Mains €9.50–21 (£6.37–14.07). Open 1.30–4pm, 8.30–11pm. Reservations recommended.

SANTA EULÀRIA DES RIU

The capital of this municipality, Santa Eulària (or Santa Eulalia in Spanish) des Riu, is perhaps the most family-friendly place on the island. Gangs of children gam-bol along the main drags in the early evening, while the town beaches have clean, soft sand, shallow, calm water, lifeguards and those all-important banana boats and pedalos. Prosperous and bustling in season, the town's port also has a handful of dive shops and restaurants. Santa Eulària is also the location of two of the most happening hippy markets on the island.

While you're in the municipality be sure to stop at **Sant Rafael de Forca.** This tiny enclave has been nominated an 'artistic zone' due to the high number of potters that live and work here. You'll spot shops selling their wares and pottery demonstrations right on the main street.

The gorgeous little inland village of **Santa Gertrudis de Fruitera** is so-named because of the abundant fruit and almond trees that grow in the vicinity. The centerpiece is the late 18th century church, with its original wooden altarpiece dedicated to Saint Gertrude, and a fine bell tower. Surrounding it, the clutch of artesan shops, galleries and

Fig Trees

counter-culture cafes might also hold you interest for an afternoon. Possibly not your children's, though.

Essentials

To get here by **car** from Ibiza Town, head along the C733 north for just over 21 km. **Bus 13** from Ibiza Town and **bus 19** from Sant Antoni de Portmany will also take you to Santa Eulària. Check *www.ibizabus.com* for timetables. The **tourist office** is at Marià Riquer Wallis s/n, Santa Eularia des Riu (971 330 728 *www.santaeulalia.net*). You can call a local **taxi** on 971 333 033.

Hippy Markets

Punta Arabí Hippy Market ★
Started in the early 1970s with a handful of stalls, over 600 now take over this resort, hawking wares from all over Asia. The market is incredibly well organized (vendors are divided into sections, according to the goods they sell) and there are plenty of food and drink options, from

Hippy Market

Festes Santa Eulària

The first Sunday of May sees a wonderfully colourful festival of horse-drawn carriages in celebration of the town's patron saint.

pizzas to organic juices. Parents can even drop off tired toddlers at the crèche (10am–5pm, apartment 36). Go in the afternoons to avoid the crowds.

Club Punta Arabí 📞 *971 330 650* **www.hippymarket.com**. *Wed 10am-7pm, May-Oct.*

Las Dalias Hippy Market & Restaurant ★

In truth, the restaurant isn't really worth bothering with, so save your pennies for lunch elsewhere. However, the hippy market itself will remind those old and travelled enough of the markets of Goa in the 1960s, with its flower-power vibe and wafts of incense. The wares here are more up-market than most, with colourful kaftans and woven straw hats mixed in with the tie-dye. It also has some decent crafts, which make good gifts, but above all it's simply a great place to soak up the atmosphere. Children tend to wander round wide-eyed at the magic of it all. Just be prepared for some 'swinging-60s' questions afterwards.

Ctra. De San Carles Km 12 📞 *971 326 825. Restaurant* 📞 *971 335 156* **www.lasdalias.com**. *All day Sat, year round. Special markets at Christmas and Semana Santa (Easter). Night market Mon, June–Oct from 6pm–1am; live performances every Wed at Namaste (within the market), 9pm–6am.*

Beaches

The 400-metre-long stretch of sand with rocky inlets at **Es Figueral** ★ is considered one the prettiest on the islands, and is popular with watersports enthusiasts. A full range of amenities includes a dive school, volleyball, parasailing, jetskis, showers and umbrellas and hammocks for hire. It's just 14 km from Santa Eulària: take the Sant Carlos village turn at the north end of Santa Eulària and follow the signs. **Santa Eulària's main beach,** meanwhile, is blue-flagged. Its shallow waters and sheltered location make it ideal for children. You'll find restaurants, hammocks, umbrellas, sailboats and jetski hire.

Museums & Monuments

Ibiza and Formentera Ethnological Museum

This small but interesting collection of artefacts is displayed in **Can Ros,** a near-perfect example of vernacular rural architecture. The old home consists of the *porxo* (main room) a balcony, olive mill and bedrooms as well as an exterior cistern and well. Displayed throughout (often *in situ*) are old clothing, jewellery, musical instruments and everyday tools used in the *pages* (peasant) life of old. The experience is

Barrau Museum

complemented with regular handicraft demonstrations.

Can Ros des Puig de Missa, Santa Eulària des Riu 📞 *971 332 845. Apr–Sep, Mon–Sat 10am-1pm and 5pm-8pm; rest of year, Mon 4pm-6pm, Tue–Sat, 10am-1pm and 4pm-6pm. Closed Sun.*

Barrau Museum ★ Painter Laureà Barrau i Buñol (1863–1967) was an early figure in Barcelona's *modernista* movement who had considerable influence on well-known artists like Roman Casas. He arrived in Ibiza in 1912, and for the rest of his life painted street scenes, local characters and the *marinero* life in the impressionist style. Although the bulk of his work is now in private collections and larger museums, this lovely gallery (founded by his wife) is worth visiting for the picturesque setting: it's in an old *masia* next to the **Puig de Missa church** (admission free). The church itself, 52 metres above sea level at the heart of Santa Eulària,

was built in the 16th century. It is attached to an unusual watchtower in the shape of a half-moon.

Puig de Missa, Santa Eulària des Riu 📞 *971 339 411. Admission free. Tue–Fri, 10am-1.30pm.*

Fun for Active Families

Horse Country Club ★★

AGES 8 AND UP This is the best place on the island to ride, whether you're a beginner or more experienced. The horses are gentle, well cared-for and suited to all levels. Fully-qualified instructors (BHSAI) offer a range of tuition, including dressage and jumping for those who want to hone their skills. Saturday is Children's Summer Riding Camp day, dedicated to young equestrians: tots from all over come together to spend the day learning about, caring for and riding horses. Lunch and a lesson are included. Other options range from one-hour lessons to week-long riding holidays. Depending on the age of your children and how independent they are, a riding holiday could prove a perfect way for you to get some time alone, too. Canadian-born Michel and her team are fun, friendly and guarantee the time of their lives for young horse-lovers.

It's a Fact!

Santa Eulària's S'Argamassa Aqueduct is 425 metres long and dates back to the 1st century AD. It was originally used to transport water for the production of salted fish.

Santa Gertrudis s/n 📞 649 457 718 (Michel). Prices change every year; call ahead for more information. Open all year.

Punta Dive ★★ AGES 8 AND UP

Punta Dive has the best facilities on the island. This is a full water-sports service centre, offering windsurfing, kayaking and cata-maran classes. Reportedly this is the best beach for learning kite-surfing in the winter, too. Even if you've no wish to get your toes wet, it is a great place to hang out while the children get down to it. Diving is their core business, and the outfit offers numerous sites for all levels, including some off nearby Formentera. Courses are friendly and upbeat with cama-raderie encouraged from the off. 'Bubblemakers' courses (children's diving) are also available.

Cala Martina s/n, Punta Arabí 📞 971 336 726. Fax: 971 319 413 www.

puntadive.com. One-tank dive, all equipment €45 (£30.15); 5 dives, all equipment €200 (£134); 10 dives, all equipment €380 (£254.60).

Ibiza Diving AGES 12 AND UP

Friendly and very professional, this dive outfit has companies in France and a well-earned reputation for safety. They offer a good range of dives; those around the island of **Tagomago** are particularly good. As are their day trips to the island of Formentera that include two dives and a paella lunch. Open-water junior courses are offered for the over-12s to a maximum of 12 metres.

Local 14, zone 4, Puerto Deportivo, Santa Eulària des Riu 📞 971 332 949. Mobile: 659 018 221. Fax: 971 332 899 www.ibiza-diving.com. One-tank dive with all equipment €45 (£30.15). Day-trip to Formentera incl. lunch and two dives €115 (£77.05).

Santa Eulària

It's a Fact!

The world's biggest and oldest living organism, a plant, was found off the shores of Ibiza in 2006. The *Posidonia Oceanica* is an incredible 8 km long. It's also 100,000 years old. For more on *posedonia*, see p. 244.

Shopping

Julio Bauza Julio Bauza is one of Ibiza's better-known designers, artists and ceramicists. He designed the striking 'Columbus Egg' sculpture in Sant Antoni, and this small shop in San Rafael sells his singular creations, as well as reproduction pieces and original works from the community's artists.

C/ San Antoni s/n ☎ 971 198 136. Open Jul–Sep, Mon–Sat 10am-2pm and 6pm-8pm.

Can Daifa This small collection of paintings, displayed in the palm-filled garden of a private home, also has an outdoor cafe next door.

Plaça de l'Església s/n, Santa Gertrudis de Fruitera ☎ 971 197 042. Call for opening times.

Family-friendly Accommodation

S'Argamassa Palace ★ If you think the terms 'family-friendly' and 'four star' don't belong together, think again. This quiet hotel, located amongst the pine trees just 80 metres from the beach, offers all the luxury trimmings together with a children' pool, playpark and mini-golf. The spacious rooms are well thought-out with soft furnishings and edges, many with separate TV rooms. The rooftop garden makes a pleasant place for some time to yourself.

Urbinización S'Argamassa s/n ☎ 971 330 271 www.sargamassa-palace. com. Double €219–420 (£146.73–281.40). Breakfast included. Cots free, extra bed add 30%. Amenities: restaurant, shop, bar, swimming pool, boat and car hire. In room: A/C, heating, hairdryer, satellite TV, telephone.

Hostal-Restaurante Cala Boix VALUE This friendly, family-run restaurant and *hostal* is a no-frills place, its biggest luxury the fantastic dark-sand beach of Cala Boix. Rooms are clean and comfortable, with plain furniture and simple linens. If life's simple pleasures are all you require for a happy holiday, then this is a great getaway for anyone travelling on a budget.

Cala Boix s/n ☎ 971 335 408 www. hostalcalaboix.com. Double with breakfast €51–60 (£34.17–40.20); double half-board €73–82 (£48.91–54.94); double full-board €95–104 (£63.65–69.68); menù del dia €9 (£6.03); main courses €7–15 (£4.69–10.05). In room: basic with fan.

Hotel Miami VALUE With 335 rooms, the three-star Miami fits squarely into the resort category:

it has tennis and squash facilities and a large selection of restaurants and bars on-site. The hotel does its best to ensure you and the children are entertained 24/7 with games, competitions and myriad activities. The beach at **Es Cana** (500 metres from the hotel) is safe and sandy, and there are plenty of other coves along this stretch to explore. Meals (including the daily BBQ) are taken buffet-style in the garden. Rooms are basic but light, spacious and comfortable.

Playa Es Caná s/n, Santa Eulària 📞 *971 803 464 www.ibiza-spotlight. com/miami. Double €30–70 (£20.10–46.90) per person. Discount for 3rd person in double room: 30% Discount for children 2–12 sharing with 2 adults: 1st child 80%, 2nd child 50%. Supplement for sea view €12 (£8) per day. Amenities: buffet restaurant, swimming pool, entertainment, TV room, open-air barbecue, table tennis, children's play areas. In room: A/C, heating, TV, telephone.*

Family-friendly Dining

Daffers ★ ★ **VALUE** Practically an institution, Daffers is possibly the most family-friendly dinner spot on the island. With its cavernous interior strung with Moroccan lanterns and intimate nooks, it's a cut above the plastic places seen elsewhere – and you can tell from their friendly smiles that the staff really care about what they're doing. Early-bird menus from 6.30pm to 8pm get a €2.50 (£1.68) discount, otherwise it's all systems go on an extensive fixed-price, three-course menu. Starters range from Thai wantons to avocado and crab cocktail and chicken liver paté; mains include rump steak with garlic butter, Thai chicken curry and fresh fish; desserts run the gamut from banana splits to mango mousses and all manner of chocolate delights. As 11-year-old Alice remarked on the table next to mine, "It makes such a change to go somewhere where the children's choice is as wide as the adults." Hear, hear.

C/Sant Vincent s/n, Santa Eulària 📞 *971 336 709. Mon–Sat, 6.30pm– 11pm. Closed Sun. Three courses €10–15 (£6.70–10.05).*

Pier 1 A fish-and-chip shop with a difference, Pier 1 offers a huge range of fresh fried fish, as well as curries, burgers, ribs and pasta. Its speciality, though, is a pint of shell-on prawns for dipping in mayonnaise. It's a good way to introduce children to the idea that shellfish can be fun, and its laid-back, jolly atmosphere

---

TIP ⟩ ## Self-catering Holidays ⟨

Eating out on Ibiza can get expensive, especially when you have many mouths to feed. It may be worth considering self-catering accommodation if you want to be able to cook and prepare food and picnics for yourself. Most self-catering places advertise online. Some reputable websites include *www.ibiza-spotlight.com*, *www.ibizahideaway.net* and *www.ibizahouserenting.com*.

overlooking the sea make it a winner for lunch or dinner.

Passeig Marítim 6-8, Santa Eulària 📞 *971 331 529. Open 11am–11pm. Pint of prawns €11.95 (£8). Mains €6–10 (£4–6.70). No credit cards.*

Ca Na Ribes Founded in 1926, this old farmhouse is a fitting setting for home-cooked Mediterranean cuisine like rice and *burrida* (stewed skate with almond sauce) and roast lamb. Children will love the garden filled with plants, hanging lanterns and stone statues.

C/San Jaime 67, Santa Eulària 📞 *971 33 00 06. Open 1.30–4pm, 8–11pm. Mains €11–22 (£7.37–14.74). V, MC.*

SANT JOAN DE LABRITJA

Away from the madding crowd, the far north-west of the island is where most of the counter-culture is concentrated. The interior, between the villages of **Sant Llorenç de Balàfia** and **Sant Carles de Peralta,** is replete with orange and olive trees and dotted with rural restaurants. **Els Amunts,** this low-ish mountain range, lies more or less in the middle of the municipality and has been a hippy Mecca since the early 1970s. Sant Llorenç has one of the municipality's more unusual sites: a clutch of rural homes with in-built **defence towers.** Peculiar to the Ibiza, these towers were originally used to look out for pirates. Half-way up

Local Fruit

there's an opening that was used to escape via a rope, if required.

During the 1960s and 1970s, hippies emigrated to Sant Carles by the handful, making homes and communes in the surrounding countryside. **Bar Anita** (next to the church) is the most visible sign that they're still here. Its legendary postbox was where the first wave of New-Agers collected their mail to touch base with the 'real world'.

Organic farms have given a new lease of life to a floundering agricultural industry, largely thanks to a population that embraces alternative lifestyles; and the coastline is largely free of resort development and the kind of monster greenhouses you see on the mainland. **Sant Joan de Labritja** itself sports an 18th century church surrounded by a pretty plaza and pedestrianised streets. On June 24th it is the epicentre of the fiery **San Joan fiesta,** celebrated all over the island but particularly in his namesake village.

Essentials

Sant Joan de Labritja is about 16 km north of Ibiza Town. To get here by **car**, take the C733. There is no bus service. For tourist information check *www.sant-joan.com*. You can call a local **taxi** on ☏ *971 398 340.*

Beaches

As you approach where the road ends at **Cala de Portinatx ★**, the hub of the region's tourism, it's easy to feel somewhat under-whelmed. Built on a narrow ledge that separates sea and mountains, most of the build-ings here are fairly new, white-concrete boxes designed with one purpose: tourism. Take heart, though: the small cove of golden sand, backed by rocks is lovely, especially as the sun goes down beyond the bobbing fishing boats. On a far and inac-cessible cliff is a fairytale light-house: black and white striped, like a mint humbug. With safe, shallow paddling for little ones in the bay, and plenty of snorkelling opportunities for older children around the rocks,

as well as a whole strip of shops, it's a bit of a winner for keeping everyone happy.

Great for snorkeling, the small pebble beach at **S'illot** has long been popular with Catalan families. It's backed by rust-coloured, shallow cliffs formed into fairytale shapes by the con-tinuous pounding of the waves. When the tiny strand is full, most head over on to the gently sloping ramps of the boathouses and wait for the fishermen as the sun sets. Children are particularly enamoured by this prospect, and love examining the catch from tiny, thumb-sized squid to silvery sardines.

The beautiful, virgin **Cala Xarraca,** only 75 metres long, will suit those wanting a day out away from the **Portinatx** crowds. Old fishing huts line the shore; there are also pedalos, hammocks and umbrellas for hire.

The gorgeous cove at **Cala de Benirràs** (baptized 'Madonna Rock'), dominated by a central rock on the sea, hosts legendary full-moon parties. If the children are itching to bang a bongo or

---

Church hopping

The largest and possibly the loveliest church in Ibiza, the interior of the 16th century **Sant Miquel de Balansat ★** features two chapels, one painted in exuberant blue and red frescoes. Entrance is free. The solitary church of Sant Vicent de sa Cala may look familiar. After Christian forces took the island, they decided to model other churches on its 14th century structure. Thus the whitewashed façade, simple bell tower and arched entrance became the norm across Ibiza. The church is still very much in use, hence its pristine state. Again, entrance is free.

Portinatx

just let off some steam, come here on a Sunday evening for a musical free-for-all.

The Cova de Can Marçà ★ ★ ★ AGES 5 AND UP One

of the island's must-sees, the first thing you notice even before entering the Cova de Can Marçà is the view. The island of Muarada peeks over the waves, home to the unique Muradensis lizard. Follow the signed path from Port de San Miguel along the rocks to get to the mouth of the cave. It is over 100,000 years old, and today is almost entirely fossilized, so the dripping that grows the stalactites has stopped. In former times the cave was used by smugglers to stash their booty, and thanks to the restoration of some of the ancient water pools and waterfall that once gave life to this ancient grotto, your children will still sense the magic and wonder.

Port de San Miguel s/n ☎ 971 334 776. Fax: 971 334 615. €7.50 (£5), €4.50 (£3) children under 11. Open daily.

Shopping

Pistachio ★ Aside from the fact it's located in a cute village house, with painted pistachio-coloured shutters, there's not much to distinguish this shop from all the others in Ibiza's villages. Except, that is, for the beautiful hand-made, buttery soft handbags and saddlebags by local gal, Angela Marti Perez.

Plaza de la Iglesia 5, San Miguel ☎ 971 334 654. Fax: 971 334 631. V, MC. Opening erratic, usually 10am–1.30pm, 5–8pm.

Papillón Papillón stocks a lovely selection of casual clothing using hand-made and woven fabrics,

White Dresses

including silk shawls, linen drawstring trousers and floppy tunics.

Plaça de l'Església s/n, Sant Carles de Peralta. Open Easter–Oct, Mon–Sat 10.30am–2pm and 5–9pm. V, MC.

Artesan Market Jewellery, ceramics, leatherwear and the usual baubles, bangles and beads are sold in the main square of Sant Miquel de Balasant every Thursday evening (6pm–10pm), May to October. It's also a good place to pick up local organic delicacies like marmalades, cakes and charcuterie.

Sant Miquel de Balasant. No phone. May–Oct, Thu 6pm–10pm.

Family-friendly Accommodation

Hotel El Greco Parents may think they have died and gone to heaven when they check into this hotel, the only one on the island with its own water park. Three giant slides give hours of pleasure for children, whilst two smaller slides and a playpool will keep toddlers happy. Located right on the beach, other activities include volleyball, darts, daily child-focused competitions and nightly shows. Suites have benefited from a recent overhaul, or for something a little more *luxe* book one of the three apartments that share their own private pool.

Cala de Portinatx s/n ☎ 971 320 570 www.ibiza-spotlight.com/elgreco. Open May-Oct only. Suites €120–240 (£80.40–160.80). Extra bed 50% of full price. Breakfast included. Cot free. Amenities: restaurant, bar, entertainment, swimming pool, children's pool, sun terraces, waterpark, table tennis, free bicycles, pool tables. In room: A/C, heating, telephone, TV.

Hotel Hacienda Na Xamena ★★★ Perched on top of a cliff and overlooking the sea, this hostelry is one of the few boutique offerings on the island that welcomes children. The interiors are eclectically fitted with Indian and Asian artefacts, and the terrace and pool offer some of the most spectacular views in the entire Med. Though it may not suit large families, older children and posh tots will

TIP ≫ **A Picnic Stop** ≪

If you're packing a picnic for a day at the beach, the Ca'n Sort farmer's market (Ctra. de Sant Joan (C733) km 17.5. No phone. Sat 10am–5pm) is worth a stop. It sells local organic produce, from fruit and vegetables to cheese and farm-fresh milk, and plenty more besides.

get a kick out of its celebrity air. Best of all, it's a bargain for what you get.

Port de Sant Miguel s/n ℂ 971 334 500 www.hotelhacienda-ibiza.com. Double €141–250 (£94.47–167.50). Extra bed 50% of total price. Closed Nov–Mar. Amenities: swimming pool, restaurants, bar, gardens, Thalasso spa, gourmet cooking lessons, child-care, tennis, heli-port. In room: A/C, heating, satellite TV, telephone.

Family-friendly Dining

Restaurante Port Balanzat ★

This staunchly Spanish eatery has a deserved reputation for the best fish and rice dishes in the area. While not particularly engaging on the inside, the terrace is pleasant enough with solid cane furniture and delightful sea breezes, making it the hottest lunch spot in town. Accordingly, tables, especially those on the terrace, are hard to come by: it pays to reserve yours in advance. Neither is it cheap, with lobster specials running to €120 (80.40) for two. The mixed fish *parillada* (grill) offers a sumptuous selection of the season's best catch and is superlative.

Port de San Miguel s/n ℂ 971 334 527. Main courses €15–50 (£10.05–33.50). Reservations recommended. V, MC. Open 1pm–4pm, 8.30pm–11pm.

Cas Mallorquí Nestled in the crook of the elbow of Cala de Portinatx, this is one of the cheaper Ibizan seaside options and a good place to watch the sun go down. The menu runs the gauntlet of pedestrian, though no less delicious,

maritime treats like grilled sardines, baby squid dredged in flour and deep fried, and traditional Spanish *tortilla* (potato omelette). Washed down with gallons of sangria while the children play on the beach, and the teenagers prowl the shops and corners that only teenagers can get a kick from, there is something refreshingly unfashionable, un-cool and distinctly unbeautiful about Cas Mallorquí. That's what makes it so very perfect for a family holiday. It doubles as a reasonably-priced *hostal*, too.

Cala de Portinatx s/n ℂ 971 320 505. Fax: 971 320 504 www.casmallorqui. com. Open 1–4pm, 8.30–11pm. No credit cards. Reservations recommended.

S'illot des Renolí ★ This wonderfully basic seaside *chiringuito* (beach bar) seems as if it's built into the side of the cliff. Whitewashed, with a simple gravel terrace shaded by pine trees and plain paper tablecloths, it has a taste of old Ibiza, before the clubbers and models and pop stars arrived. It's got a great vibe, a real weekend meeting place for family and friends (mainly Catalans who've been coming for years). It's also more reasonably priced than most of the beach bars around the island. Specials include classic *bullit* (the sumptuous Ibizan fish stew enriched with saffron); mixed fish grills; and whole *dorada* (gilt-head bream) or *lubina* (sea bream) baked in salt.

Ctra. Portinatx km 25.3 ℂ 971 320 585. Open 1pm–4pm, 8.30pm–11pm.

Sant Antoni

Bullit €25 (£16.75); mixed fish grill €25 (£16.75); salt-baked fish €15 (£10.05). No credit cards.

SANT ANTONI DE PORTMANY

Once a small fishing village, **Sant Antoni** is now the centre of the island's package holiday and club scene. Its reputation as a party town ('San Antonio') was unrivalled during the 1990s. Recently, however, the local council has put efforts into improving its bad reputation, with a focus on the region's cultural attractions. The Romans called the place **Port Magus** because of the bay's size, and although Sant Antoni has lost much of its maritime air to the high-rise and burger joint, it lacks the pretension of Ibiza Town.

There are some lovely beaches in the immediate vicinity: try **Cala Salada** ★ (north of Sant Antoni on the road to Santa Agnès de Corona), a postcard-perfect cove with crystalline waters, old boat moorings and thick pine forests. The fine golden sand is only 25 metres wide, so get there early to claim your patch. **Cala Gracioneta** (also on the road to Santa Agnès), the smallest cove on the island at just 25 metres long, is also a fine spot to catch the rays. All beaches are clearly signposted from Sant Antoni, though they may not be marked on your map.

If you're on Ibiza for the watersports, Sant Antoni makes a good base. Your teenagers might also get a kick out of visiting the **Cafe del Mar** ★ (C/ de la Mar 1, Sant Antoni ☎ 971 342 516), the birthplace of the Balearic Beat.

Of the surrounding villages, **Sant Mateu d'Alabarca** is the best known, mostly for its heady red wine sold all over the island. Vineyards dot the surrounding terrain, and are best viewed before the September harvest. **Santa Agnès de Corona,** on the other hand, is a good starting point for walks down to the coast on easy roads. It's worth seeking out the small, white sanctuary in the village square before you do.

Essentials

To get here by **car** from Ibiza Town, head north-west along the C731. **Bus 3** from Ibiza Town and **bus 8** from Sant Josep

It's a Fact!

Your children had better behave on the beach in Sant Antoni. The town's 19th century church is equipped with a cannon that can still hurl four-pound balls into the bay. It's hard to believe that this church was the main feature of Sant Antoni's topography until the tourists arrived.

de Sa Talaia will also take you to Sant Antoni. Check *www.ibiza bus.com* for timetables. The **tourist office** is at Passeig de Ses Fonts s/n (📞 *971 343 363 www. santantoni.net*). You can call a local **taxi** on 📞 *971 343 764*.

Child-friendly Events & Entertainment

Between 24th and 28th May, take the children to Cala Bou, a residential area on Sant Antoni's periphery, for **Magic Clown** ★ **ALL AGES** (📞 *971 800 040 / 800 125 www.magiclown.org*). It's a huge

Cala Salada

event celebrating the art of buffoonery, with clown processions on the beach, face-painting workshops, theatre and general silliness. Events are held outdoors, in bars, hotels and a special tent. It attracts clowns from all over the world.

For razzle-dazzle entertainment year-round, the newly opened **Ibiza Marquee** (C/Es Calo s/n, Sant Antoni 📞 *971 344 532 www.ibizamarquee.com*) has everything from *Mardi Gras* dancing girls to Vegas-style singing and dancing. All shows are extremely well-produced (often featuring a West End cast) and performed in English.

If you're here during the summer months, your children might enjoy Sant Antoni's **night market,** held daily behind the main church. It sells arts, crafts and gifts for grandma – all made on the island.

The Best Family Attractions

Aquarium Cap Blanc **ALL AGES**

Also know as the 'cave aquarium', this natural fish tank located in an underwater cave holds a sizable collection of fish and sea plants native to the island. At any one time you can see up to

30 different species in the cave, and knock back an ice-cold beer while you're at it. Only in Ibiza.

Cova de ses llegostes, Cala Gració, Sant Antoni ☎ 971 340 460. €15 (£10.05), children under 11 €7.50 (£5). Open 10am–1.30pm, 5pm–8pm.

Cruceros Portmany ★

AGES 7 AND UP There are several glass-bottomed boats operating out of Sant Antoni, with little to choose between them. Cruceros Portmany, though, is reliable with an on-board bar and toilets, and has most of the island covered. They run trips to the monolithic rock of **Es Vedrà** (three hours) with swim stops. The Neptuno cruise (two hours) focuses on the underwater world and includes a stop-off at the Ibiza aquarium. The Portinatx cruise takes you and your little Nemos along the craggy north coast, stopping at **Cala de Portinatx** (see p. 224) for lunch and swimming. The top cruise is over to neighbouring **Formentera,** with its virgin beaches, pearly white sand and gin-clear waters. The cruise heads along Ibiza's west coast before crossing to the munchkin-sized port of La Savina. Visitors have a choice to get off here to spend the day exploring the island, or to continue to the nudist beach at Illetes. Chapter 11 has ideas for passing a day on Formentera.

Port de Sant Antoni ☎ 971 343 471. Fax: 971 345 232 www.crucero sportmany.com. Prices vary according to tour, from €30 (£20.10) upwards. Children half-price.

Capella de Santa Agnès

ALL AGES One of the island's curious places, this underground chapel discovered in 1907 was a place of worship under Islamic rule. Mass is still celebrated here every 12th August.

Camí de Cas Ramons s/n. Open Sat 9am–noon. Just south-west of Santa Agnès de Corona.

Family-friendly Accommodation

Club Stella Maris Paraiso

One of the quieter options near Sant Antoni, the Stella Maris is a 300-room resort-hotel just 300 metres from Cala Grassio cove, and about 4 km from the hustle and bustle of Sant Antoni town (connected by an hourly shuttle). Its location and natural setting keep the lager-louts away, leaving guests to enjoy the spacious rooms, three pools,

---

Look Out!

Perched on the coast near the popular Platges de Comte, the 18th century **Torre d'en Rovira** is another relic from the period when pirates regularly attacked Ibiza. Directly in front is the island of **Sa Conillera** ('Rabbit Island').

TIP **Wanted: Sporting Goods**

If you've forgotten, or need to replace, some sports equipment, pop down to **Deportes El Coral** ★ (C/ Sant Antoni 23 and C/ Balanzat 16 ☏ 971 340 517). Whether it's a bathing costume, snorkelling gear or a new tracksuit, you'll find it at one of two branches of this sporting megastore.

---

tennis courts, cycling facilities, huge garden and kids' club. After the little ones are tucked up in bed, there is even a cabaret and flamenco show for the grown-ups. The range of stuff going on here is staggering, putting it among Ibiza's most family-friendly places.

Cala Grassio, Sant Antoni www.ibiza-hotels.com/stmaris. Doubles from €60 (£40.20) and bungalow (for up to 5) from €75 (£50.25). Amenities: pool, restaurant, sports, games. In room: A/C, heating, telephone, TV.

Riviera Hotel and Apartments

With outstanding views of the Bay of Portmany from all its rooms, as well as three pools, this comfortable, recently-renovated three-star is a good bet. It's just 3 km from Sant Antoni. All 160 rooms are air-conditioned, with balconies and in some cases terraces. Facilities include table tennis, mini-golf and pool tables, though most of the action takes place on the beach itself, a 150-metre stroll away.

Es Calo 47-51, Sant Antoni www.ibiza-spotlight.com/riviera. Doubles from €70 (£46.90). Extra bed €35 (£23.45). Cot free. Amenities: games and three pools. In room: A/C, heating, TV, telephone.

Es Cucons ★ This charming rural hotel, in the valley of Santa Agnès, has been beautifully converted from a 17th century *masia* (country home). The seven double rooms and three suites all have en suite bathrooms, as well as TVs and DVD players. They've been decked out in soothing Ibizan style with floating gauze curtains, stripped-back furniture and eclectic linen and fittings. There is a large pool in a lovely garden with gorgeous views of the surrounding countryside.

Camí des Plá de Corona 110, Santa Agnès de Corona ☏ 971 805 501 www.ibiza-spotlight.com/escucons. Doubles from €240 (£160.80); suites from €290 (£194.30). Children under 12 extra €25 (£16.75), over 12 extra €40 (£26.80). Breakfast included. Amenities: swimming pool, gardens. In room: A/C, heating, TV, DVD, telephone.

Family-friendly Dining

Club Sandwich ★ Since opening five years ago, childhood friends Pam and Barbara's Club Sandwich has become something of an institution. Decked out like an American diner with a genuine jukebox, peppermint walls and chrome-and-black diner chairs, this is no ordinary eatery. While the wall signs read Marilyn Monroe Drive and James Dean Avenue, the black-and-white photos show a history of girlie holidays and family get-togethers. It's a formula that works, more so because the food is top notch thanks to a simple, no-fail formula. Everything is freshly made – including sausage rolls, cheese pies, cakes and crumbles. The famed 'Potbelly Breakfast' (a heaven-sent hang-over cure for clubbers) and the sandwiches stuffed with as many fillings as you can handle, are as good as any New York deli. Eat in or take it away.

C/Ramón y Calal 44, Sant Antoni ☏ 971 341 789. Open 9am–5pm. Sandwiches €4.50–5.50 (£3–3.69)

with as many fillings as you like; 'Potbelly Breakfast' €7.95 (£5.33); fruit smoothies €5 (£3.35). No credit cards. No reservations.

Sa Capella For something more than packaged paellas and pub food, head to this old monastery on the outskirts of Sant Antoni. The dining is fine, but children will love the rural setting, outdoor terrace and 16th century, cave-like dining room replete with rose windows and cast iron chandeliers. Mediterranean food is the order of the day: freshly grilled fish, meats and salad.

Acor Complex, Sant Antoni ☏ 971 340 057 www.ibiza-restaurants. com/sacapella. Open 1.30pm–4pm, 8pm–11pm. No credit cards. Mains €9.50–22 (£6.37–14.74).

11 Formentera

FORMENTERA

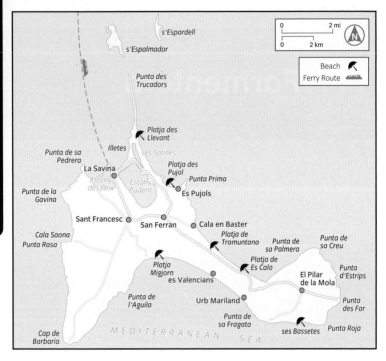

Formentera

Formentera isn't quite as unspoilt as the natives make out, but hit it at the right time and it's still one of the most relaxing holiday destinations in the Mediterranean. It is easily the smallest inhabited Balearic island, and by far the most chilled out. In the 1960s and 70s it became the hippy destination *par excellence,* and while most of the flower-power generation have moved on, the place retains an aura of devil-may-care, do-what-you-willness about it. You notice it as soon as you step off the ferry. Out of peak season, on many beaches nude sun-bathing is the norm; life in general moves at a slower pace than almost anywhere in Europe. After a while here you start to wonder: was the hippy movement informed by Formentera, or vice versa? The truth clearly lies somewhere in the middle.

If you avoid high season, in August, it's an excellent family destination. There are beautiful, safe, clean, shallow-shelved beaches all round the coast; the food is excellent; the skies are almost always blue; and because it's so small there's very little travelling to get from place to place. In fact, unless you have small children you can negotiate virtually the whole island without much trouble on a bike.

While the eco-savvy authorities are trying hard to keep a lid on development, the island is changing fast, and will continue to do so while it maintains its 'last Paradise in the Mediterranean' reputation. A double-edged sword this: while it's not the completely unspoilt beauty of yesteryear, there are now plenty of amenities and ready-made family-oriented activities to augment the natural beauty and justify the higher prices you pay for most things compared with the other Balearic islands.

One thing to note: Formentera has a 'season' that runs from the beginning of May to the end of October. It is advisable, if you want to find the sort of amenities you generally expect from a beach holiday, to go in season. Otherwise most of the restaurants and hotels are closed: many of the islanders, after working hard all summer on other people's holidays, go off for their own. That said, going off-season is the best time to enjoy the island's unspoilt nature. Take your pick.

ESSENTIALS

Getting There

Unless you have a yacht, to get to Formentera you have to take the ferry from Ibiza Town, or from Denia or Valencia on the Spanish mainland. The only point of entry is the port of La Savina. The peace and well-conserved nature of the island are a direct result of this relative isolation. Having said that, a trip from Ibiza is an easy task. Ferries run every hour or so from the harbour in central Ibiza Town to La Savina in the north of Formentera (from 7.45am to 10pm between April and October, and 10.30am and 8.30pm November–March). The journey takes around half an hour. There are two companies that run boats, Formentera's own **Pitiusa** (Mediterranea-Pitiusa, Paseo de La Marina, Ed. Vicente Lluquinet s/n, La Savina ℂ *971 322 443/322 224 www.medpitiusa.net*) and **Balearia** (ℂ *902 160 180/971 312 071 www.balearia.net*). Just go to the ferry terminal and wait in

A Tall Tale

In 1974 a megalithic sepulchre was discovered in Ca Na Costa, with the remains of six Stone-Age people. It dates from 1900 to 1600 BC, some 1,000 years before the arrival of the Phoenicians in Ibiza. Archaeologists were stunned to find that the skeletons of the men were nearly seven feet tall. This fact alone makes the tomb worth a visit with the children. You can still see the (fenced off) limestone tombs from every angle. There is no charge. The tomb is situated near **Estany Pudent,** just off the road between Es Pujols and La Savina. Look out for signposts as you leave Es Pujols.

Formentera in a Nutshell

2000–1600 BC The first known inhabitants of Formentera make pottery and build elaborate tombs, one of which, **Ca Na Costa** (see 'A Tall Tale', p. 235), is still visible.

200 AD A permanent detatchment of Roman soldiers is based on Formentera. We know this from the remains of their base in **Can Pins** near Es Calo. They give the island its name (from *Frumentum* which means 'grain').

10th century Formentera prospers under Moorish rule. The Moors pushed out the Vandals, who'd pushed out the Byzantines, who pushed out the Visigoths. They irrigate the island, and call it "Koluyunka" (full of sheep).

1235 Guillem de Montgri, the Bishop of Tarragona, invades the island. From this time Catalan has been the indigenous language, spoken in the local *formenterenq* dialect.

14th century The island is deserted because of the constant threat of pirates. It is used by pirates as a stop-off point, as a place for storage, and as a springboard for raids on other islands.

1695 Marc Ferrer and Toni Blanc, from Ibiza, are given permission by the King of Spain to reinhabit the island.

1719 Formentera becomes part of the Kingdom of Spain.

1726 San Francesc, the first stable settlement, is founded.

1749 The first watchtower is built.

19th century Formentera becomes known in Ibiza as 'The Island of the Women' because men have to leave it to find work.

1930s During the Spanish Civil War, Franco uses the island as a concentration camp for political prisoners awaiting execution.

1963 The first hippies arrive on the island, which soon becomes known as an out-of-time idyll.

1970s–present day Formentera grows as a holiday destination. Now virtually all the 5000–7000 inhabitants are involved in the tourist industry.

---

front of the window which advertises the next boat; they will start selling tickets half an hour before departure. An adult single costs €16 (£10.70) or €18.50 (£12.40), under 16s €8.50 (£5.70) and €11.50 (£7.70). Returns for adults are €30/34 (£20.10/£22.80), and €17/23 (£11.40/15.40) for children. The cheaper prices are for 35-minute trips, the more expensive for 25-minute trips. If you are lucky you'll get a ferry that allows you to stand on deck, making the journey quite an adventure for children as you buzz from one Balearic to the

Fig Trees & Poppies

next. Alas, normally you're closed inside the hull, and have to witness arrival in La Savina through the (usually steamed-up) windows.

You can take your car on a ferry from Denia or Valencia, on mainland Spain, or Ibiza Town. From the mainland the journey takes four hours. From Ibiza, the bright yellow Iscomar (☎ 902 119 128 http://www.iscomar.es) car ferries take an hour and

20 minutes. Alternatively, try Trasmediterránea (☎ 902 454 645 http://www.trasmediterranea.es)

Visitor Information

There is a small but excellent Tourist Information office at the port of La Savina (Calle de Calpe s/n ☎ 971 322 057. Fax: 971 322 825 www.formentera.es. Open Mon–Fri 10am–2pm, 5pm–7pm; Sat 10am–2pm all

Fiestas!

Folk music, dancing and vast paellas are par for the course during Formentera's fiestas, when the locals let their hair down, big-time. These are family occasions, enjoyed by islanders of all ages.

- San Ferran, 30th May
- Nostra Senyora del Carme, 16th July
- San Jaume (the patron saint of the island), 25th July
- Santa Maria, 5th August
- El Pilar, 12th October
- Sant Francesc, 3rd December

year round), which will offer you advice on what to do on the island. They can't book your accommodation, but can offer suggestions. It is advisable to book ahead in Formentera, especially in July, August and September, otherwise you may find the island completely 'full'. Another small tourist office is located outside the **Town Hall** in the Plaza de la Constitution in **San Francesc** (open same hours during May–Oct); there is another fully-equipped glass-walled office in **Es Pujols** (Calle Espalmador esquina Avenida Miramar. Open same hours during May–Oct) with a little sandpit playground in a mini-park outside. The island lives almost entirely off tourism, and the authorities have developed a highly competent system to help visitors get the most out of their time on Formentera.

Getting Around

By Bike The best way to tour the island is on a bike, and there are plenty for hire all over the island, particularly in La Savina. **Motorent Mitjorn** (Port of La Savina ℂ 971 328 611, 24-hour service ℂ 696 014 292. Fax: 971 328 350 www.motorentmitjorn.com) offers bikes for €8.10 (£5.43) a day with a sliding scale so you pay less per day the longer you keep the bike (down to €4 (£2.68) a day for 21 days). They also rent smaller bikes for children at €6.10 (£4.10), and you can ask for a baby chair at no extra cost. Formentera is only 11 miles long, most main roads have a cycle lane, and there's a network of **'green' pathways** if you want to avoid the traffic, though the narrower of these can be difficult to negotiate. You can get a map at the tourist office though when we tried to follow it we did get lost several times. Plans are afoot to connect all the major towns with a circular 'green route'. Note, in July and August the roads are clogged with Italians on mopeds, which makes life a little dangerous. Otherwise it feels quite safe to pedal your way around the place. Ask for lights if you're planning evening journeys, and make sure to carry plenty of water during the day. Formentera is mostly flat, but in the heat you'll notice the slightest slope.

By Car Obviously two wheels are not an option for every family. While there is a regular bus service connecting the major towns (see p. 239), a rental car remains the next most convenient way of moving everyone from place to place. Again, La Savina is the best place to arrange this. There are a number of offices in the complex in the port. Try **ProAuto Rent a Car** (Calle Edificio Boulevard Local 1, Puerto de La Savina ℂ/Fax: 971 323 226 www.proautorent acar.com), which offers basic cars from €50 (£33.50) per day. You'll never end up doing too much driving in Formentera, because it's so small, but the roads between the main villages are all well-built and you can travel between each place in a matter of minutes. **El Pilar de la Mola,** at the far east of the island, is about 15 minutes' drive from San Francesc. Note: in the summer roads do tend to get clogged up with those Italian motorcyclists, who like driving in packs and are sometimes hard to overtake. Some of the 'green' paths are usable, but don't go too far off the beaten track, for the sake of your suspension.

By Bus There is no railway in Formentera, but there is a regular bus service which connects all the towns and villages every hour or so from about 8.45am to 7.15pm. The vehicles are comfortable luxury coaches. Buy your ticket (€1.20 (£0.80), half price for under-16s) on the bus. There is room for pushchairs in the hold. The driver will help you load it, and get it out afterwards.

By Taxi There are taxi ranks in **La Savina** (at the port), **Es Pujols** (Avinguda Miramar) and **San Francesc** (Carrer Sta Marina), but you can call **Radio Taxis Formentera** from anywhere. In La Savina call ☎ 971 322 002, in Es Pujols or San Francesc ☎ 971 322 016 or ☎ 971 322 342. A journey from La Savina to Es Pujols, three miles away, costs around €12 (£8).

FAST FACTS: FORMENTERA

Area Codes As in the rest of Spain, prefix 0034 from outside the country, followed by the full six-digit number. Formentera numbers start 971.

Baby Chairs Most restaurants do not offer baby chairs.

Baby Change There are no public baby change facilities in Formentera.

Business Hours Generally 9am–2pm and 5pm–8pm. Don't plan any commercial activity around lunchtime, as the streets empty and most shops close: the locals are still quite religious about maintaining the traditional Spanish hours, which means a long lunch break followed, if possible, by a siesta. It is advisable to get into the same habit, especially in the summer, when a power nap at lunchtime can revitalise the whole family. This is also the best time to avoid the most dangerous rays of sunlight on the beach.

Chemists There are three on the island: in **San Francesc** (C/ Sta Maria s/n ☎ 971 322 419), **Es Pujols** (Avda Miramar s/n ☎ 971 328 663) and **San Ferran** (Avda Juan Castello 21 ☎ 971 328 004). Wherever you are in Spain, it is worth noting that chemists offer medication, which in the UK would need a GP visit and prescription. They are often the first port of call for people with minor ailments. Chemists take it in turns to open on a Sunday and after hours; if your local one is closed, a board outside will give you information about the closest open.

Consulate The nearest British consulate is on **Ibiza** (Isidor Macabich 45 ☎ *971 301 818*).

Credit Cards Most hotels and restaurants on the island take Visa and Mastercard.

Electricity The current in Formentera is 230 volts and 50Hz.

Medical Emergencies ☎ *061*. There's one **Medical Centre** on the island, at Ctra. La Savina (km 3.1) on the road between La Savina and San Francesc (☎ *902 079 079/971 322 369;* emergencies ☎ *971 322 357*). A hospital is being built, scheduled to be complete in Spring 2007. Until then, patients whose needs cannot be met in the medical centre are helicoptered to Ibiza.

Internet Access **Café Formentera** offers Internet access in **San Ferran** (Crta La Mola km 5.5 ☎ *971 321 842. Fax: 971 328 129*) and **Es Pujols** (C/ Espalmador 98 ☎ *971 328 806 www.cafeformentera.com*). Both have broadband connections, as well as fax, photocopying and scanners.

Laundry Laundry facilities are only offered in hotels and hostals.

Newspapers & Magazines You can buy English newspapers at the newsagent on the harbour front in **La Savina,** as well as in various newsagents in **Es Pujols.**

Nudity Nudity is allowed on all beaches at all times in Formentera, though it isn't the norm for naturists to bathe in Es

Pujols, so if it offends you stick to this beach. Otherwise the general rule of thumb is: the more off-season it is, the bigger the proportion of nudity on the beach. Note: there is nothing predatory or exhibitionist about nude sunbathing in Formentera. Many families go bare on the beach.

Petrol Petrol stations sell unleaded (95 and 98 octane) petrol and diesel.

Photography A one-hour developing service is available at **JJ Fotograf,** C/Ramon Llull 12, San Francesc (☎ *971 321 130*). They will also print digital photos for you.

Police There are two separate police forces working on the island, the **Policia Local** (☎ *092* or *971 322 087*) and **Guardia Civil** (☎ *062* or ☎ *971 322 022*). The police emergency number is ☎ *112*.

Post Office There is only one in the island, situated in Plaza del Rei 1, San Francesc (☎ *971 322 243*).

Safety The nature of Formentera means that there is very little crime, though bag-snatching is not unheard of. Keep an eye on your belongings, as you would in any touristy area.

Tipping Tipping is not considered compulsory (the Spanish often only leave a few coppers), but it is considered polite for foreigners to leave 5–10% in bars and restaurants.

Time Zone GMT + 1.

Orientation

It was once pointed out to me by a 12-year-old that Formentera is shaped like the head of Wile E. Coyote, and I have never been able to look at it any other way since. The four main towns (**La Savina, San Francesc, Es Pujols** and **San Ferran**) are located very near to one another in the north, connected by single-lane roads, most of which have cycle paths alongside. It takes a few minutes to travel between them. There is another main road, heading west to **El Pilar de la Mola** and beyond, which is difficult to negotiate on a bicycle unless you have a lot of energy: La Mola sits on top of a cliff. Roads lead off to various beaches and restaurants, all well signed. Another main road leads due south to **Cap de Barbaria**, but turns into a track before you reach the lighthouse. To get to **Cala Saona** turn right on the way south. There is also a network of smaller roads that the locals use to get to their further-flung houses, but it is not advisable to drive them without local knowledge. Some are virtually impassable.

WHAT TO SEE & DO

If You Have One Day in Formentera

● Visit **Illetes** beach before 10am when it will be virtually deserted. You'll find fine white sand and shallow turquoise water stretching out to the bobbing superyachts in the distance. Take photographs of your feet in the clearest water you've ever seen, and make a mental note of one of the most beautiful beaches in Europe. You'll want to come back.

● Rent a bicycle and pedal *en famille* to the **Cap de Barbaria lighthouse** and watchtower. It'll take about half an hour. This truly wild spot, where they used to look out for Barbary Coast pirates, is like the end of the earth. But take provisions: there are no bars or shops, only rocks and scrub.

● Stop off on the way back and hire a pedalo on **Cala Saona** beach, flanked by rocky outcrops harbouring fishing boats in ramshackle huts.

● Have lunch in the capital, **San Francesc.** Watch the world go by on the pretty terrace of the **Fonda Plate** restaurant. The children will love the imaginative sandwiches, and can run down the pedestrianised market

Cala Saona

outside looking for hippy-style fashion accessories.

● Spend the afternoon getting serious about your shopping in the hippy market in **El Pilar de la Mola,** open Wednesday and Sunday afternoons, with hand-made stuff to suit all ages. Make sure you buy something with the island's trademark symbol, a lizard.

● Have an aperitif in the famed 'Hippy Bar' **Fonda Pepe,** in San Ferran, admiring the eclectic hit-and-miss art on the wall left by customers through the decades.

● Head back to the top of the Illetes peninsula to watch the sunset from the **Es Minestre** restaurant. An unforgettable experience for the whole family.

Ses Salines Nature Reserve ★

AGES 5 AND UP The salt pans in Formentera, near La Savina, were in use from the Phoenician era, in the 7th century. That's no longer the case, but they are preserved to help maintain the wealth of native flora and fauna. The area is perfect for the pro-duction of salt: it's flat, one metre above sea level, with all-year sun to help evaporate the water. It's a really atmospheric place, and you'll have to work hard to stop your children from trying to jump over the little walls to walk on the flats. These salt pans form the heart of the Formentera side of the **Ses Salines Nature Reserve** (which also includes part of southern Ibiza). On Formentera it includes the Illetes peninsula, the island of **s'Espalmador** and the inland lagoons of **s'Estany d'es Peix** (Fish Lagoon) and **Estany Pudent** (Smelly Lagoon). The latter doesn't smell any different to the former, but you can have fun pretending it does, and holding your nose in mock horror as you drive or cycle past. The area is excellent for bike excursions: there are many traf-fic-light green routes in the area. It is notable for its fragile dune systems and abundant bird life. Migrating birds use the area as a resting point in winter and sum-mer; flamingoes can be seen all year round. If you're vigilant and patient you'll definitely see some of these wonderful birds, with their characteristic John Cleese walk. The children will love them. Get a map from the tourist office, or contact the nature reserve office.

Ses Salines Nature Reserve ☎ *971 323 283. Open 9am–1pm and 4pm–8pm.*

TIP ⟩⟩ **Mozzies** ⟨⟨

Mosquitoes like loose clothing, but find it hard to get through tight-fitting materials. They like sweat and strong perfumes, too, so keep dipping in the water, and have a shower whenever you can. Insect-repellants like **Autan** help keep them off.

Getting Wet: Having Fun with Water

Wet4Fun AGES 6 AND UP Based on a shack on Es Pujols beach, Wet4Fun offers windsurf and catamaran lessons, from a one-off taster to week-long intensive courses, in various languages including English. I tried out a windsurfing lesson from a rookie instructor, at the same time as a 12-year-old German child. The child was a natural – most are – and was off within minutes. I never managed to get going, though I did realise I had a great propensity for swallowing seawater. It was a tiring and frustrating experience for me, but the child seemed to love it, and his parents booked more lessons. A basic, three-day (two hours per day) course for 8–14-year-olds costs €125 (£83.75), and teaches everything from balance on the board to tacking and jibing... and safety. The equivalent catamaran course for children (aged 6–14) costs €150 (£100.50).

Office: C/ Roca Plana 51-69, Es Pujols ☎/Fax: 971 321 809. Open Mon-Fri 9am-1pm. Centre: Es Pujols beach. Open Mon–Sat 10am–1pm, 2pm–6pm; Sun afternoon only.

Vellmari Scuba Diving School ★ AGES 12 AND UP This well-established school offers PADI (Professional Associates of the Diving Institute) courses at different levels in different languages, and takes students from the age of 12. The basic three-day course, which costs €185 (£123.95), constitutes three video and theory sessions, three swimming pool sessions and two open-water sessions, to a depth of 12 metres. Students, rest assured, are accompanied at all times by instructors. You will need to produce a medical fitness certificate, so it's worth getting this sorted before you leave home. It should be worth it. The seas off Formentera are extremely clean and teeming with aquatic flora and fauna. The island is the ideal place to learn to dive.

Av. Mediterraneo 90, La Savina ☎ 971 322 105. Fax: 971 323 198 www.vellmari.com. Courses from €185 (£124).

Escuela Municipal de Vela ★★★ AGES 6 AND UP If you want your children to learn to windsurf or sail, this is the best place on the island, and one of the very best in Spain. Run with passion by a young man (Asier Fernandez) who was once the Spanish Olympic windsurfing instructor, the school has a very strong philosophy of instilling good habits in students from the beginning. The method clearly works: the school has produced a number of Spanish and international champions in both sailing and windsurfing. Courses, at five different levels, last a week, in five two-hour sessions, costing €120 (£80.40). There are courses for adults, too. They also run kayaking trips.

Avda Mediterraneo 23, La Savina ☎ 627 478 452. Fax: 971 323 326 www.4nomadas.com. Courses from €120 (£80.40).

Posidonia

The underwater Posidonia prairies ★★ around Formentera are considered some of the most important in the whole of the Med: they give the sea its turquoise colour, help to protect the beaches and provide the habitat for countless species of sea life. *Posidonia* is often referred to as seaweed, but in fact is a species of sea grass, a genuine plant with its own roots, leaves, stem and even fruit. A square metre of *Posidonia* gives off the same amount of oxygen as a square metre of rainforest, and the island is surrounded by 800 square kilometres of this stuff. The species is vital to the welfare of the island, and also provides a big incentive for tourists to visit: snorkellers and sub-aqua divers get to view the teeming life that calls these underwater pastures home.

Tiny Towns

La Savina

If you arrive in Formentera on a **ferry,** which virtually everybody does, the bobbing yachts in the functional-pretty harbour-front of La Savina will be the first you see of the island. It's a pleasant enough introduction to the place, and home to a number of vital tourist amenities, but, truth be told, a few hours is enough to witness its charms. The first time we stayed on the island we booked into a hotel here, thinking its ferry-side location would make life easy. After a couple of days we realised this wasn't a great idea. It's the best place to **rent a car or a bicycle** (see 'Getting Around', p. 238), and there are plenty of child-friendly activities, including excursions and windsurfing, sailing and scuba diving (see 'Getting Wet', p. 243). But there are far more pleasant places to stay. That said, La Savina does boast a handful of good restaurants (see 'Family-friendly Dining', p. 253), and a pleasant little **market** open daily on the harbour front. And it would be a shame to leave the place without taking the family up to the new state-of-the-art **harbour bar,** all big windows and minimalist furnishings, even if just to watch the ferry arrive.

San Francesc (San Francisco) ★ San Francesc is the capital of Formentera. You might think it weird then, on such a small island, that it's not on the coast. You realise the reason when you visit the church that dominates the central square, **Placa de la Constitucio.** It's a virtually windowless white cube, more military than ecclesiastical. With good reason: this is where the townspeople would hole themselves up when pirates invaded. San Francesc is a lovely, buzzy best-in-the-daytime place with a colourful **daily street-market** (C/ Ramon Llull. Open 10am–2pm) where it's hard to resist going with the flow and

buying you and yours the sort of semi-hippy clothing so in keeping with the island. There are some great bars and restaurants, too, to suit every pocket. And the main shopping drag in town is pedestrianised, which means you can sit and have a quiet beer with the luxury of not having to keep *too* close an eye on the children. A great antidote to the beach, a nice place to have lunch, and an essential key to understanding Formentera.

San Francesc Xavier Church ★ AGES 6 AND UP

For children this is a more exciting church than most: not only is its façade completely whitewashed and windowless, it is a fortress church, built with the dual purpose of offering the locals the opportunity for worship, and being a place to go if the island was invaded, a common danger until the 19th century. The door was protected by a vertical hollow, armoured with wooden plates, from which missiles could be hurled. The church's first stone was laid in 1726, and by 1738 it had been consecrated as a vicary. In those days it boasted a golden altarpiece, which has sadly disappeared. Inside now it is rather bare and austere, though the Baroque-like font, of mysterious descent, is of interest to connoisseurs of such things. The steps outside provide a great place to hang out for a while, watching life go by in the pretty little square which, in effect, constitutes the bureaucratic epicentre of the island: the Town Hall is directly opposite.

Plaza de la Constitucion 8–10, San Francesc ☏ 971 322 498.

San Francesc Church

Pirates!

Formentera's position in the Mediterranean made it vulnerable to attack, particularly from the Barbary pirates of Morocco, who give the southernmost point of the island, Cap de Barbaria, its name. The island didn't have many resources – it was barely inhabited between the 12th and the 17th centuries – but it was strategically important as a base to attack Spain and the other Balearic islands. In 1697 a resettlement charter was awarded to Marc Ferrer. Subsequently, between 1749 and 1800, five watchtowers were built around the coast, with lookouts who would warn of invaders by lighting a fire. The towers were built so each could be seen by another. The lookouts themselves lived in the top floor of the towers, and used a ladder to get in and out. The most fun watchtower to visit is at **Cap de Barbaria** in the far south. You can't get into the building, but you can stand alongside it and look out to sea for pirates.

San Ferran (San Fernando)

There's not really much point in visiting scrubby, road-surrounded San Ferran if you don't want to eat there, or go for an evening drink. But it would be a pity not to do this, because this is where many locals go to relax and let their hair down at night. Not the best place for children, then, you might think, but it's not the worst either. The action centres around **La Fonda Pepe** ★★ (C/ Mayor 51–55 ☎ *971 328 033*) otherwise known as 'The Hippy Bar', which is on a pedestrianised *rambla*: the evenings are usually warm enough for you to sip drinks outside and watch the world go by. It's one of those spots that enjoys the "*Simpsons* effect" of being enjoyable for all generations: your children are likely to meet friends and have fun, and so, if you're open to it, are you.

Es Pujols Es Pujols is the most touristy spot in Formentera, where most of the hotels and hostels are based and where most of the nightlife goes on. More discerning adults might find it a little tacky, but the children will love it. And everything's relative: the beaches might be crowded, but they are characterful, too, full of fishing boats on wooden railings in their ramshackle huts waiting to be called into action. It's noisier than the rest of the island, but there's only one

Es Pujols Cove

nightclub (the only one on the island), a modest affair on the outskirts of town, so it's not *that* noisy. For 11 months of the year, anyway. In August Es Pujols is the epicentre of the 20-something Italian invasion, and best avoided. Otherwise, it's a great centre for activities, mainly because you can get anything you need here, and get out fast when you've had enough.

El Pilar de la Mola ★ Situated far from the madding crowd in the middle of the south-east 'nose' of Formentera, El Pilar de la Mola is the village that most retains that hippy spirit that attracted so many alternative visitors in the 1960s and 70s. A few of them are still here. El Pilar is famous for two things: The wonderful **lighthouse** built on the cliff-face where the eastern cape of the island meets the sea, and the **hippy market** (see 'Shopping the Hippy Market',

Wares from the Market

below). The former overlooks an unforgettable end-of-the-earth viewing experience (you'll find yourselves telling them not to go too near the edge), a great photo opportunity. The latter is perfect for all ages. There's food and music, and fantastic views of the rest of the island on the way up. Warning: it's quite a feat getting to El Pilar on a bicycle. No matter, regular buses run from all the main towns.

Shopping the Hippy Market

Officially called La Fira de la Mola ★★ AGES 5 AND UP this collection of artesenal stalls is a must-see for any visitor to Formentera. It runs between May and October, every Wednesday and Sunday, between 4pm and 9pm. You can't miss it as you drive into the village: it's right on the main road in the centre. Started by the hippies who colonised the island in the 1960s (Bob Dylan spent the summer here in 1967), stall-holders are obliged to produce hand-made products to get a licence – though sometimes they are a little liberal in their definition of 'hand-made'. You can buy clothing and jewellery, soft toys and artworks, belts and hats, and much more. Check out the store selling mince-filled doughnuts with an extraordinary taste. Your children will love the place, particularly the central plaza where a 60-something hippy sits on a high-stool playing a slide guitar on his knees.

Beaches

Es Pujols This is the most commercial, least far-from-the-beaten track beach in Formentera, but it still has plenty of character, and is a great place for children of all ages. The beach starts in front of the city centre, and while the fishing boats give it picture-postcard credibility, those who dump themselves down here are missing a more enjoyable experience if they take a five-minute walk north-west, where the sand is whiter, the beach broader, and there are fewer people around. If you want a beach where facilities are never far away, where your children can get an ice-cream within five minutes, where you can enjoy that anonymous feeling that is born of living in a crowd, this is the place for you.

Beach facts: 300 metres wide, 30 metres deep, east-facing.

Cala Saona ★★ Cala Saona is a wonderful little covey beach, and an excellent place for a day-trip. In peak season entrepreneurs hire out colourful pedalos to enable up to five people to escape out to sea and away from the many neighbours also enjoying the 'secluded' nature of the spot. Off-peak it's a different affair entirely, an off-the-beaten-track destination for discerning (and often naked) sunbathers. It's well serviced by two restaurants and a hotel, and hosts a small fleet of fishing boats on the rocks off its southernmost side, sitting in their rickety huts, reminding you that not all the locals make their money servicing tourists. The beach is perfect for children: it's shallow-shelved and calm and there are plenty of snorkelling opportunities on the rocks to either side of the sand.

Beach facts: 140 metres wide, 200 metres deep, west-facing.

Platja de Ses Illetes ★★★

This is such a beautiful beach that a joke goes round that the Seychelles Tourist Board uses pictures of it to illustrate its brochures. Situated on the west (and thus calmer) side of a spit of land stretching from the northern coast of the island, Illetes is the sort of place you'd take a Martian if he wanted to know what a perfect beach should look like. Backed by dunes, it boasts pale beige sand, and water so clear that if you go in up to your knees you'll see the clearest image of your feet magnified under you. This is where the rich and famous anchor their yachts and come to take some sun: you can see their vessels out to sea and, if you care for that sort of thing, often spot them lying near you, too. Though if anyone A-list is around, you'll notice the paparazzi hiding in the dunes first. A wonderful beach, woefully overcrowded in peak season, and a great place for sandcastles, too, especially at sunset.

Beach facts: 500 metres wide, 40 metres deep, west-facing.

Platja de Llevant ★★ This

beach is on the eastern side of the spit of land that also harbours Illetes. At one point the spit is so narrow that the beaches join in the middle, with the sea lapping both sides. But, because of the nature of that sea, Llevant is very different from its posh neighbour. The waves come in more choppily, and the colour is much darker than the pale turquoise that makes Illetes so popular. It's not such a good destination for smaller children, then, though the older ones might prefer the feel of it. It's certainly a less crowded stretch of sand, and there are lifeguards when the flags are amber.

Beach facts: 1500 metres wide, 30 metres deep, east-facing.

Platja del Migjorn ★ 'Midday Beach' is the name for a vast stretch of shore that covers much of the southern coast of Formentera. Of course, one part differs significantly from another, but without doubt this is the island's least commercial stretch of coast. Even in August, if you walk far enough (especially towards the western area known as **Es Arenals**), you'll be able to find a stretch where you can't hear what your nearest neighbours are saying, or see what they are (or aren't) wearing. It's a little rockier than most of the other beaches, with deeper shelving than is normal on the island, so be careful where your children bathe.

Beach facts: 5000 metres long, 10–15 metres deep, south/south-west facing.

Platja de Es Calo Es Calo is a small beach just off the main road to El Pilar de la Mola, in the east of Formentera. It's rockier than most, and quite secluded, making it a popular spot with naturists, even in high season. The west end of the beach runs to a pretty harbour, which the

Jellyfish

Like everywhere in the Mediterranean, the sea off Formentera is home to various species of jellyfish (*lamedusa* in Catalan), especially after a storm. Scientists report that changing sea temperatures are bringing more of these beasts floating into shore. I got stung one summer, and it's a short, sharp shock for an adult, let alone a kid. If you *are* stung, it is an extremely painful experience ('A fish bit me!' screamed one kid I know), and will smart for an hour or two; but treatment can help. If the sting is serious, make your way to the nearest chemist (see 'Fast Facts: Formentera', p. 239), who can advise you about appropriate further action. Otherwise do as locals do: go to the nearest bar, restaurant or shop, and rub on some raw lemon or (even better) vinegar, which will eventually ease the pain, though a red mark may be visible for days. Be warned: I was charged a few cents for the lemon. By the way, the old wives' tale about urine being the best remedy holds no scientific water, and can be extremely embarrassing to administer.

Fig Trees

All over the island you'll see fields divided by dry-stone walls, and containing several fig trees. Look closer and you will spot that the branches of the trees are held above the ground with wooden supports. There are two reasons for this: to protect the fruit, and to give the sheep that graze in the field some welcome shade. These provide excellent photo opportunities with the kids. We once set up a 'best fig tree in the island' competition that became a theme for the holiday.

villagers use as a makeshift swimming pool. Not the best place for hyperactive children, then, but a nice change if you want a more chilled-out vibe.

Beach facts: 100 metres wide, 25 metres deep, north/north-east facing.

FAMILY-FRIENDLY ACCOMMODATION

Hostal Costa Azul This very reasonable, big, whitewashed hostal at the end of a dirt track has the advantage of being right on Platja de Migjorn. The rooms are clean and spacious: don't forget to ask for a sea view, because it makes a difference. The hotel runs a rather good restaurant overlooking the beach; there is an English menu that includes the boast that the restaurant catches all its own fish. Arrive early and reserve the best table sheltered by a wicker roof with great views of the sea. There are several card tables and a pool table to help while away the pre-bed hours.

Apdo. 56, Platja de Migjorn 📞 *971 328 024. Fax: 971 328 994. 27 rooms: high season double €44.15 (£29.58) per person with breakfast.*

Third child occupant, 2–12 years, 50% discount. Cot €3.60 (£2.41).

Hostal Entre Pinos ★ FIND

Another family-run establishment, with an extremely friendly husband–wife team running it in shifts, the Entre Pinos is situated on a small road 100 metres from Es Arenals beach. It has 54 rooms in a block overlooking a large swimming pool, and a pleasant, air-conditioned bar with terrace. The only drawback is that at night you can hear the loud music from the large beachside package holiday hotel on the seafront.

Es Calo, Ctra. La Mola Km 12,3 📞 *971 327 019. Fax: 971 327 018* **www.hostalentrepinos.com.** *54 rooms. High-season double €50 (£33.50) with breakfast.*

Hostal Tahiti ★★ A smart, recently refurbished option at the right end of Es Pujols beach, Tahiti is a great place for the family. Sitting across the road from the sand, this 74-room, family-run establishment has its own (kidney-shaped) swimming pool where you can take a dip to the insistent sound of cicadas chattering away in the scrubby bushes. The inside bar, too, is worth checking out – all white-washed neoclassical pillars with stainless steel bases.

Cl. Fonoll Marí, Es Pujols ☎ *971 328 122. Fax: 971 328 817. 74 rooms. High season double €150 (£100.50).*

Hostal Roca Bella If you want to be near all the tourist facilities in Es Pujols, but a little out of the way of all the noise and traffic, then the Roca Bella, just 15 minutes' walk from the town centre, is the place for you. We liked it from the moment we walked through the entrance, which is guarded by chunky palm trees. There's a terrace surrounding the hostal; from one side you get a view of the whole of Es Pujols bay, from the other the calm little cove that most tourists wouldn't dream was so near such a popular tourist spot. The whole experience of staying in the place makes you feel that you've stepped back a little in time. There's a children's playground, too, with swings, slides and a strange Zebedee-like horse, and a swimming pool with separate adult and children's areas. The Roca Bella has been run by the same family since 1956, and is one of the oldest hostals in Formentera.

Platja Es Pujols s/n ☎ *971 328 019. Fax: 971 328 002 www.roca-bella. com. Double in high season €126.15 (£84.52). Breakfast €8.70 (£5.83).*

Hostal Rosales This family-run, 45-room hostal is right in the centre of Es Pujols, but as soon as you step inside you feel you've entered a haven. It's been run by the same family for 25 years and was restored four years ago: we disagreed on the wisdom of choosing mottled-pink walls in the foyer, but loved the room,

Apartment DIY

A dependable and extremely helpful team runs Astbury Self-catering Accommodation ★★★ from Es Pujols and Middlesbrough. The company rents islanders' accommodation to tourists from the beginning of April to the end of October. Prices vary from €200 (£134) to €400 (£268) per week. Astbury Formentera has been in business for 25 years, renting everything from bungalows to villas and apartments. There are houses all over the island. We stayed in a two-bedroom place on the outskirts of Es Pujols that, though a good 10-minute walk to the beach, was perfect for our needs, with a spacious kitchen and living room, and two double bedrooms. There was a large terrace outside where we hung out and ate. Having your own place eases the stress of hostal-dictated life and enables you to move at your own pace, in a place that soon feels like home.

☎ *016 42210163 from the UK. Fax: 01642 222210 www.formentera. co.uk* which was clean and spacious. Try to bag a room on the first floor, which offers sea views. The staff are very friendly indeed; there is a courtesy room at the disposal of guests who are leaving the island late in the day. It's open all year round, too.

Avd. Miramar s/n, Es Pujols ☎ 971 328 123. Double in high season with breakfast €143 (£95.81). 50% reduction for extra person in room. Cots available.

Hostal Bellavista However much you might try to entice them, the two large grey parrots in the lobby of this 40-room, harbour-fronted hostal won't talk. No matter, they are enough to make a stay in the place memorable for your children, though La Savina isn't really the best place to settle on the island unless you need to get an early boat to Ibiza. Most rooms are doubles, but you can rent a cot

or folding bed for extra family members for a little extra, a feature which is common to most hostals on the island.

Harbour Front, La Savina ☎ 971 322 236/322 255. Fax: 971 322 672. Double in high season with breakfast €120 (£80.40). Extra bed €25 (£16.75). Cot €12.50 (£8.38).

Hotel Cala Saona From pictures in the lobby of this modern-looking, three-storey, 114-room hotel perched above one of the prettiest beaches on the island, you can chart its progress from the time it was a converted single-storey house in 1958. Now it's one of the most pleasant and well-facilitated places to stay on the island, with a large, oblong swimming pool backed by a paddling pool where you can take a dip or relax in green-and-white-striped loungers. There's a library stocked with English-language books (though none are for

Hostal Bellavista, La Savina

children) and a large plasma screen for unmissable sporting occasions. A good option, particularly out of high season when you can enjoy the off-the-beaten-track feeling that comes from its beautiful location without missing out on facilities that will fill the hours for the children. Make sure that you ask for a room with a sea view.

Playa Cala Saona 📞 *971 322 030. Fax: 971 322 509* **www.hotelcala saona.com**. *High season double with breakfast €160 (£107.20). Extra child in room with breakfast €40 (£26.80).*

FAMILY-FRIENDLY DINING

San Ferran

Can Forn San Ferran is a scrubby little town, worth visiting for just one pedestrianised street where discerning tourists and locals hang out. Can Forn is at the top end of this street, and is a perfect place for a family meal, as the area in front of it is pedestrianised – if you forgive the odd cyclist taking a short-cut. Inside it's all hanging gourds, old pictures of Formentera and wooden ceiling fans. There's an interesting table made from a barrel. The menu offers a good range of food, some of which your children will jump at, some of which they will enjoy being disgusted at the idea of. In the former category try the fried squid and chips; in the latter the *peus de porcs guisats* (stewed pigs' feet) or the pigeon

with cabbage. There is also spag bol, and you can pre-order paella.

Major 39 📞 *971 328 155. Open Mar–Dec, 9.30am–2am; closed Sun in winter. Main dishes around €12 (£8).*

La Savina

Restaurant Hostal de la Savina This place doesn't look promising from its road-fronted façade, but walk through the door and you'll find a little restaurant at the back that is just perfect for a family lunch or early dinner. The terrace overlooks the beach, so after they get down the children can play in the calm, clean, gently shelving water in full sight, as you sip your *digestivo* (tip for the brave: try *orujo*). There's jazzy music, a pool table and an indoor fountain to enjoy; even in peak season it doesn't get too packed. The menu might please your children more than you, but there's plenty to choose from, with an Italian flavour. *Farfalle* with prawns and tomato sauce is good, as are the *tallarine* with Bolognese. There are also 'stone-oven' cooked pizzas. Don't leave without at least one family member trying out a *batido*, creamy fruit juice sucked through a bendy straw.

Avda Mediterranea 22-40 📞*/Fax: 971 322 279. Main course around €10 (£6.70).*

Platja Migjorn

Las Banderas Las Banderas means 'the flags' in Spanish, and its presence is flagged up with colourful sail-like banners along the dirt track down to Platja Migjorn beach. This is an off-the-beaten-track option, but one well worth going for; it's a great lunchtime spot for children, who can run straight from the table to the beach. There's a cool ambience; it's got a very Asian-hippy look with Indian deity statues, elaborate hanging lanterns and crazy-paved tiling floors. There's also a touch of Gaudi about the decor, to place it in the Catalan Western Mediterranean. The food gives options for children and adults: there are child-sized portions on offer, and while transcontinental fusion dishes might please mum and dad, chicken nuggets or fish and chips are a sure-fire hit for the children. It's run by an English couple, if that makes any difference.

Platja Migjorn ☎ 666 559 027. Daily menu €18.50 (£12.40). €6 (£4) children's version).

Blue Bar ★ Any local will tell you that Pink Floyd played a gig in the Blue Bar back in the 1970s. It's difficult to believe now, though what was once a hippy shack *par excellence* has transmogrified into a well-organised bar that's heaven for children. Outside, everything is painted blue, from the floor to the walls, perhaps as an antidote to the turquoise sea. Inside the place looks like a teenager with a sci-fi obsession did the decor. It's all flying-saucer mobiles, paintings of stars on the ceiling and effigies of *ET*. The salted almonds make a great pre-starter;

the menu is extremely child-friendly with plenty of pasta and chicken-and-chips-style options for under €10 (£6.70). Have an aperitif on one of the (inevitably) blue plastic seats on the sloping terrace in front where you can keep half an eye on the children until they disappear down the track leading to the beach below.

Platja Migjorn km 8 ☎ 666 758 190 www.bluebarformentera.com. Open 12pm–4pm, 6pm–midnight. Main course around €12 (£8).

San Francesc

Bar Restaurant La Estrella ★ VALUE All over Spain, working people who can't get home at the (decreasingly) extensive lunchtimes the country is famous for, tend to spend at least an hour in an inexpensive restaurant. On offer is the ubiquitous *menu del dia*, a three-course meal with a drink (including wine), which is affordable as a daily option to most. Of course, these places exist even in the most touristy areas, and La Estrella in San Francesc is a good example. It's a great place to take the family for a meal, and you'll leave having had a great feed for your money. It's right in the centre of town, in a little square shaded from the sun by a vast awning of black and white cotton, next to a tiny section of the market. A typical *menu* might include pasta with tomato sauce as a starter, squid and chips as a main and a slice of melon for pudding, with wine and/or water and lemonade to drink. But there are always two or three choices.

C/Jaume 8 ☎ 971 322 592. Open all year round, 10am-10pm. Daily menu €10 (£6.70). No credit cards.

Fonda Platé ★ VALUE A wonderful place to watch the world go by while you grab lunch during a shopping trip in the capital. The bar has a spacious juniper-shaded terrace, where on sunny, in-season days you'll have to be alert to bag a table. Once you've got one, you won't want to move for a while. The menu is simple, child-friendly and relatively cheap. If you don't want a bowl of pasta, try a sandwich, including the 'Beach Boy' (tuna, ham and mayonnaise), the 'Bikini' (ham and cheese) and the Plate (ham, cheese, sausage and mayonnaise). There are also great milkshakes and juices; most adults opt for a cold *canya* (beer). The green wooden tables, nestling in the shade, look over one end of a pedestrianised street market where everybody buys the hippy gear that makes life comfortable in the hot summer months. The pester factor is high here ('I want a straw hat'; 'I want a lizard sarong'), but what the hell.

San Jaime 1-3 ☎ 971 322 313. Open Mar to end Oct, Mon–Sat 10am–2am. Closed Sun. Pasta dish €6.50 (£4.36).

Cala Saona

Chacala This restaurant looks out over Cala Saona, and is the most family-friendly place to eat if you spend the day at the island's worst-kept-secret secluded beach. There's a great view of the sandy cove below, and you're likely to get a table here however crowded the beach gets; most punters opt for waiting in line for the more popular, but much more snooty restaurant at sea level. The place is shaded by pine trees, which lend it a lovely smell and means that when you eat here you inevitably find pine needles in unusual places days later. The food is great, with possibilities for both children and adults, and those whose tastes meet in the middle. There are child-sized portions, too. The staff are a laugh, especially the guy who wanders the terrace with a vast platter of exotic-looking fresh fish: if you fancy one you can have it fried on the spot. These are usually more expensive than the staple options: the squid and chips is particularly commendable at €13.50 (£9.05).

Venda de Sa Marina ☎ 971 323 468. Open 12pm–5pm and 8pm-midnight. Closed Tue and Wed afternoon. Main course around €13 (£8.71).

Platja Illetes

Es Minestre ★★ FIND In high season in July and August, Italian youths crowd to the 'Big Surf' bar on Illetes to watch the sunset, and it's quite an experience to witness them whooping and clapping the close of the day. But you actually get a much better and more peaceful view from this restaurant-bar at the top of the peninsula. It's a good spot to bring your family to see the sun drop into the sea, if a bit pricey

Sunset at Platja Illetes

(squid rings in batter with chips, a perennial favourite, will set you back €15 (£10.05)). Try, of course, to get a table on the beach side of the large terrace, which affords the best view as the sun grows large, luminous and orange, then cools itself and disappears in the ever-darker turquoise water. Yachts turn into exotic silhouettes in the mid-distance. The children will love the experience as much as you, and the food is fresh and well cooked. Go for a paella, or, if everyone's feeling adventurous, a bowl of *sepia en su tinta* (squid cooked in its own ink) for €16 (£10.72).

At the far end of the road running up the Illetes peninsula. *971 322 366. Open 12pm–11pm, May to end Oct. Main course €15 (£10.05).*

Es Pujols

Caminito ★★★ The first thing that your children will notice when you come to Caminito, Formentera's only Michelin-starred restaurant, is the large swimming pool in the middle of the restaurant. Sadly, perhaps, guests are not allowed to use it for a dip between courses: it's there for show, along with the palm tree next to it. Caminito is an Argentine-run place with a young chef who performs interesting experiments on traditional food. Best of all, unsurprisingly, is the *solomillo* (rump steak): exquisite and affordable, at €22 (£14.74). The children might turn their noses up at some of the more bizarre stuff, but there are simple options to suit all tastes, and the menu makes for interesting reading. If you want to treat yourself to a blow-out meal in one place, this is the best option. There is a children's menu, too. *Crta. Es Pujols-La Savina * 971 328 106. Fax: 971 328 724. Open Apr–Dec 8pm–12.30am (July–August open till 2am). In Nov and Dec only open Thu, Fri and Sat, 7.30pm–11.30pm. Main course around €22 (£14.74). Booking recommended.*

Appendix: Useful Terms and Phrases

Tourism is such an important industry for the Balearics, that speaking Spanish (or Catalan) certainly isn't essential. In a few resorts – Magaluf being the main culprit – you may struggle to find anyone who is even Mallorcan. But this doesn't excuse you from making an effort, and locals genuinely appreciate it when you greet them in their own language. As a child, I spent many a summer playing alongside Spanish children on the beach, and now with a child of my own, I've seen that children are great ice-breakers. Even a handful of phrases will help you get more out of your time here.

Not only do children have little trouble communicating internationally, they also apparently have no problems absorbing new vocabulary. The BBC's award-winning language course, *Muzzy*, which includes DVDs with cartoons, is a fantastic way to take advantage of their sponge-like ability to soak it all up. Adults may even be able to learn a few words, too. *Muzzy* is available from ***www.bbcshop.com*** or ***www.muzzyonline.co.uk***. See 'Resources', below, for some other ideas.

Spanish is gaining popularity in education, and learning the language at school is an ideal way to build up interest in Spain and its culture. As your children grow older, an exchange programme with a Spanish family is a good way to put their language skills to the test – they say survival is a great teacher! Ask the language department at school whether they organise such trips. If you have friends in Spain with children of similar ages, invite them to visit, or ask if your children can come and stay.

As for Catalan, or *Mallorquin, Menorquin* or *Eivissenc* which locals will proudly explain are very different to Catalan, a *bon dia* when you enter a shop can go a long way – although be aware that these dialects are more widely used in towns and villages. In cities and resorts you're

Resources: Learning Spanish with Kids

The following language resources are all available at ***www.amazon. co.uk***.

- *First 100 Words in Spanish Sticker Book* (Heather Amery and Stephen Cartwright)
- *First Thousand Words in Spanish* (Heather Amery and Stephen Cartwright)
- *Spanish for Beginners* (Usborne Language Guides)
- *Hablo Español! Creative Activities to Teach Basic Spanish (Kid's Stuff)* (Lynn Brisson)
- *Spanish for Children (Language for Children Series)* (Catherine Bruzzone)
- *Muzzy* (BBC English)

more likely to come across workers from southern Spain unfamiliar with Catalan. For more information on Catalan, see p. 3.

A few notes on pronunciation: when reading a word you do not know, the stress often falls on the second-to-last syllable unless an accent indicates otherwise; unlike English, vowel sounds do not change, so the 'a' in *amigo* is pronounced the same way as the 'a' in *casa* or *siesta*; remember that 'h' is *always* silent (so *hola* is *oh*-la and most definitely not *hoe*-la). And if all else fails, remember the Spanish are typically expressive characters. Don't be shy to use a bit of sign language to fill in the gaps.

Basic Vocabulary & Greetings

English	Spanish	Pronunciation
Yes / No	**Sí / No**	sea / noh
Okay	**Vale**	*Bal*-i
Please	**Por favor**	paw *fa*-vore
Thank you	**Gracias**	*grah*-sea-ass
You're welcome	**De nada**	duh *na*-dah
Hello	**Hola**	*oh*-la
Good morning	**Buenos dias**	*bwen*-os *di*-az
Good afternoon	**Buenas tardes**	*bwen*-az *tar*-dez
Goodbye	**Adiós**	a-dee-*os*
What's your name?	**Cómo te llamas?**	*Ko*-mow tey *yam*-az?
My name is	**Me llamo**	me *yam*-o
How are you?	**Cómo estás?**	ko-mow es-*taz*?
I'm sorry / excuse me	**Perdón**	per-*don*

Getting Around

English	Spanish	Pronunciation
Do you speak English?	**Hablas inglés?**	*ab*-laz in-*glez*?
I don't speak Spanish	**No hablo español**	no *ab*-low es-pan-*yol*
I don't understand	**No entiendo**	no en-tea-*en*-do
Could you speak more loudly / more slowly?	**Podrías hablar más fuerte / más despacio?**	Pod-*re*-az ab-*lar* mas fuer-tay / mas des-*pa*-sea-o?
What is it?	**Qué es?**	kay es?
What time is it?	**Qué hora es?**	kay *or*-ra es?
What?	**Qué?**	kay?
How? or What did you say?	**Cómo?**	*ko*-mo?

English	Spanish	Pronunciation
When?	**Cuándo?**	*kuan*-dow?
Where is?	**Dónde está?**	*don*-day es-*tah*?
Who?	**Quién?**	key-*en*?
Why?	**Porqué?**	paw-*kay*?
Here / there	**aquí / allí**	a-*key* / a-*yee*
Left / right	**izquierda / derecha**	ith-*kier*-da / duh-*retch*-a
Straight ahead	**todo recto**	*to*-dow *rec*-toe
Fill the tank (of a car), please	**Lleno, por favor**	*yen*-o paw *fa*-vor
I want to get off at	**Quiero bajar a**	ki-*er*-o ba-*ha* a
the airport	**el aeropuerto**	ell ay-ro-*pu-ert*-o
the bank	**el banco**	ell *ban*-co
the beach	**la playa**	lah *plai*-ya
the bridge	**el puente**	ell po-*wen*-tey
the bus station	**la estación de autobuses**	lah e-sta-sea-*on* duh au-to-*buss*-ez
the bus stop	**la parada de autobuses**	lah pa-*rar*-dah duh au-to-*buss*-ez
broken down (in car)	**averiado**	a-ver-ri-*ah*-doh
by car	**en coche**	en *cot*-chey
cathedral	**la catedral**	lah ca-te-*dral*
church	**la iglesia**	lah ig-*glay*-sea-ah
driver's licence	**el carné de conducir**	ell car-*nei* duh con-do-*thir*
entrance (building or city)	**la entrada**	lah en-*tra*-dah
exit (building or motorway)	**una salida**	*u*-na sa-*lead*-ah
first floor	**el primer piso**	ell pri-*mare* pi-*sow*
hospital	**el hospital**	ell hos-pi-*tal*
lift / elevator	**la ascensor**	lah as-sense-*saw*
luggage storage	**consigna**	kon-*sig*-nah
museum	**el museo**	ell moo-*say*-o
no smoking	**no fumar**	no foo-*mar*
petrol	**gasolina**	gas-oh-*li*-nah
one-way ticket	**billete de ida**	bee-*yet*-tey duh e-dah
police	**la policía**	lah po-li-*sea*-ah
return ticket	**billete de ida y vuelta**	bee-*yet*-tey duh e-dah e *vuel*-tah
street	**la calle**	lah *cai*-yay
telephone	**el teléfono**	ell te-*lef*-on-no

English	Spanish	Pronunciation
ticket	**un billete**	oohn bee-*yet*-tey
toilets	**los servicios**	loss serve-*ith*-ea-oz

Shopping

English	Spanish	Pronunciation
How much does it cost?	**Cuánto cuesta?**	*quan*-toe *ques*-tah?
That's expensive	**Es muy caro**	es mui *ka*-row
Do you take credit cards?	**Aceptáis tarjetas de crédito?**	A-cept-*taiz* tar-*het*-az duh *cre*-di-toe?
I'd like	**Quiero**	ki-*air*-oh
I'd like to buy	**Quiero comprar**	ki-*air*-oh kom-*prar*
aspirin	**aspirina**	as-p-*ri*-nah
boots	**botas**	*bot*-az
colouring pencils	**lápices de colores**	*la*-pea-cez duh co-*lor*
a gift	**un regalo**	oohn re-*ga*-low
a hat	**una gorra**	*u*-na *goh*-rah
a map of the city	**un mapa de la ciudad**	oohn *ma*-pah duh lah thiu-*dad*
a newspaper	**un periódico**	oohn pear-ri-*od*-i-co
a phonecard	**una tarjeta de teléfono**	*u*-na tar-*het*-az duh te-*lef*-on-no
a postcard	**un postal**	oohn post-*tal*
a raincoat	**un impermeable**	oohn im-per-mi-*ab*-ley
a road map	**un mapa de carreteras**	oohn *ma*-pah duh car-ra-*ter*-raz
shoes	**zapatos**	tha-*pa*-toes
soap	**jabón**	ha-*bon*
a stamp	**un sello**	oohn *say*-yo
sweets	**caramelos**	ka-ra-*mel*-oz
swimming trunks / swimsuit	**bañador**	ban-ya-*door*
suntan cream / sunscreen	**crema solar**	*kre*-mah so-*laa*
toothpaste	**pasta de dientes**	*pas*-tah duh di-*en*-tez
shop	**una tienda**	*u*-na tea-*en*-dah
bakery	**una panadería**	*u*-na pa-na-dah-*ri*-ah
butcher	**una carnicería**	*u*-na car-nee-sir-*ri*-ah
cake shop	**una pastelería**	*u*-na *pas*-tell-er-*ri*-ah
drycleaners	**una tintorería**	*u*-na tin-tor-rer-*ri*-ah

English	Spanish	Pronunciation
fishmonger	**un pescadería**	oohn pes-ca-der-*ri*-ah
grocery	**tienda de combustibles**	tea-*en*-dah duh com-bust-*ti*-blez
laundrette	**una lavandería**	*u*-na la-van-da-*ri*-ah
market	**un mercado**	oohn mer-*car*-dough
supermarket	**un supermercado**	oohn super-mer-*car*-dough
shopping trolley	**un carrito**	oohn cah-*rit*-oh
shopping bag	**una bolsa**	*u*-na *bol*-sah
till	**la caja**	lah *ca*-ha

Children's Stuff

English	Spanish	Pronunciation
Baby changer	**cambiador**	cam-bee-a-*dor*
bottlewarmer	**calienta biberón**	kal-li-*en*-tey bi-ber-*ron*
buggy / pushchair	**cochecito**	cot-chey-*thi*-toe
child seat	**un asiento infantil**	oohn as-sea-*en*-toe in-fan-*till*
children's Paracetamol	**paracetamol para niños**	pa-rah-set-a-*moll pa*-rah *nin*-yos
dummy	**un chupete**	oohn chew-*pet*-ey
formula milk (newborn–4 months; 4 months–1 year)	**leche en polvo (primera etapa, segunda etapa)**	*lech*-ey en *pol*-vo (pri-*mayor*-ah ey-*tap*-ah, say-*gun*-dah ey-*tap*-ah)
follow-on milk	**leche de continuación**	*lech*-ey duh con-tin-u-a-sea-*on*
highchair	**una trona**	*u*-na *tron*-ah
nappies	**pañales**	pan-*ya*-lez
playground	**parque infantil**	*par*-key in-fan-*till*
seesaw / swing	**un columpio**	oohn co-*lum*-pea-oh
slide	**un tobogán**	oohn toh-boh-*gan*
sterilising tablets	**pastillas esterilizadoras**	pass-*tea*-yas es-ter-ri-li-sa-*dor*-az
wet wipes	**toallitas**	ta-why-*ee*-taz

In Your Hotel

English	Spanish	Pronunciation
We're staying for . . . days	**quedamos aquí por ... dias**	ke-*dam*-os a-*key* por ... *di*-az
Is breakfast included?	**está incluido el desayuno?**	Es-*tah* in-clue-e-doh ell des-ai-*u*-no?

English	Spanish	Pronunciation
Are taxes included?	**están incluidos los impuestos?**	Es-*tah* in-clue-*e*-dohs los im-*pues*-toes?
room	**una habitación**	*u*-na a-bi-ta-sea-*on*
double room	**una habitación doble**	*u*-na a-bi-ta-sea-*on do*-bley
triple room	**un triple**	oohn *trip*-ley
family room	**una habitación familiar**	*u*-na a-bi-ta-sea-*on* fa-me-li-*ar*
family suite	**una suite familiar**	*u*-na suite fa-me-li-*ar*
extra bed	**una cama extra**	*u*-na *ka*-mah extra
cot	**una cuna**	*u*-na *ku*-nah
shower	**una ducha**	*u*-na *do*-cha
sink	**un lavabo**	oohn la-*va*-bow
suite	**una suite**	*u*-na suite
the key	**la llave**	lah *ya*-vai
balcony	**un balcón**	oohn bal-*kon*
bathtub	**una bañera**	*u*-na ban-*yer*-ah
bathroom	**el cuarto de baño**	ell *quar*-toe duh *ban*-yo
hot and cold water	**agua caliente y fria**	*ag*-wa kal-li-*en*-tey e *fri*-oh
babysitting	**canguro**	can-*gur*-roo
swimming pool (heated; indoor)	**una piscina (climatizado / cubierto)**	u-na pis-*sea*-nah (cli-ma-ti-*tha*-do / ku-bee-*er*-toe)

Numbers & Ordinals

English	Spain	Pronunciation
nought / zero	**cero**	*their*-row
one	**un**	oon
two	**dos**	dos
three	**tres**	trez
four	**cuatro**	*quat*-row
five	**cinco**	*think*-o
six	**seis**	says
seven	**siete**	sea-*et*-ey
eight	**ocho**	*otch*-ow
nine	**nueve**	*no-e*-vey
ten	**diez**	di-*eth*
eleven	**once**	*on*-thei

English	Spain	Pronunciation
twelve	doce	*doth*-ei
thirteen	trece	*tre*-thei
fourteen	catorce	ka-*tor*-thei
fifteen	quince	*kin*-thei
sixteen	dieciséis	di-eth-e-says
seventeen	diecisiete	di-eth-e-sea-*et*-ey
eighteen	dieciocho	di-eth-e- *otch*-ow
nineteen	diecinueve	di-eth-e- *no-e*-vey
twenty	veinte	*vain*-tai
thirty	treinta	*tren*-tah
forty	cuarenta	qua-*ren*-tah
fifty	cincuenta	sing-*quen*-tah
Sixty	sesenta	sa-*sen*-tah
seventy	setente	sa-*ten*-tah
eighty	ochenta	o-*chen*-tah
ninety	noventa	no-*ven*-tah
one hundred	cien	thi-en
one thousand	mil	mill
first	primer	pri-*mayor*-o
second	segundo	say-*gun*-doh
third	tercero	ter-*ser*-roh
fourth	cuarto	*quar*-toh
fifth	quinto	*kin*-toh
sixth	sexto	*sex*-toe
seventh	septimo	*sep*-tea-moh
eighth	octavo	och-*tarv*-oh
ninth	noveno	no-*ven*-oh
tenth	décimo	*dea*-thi-moh

The Calendar

English	Spanish	Pronunciation
Sunday	domingo	doh-*min*-go
Monday	lunes	*loo*-nez
Tuesday	martes	*maar*-tez
Wednesday	miércoles	mi-*air*-co-lez
Thursday	jueves	*huey*-vez

Friday	**viernes**	vi-*air*-nez
Saturday	**sábado**	*sa*-bah-doe
yesterday	**ayer**	ai-*yer*
today	**hoy**	oi
this morning / this afternoon	**esta mañana / esta tarde**	*es*-tah man-*yar*-nah / *es*-tah *tar*-day
tonight	**esta noche**	*es*-tah *not*-chay
tomorrow	**mañana**	man-*yar*-nah
January	**enero**	en-*air*-oh
February	**febrero**	fay-*brer*-oh
March	**marzo**	*mar*-thoh
April	**abril**	a-*brill*
May	**mayo**	*my*-oh
June	**junio**	*who*-ni-oh
July	**julio**	*who*-li-oh
August	**agosto**	o-*gost*-oh
September	**septiembre**	sep-tea-*em*-brey
October	**octubre**	oct-*too*-brey
November	**noviembre**	no-vi-*em*-brey
December	**diciembre**	de-ci-*em*-brey

Food/Menu/Cooking Terms

English	**Spain**	**Pronunciation**
I would like	**Quiero**	ki-*air*-oh
to eat	**comer**	com-*mayor*
Please give me	**Podrías darme**	Pod-*re*-az dar-meh
a bottle of	**una botella de**	*u*-na bo-*tey*-ya
a cup of	**una taza de**	*u*-na *ta*-tha
a glass of	**un vaso**	oohn *va*-sow
breakfast	**el desayuno**	ell des-ai-*u*-noh
the bill	**la cuenta**	lah *quen*-tah
supper	**la cena**	lah *thenn*-ah
lunch	**la comida**	lah co-*me*-dah
a knife	**un cuchillo**	oohn coo-*chi*-yo
a napkin	**una servieta**	*u*-na ser-vi-*et*-ta
a spoon	**una cuchara**	*u*-na coo-*cha*-rah
a fork	**un tenedor**	oohn te-ney-*door*

English	Spain	Pronunciation
Cheers!	**Salud!**	Sa-*lud*!
fixed-price menu	**menú del día**	ell men-*u* del *di*-ah
menu	**la carta**	lah *kart*-a
children's menu	**el menú de niños**	ell men-*u* duh *nin*-yos
extra plat	**otro plato**	*ot*-row *pla*-toe
small portion	**una ración pequeña**	u-na ra-sea-*on* pe-*ken*-yo
Waiter! / Waitress!	**Camero! / Camarera!**	cam-a-*rare*-ro / cam-a-*rare*-ra
wine list	**la carta de vinos**	lah kar-tah duh *vee*-nose
appetizer	**un entrante**	oohn en-*tran*-tey
main course	**un plato principal**	oohn *pla*-toe prin-sea-*pal*
homemade	**casero**	ka-*sir*-oh
dish of the day	**el plato del día**	el *pla*-toe del *di*-ah
tip included	**servicio incluido**	ser-*vi*-ci-oh in-clue-*i*-doh
Is the tip / service included?	**El servicio está ? incluido**	El ser-*vi*-ci-oh es-*tah* in-clue-*e*-doh?

Balearic Specialities

English	Catalan	Pronunciation
Spicy sausage	**sobrassada**	sob-ra-*sa*-dah
Round pastry	**ensaïmada**	en-sigh-*mah*-dah
Lobster stew	**caldereta de llangosta**	cal-duh-*ret*-ah duh yan-*gos*-tah
Fish, potatoes and garlic mayonnaise	**guisat de peix**	gui-*shat* duh pesh
Meat stew	**frit mallorquín**	frit my-your-kin
Herb liqueur	**herbes**	*erb*-ez
Garlic mayonnaise	**alioli**	al-e-*ol*-e
Tomato-smeared bread	**pa amb tomàtic**	pa am to-*ma*-tik

The Basics

English	Spanish	Pronunciation
bread	**pan**	pan
wholemeal bread	**pan integral**	pan in-tea-*gral*
slice	**una rebanada**	u-na reh-bah-*na*-dah
toast	**pan tostado**	pan tos-*ta*-doe

English	Spanish	Pronunciation
butter	**mantequilla**	man-ta-*qui*-ya
breakfast cereals	**cereales**	thi-re-*al*-ez
sugar	**azucar**	a-*thu*-ka
honey	**miel**	mi-*ell*
jam	**mermelada**	mer-meh-*la*-dah
cheese	**queso**	*keh*-so
eggs: boiled	**huevo pasado por agua**	*way*-vo pas-a-doe por *ag*-wa
eggs: hardboiled	**huevo duro**	*way*-vo dur-oh
eggs: fried	**huevo frito**	*way*-vo *fri*-toe
eggs: poached	**huevo escalfado**	*way*-vo es-cal-*fa*-doe
eggs: scrambled	**huevo revuelto**	*way*-vo re-*vuel*-toe
omelette	**tortilla**	tor-*tea*-yah
Spanish omlette (potatoe, onion)	**tortilla española**	tor-*tea*-yah es-pan-*yo*-la
pasta	**pasta**	*pas*-tah
pizza	**una pizza**	u-na piz-za
pizza Margherita (with tomato and cheese, and sometimes ham)	**un pizza margarita**	u-na piz-za mar-ga-*ri*-tah
rice	**arroz**	a-*roth*

Snacks

English	Spanish	Pronunciation
ham and cheese toastie	**un bikini**	oohn bi-*ki*-ni
olives	**aceitunas**	a-they-*tu*-naz
crisps	**patatas churras**	pa-*ta*-taz *chew*-raz
nuts / walnuts	**nueces**	*no-weth*-ez
almonds	**almendras**	al-*men*-draz
cashews	**anacardos**	ah-na-*car*-doz
chestnuts	**castañas**	cas-*tan*-yaz
hazelnuts	**avellanas**	ah-vey-*yan*-az
peanuts	**cacahuetes**	ca-ca-*wet*-tez
coconut	**coco**	*co*-co
chocolate	**chocolate**	choc-oh-*la*-te
ice lolly / ice cream	**un polo / un helado**	oohn *po*-low / oohn eh-*la*-dow

Starters and Side Dishes

English	Spanish	Pronunciation
chips	**patatas fritas**	pa-*ta*-taz *fri*-taz
soup	**sopa**	*so*-pah
steamed mussels	**mejillones al vapor**	meh-i-*yon*-ez al vap-*hor*
green salad	**ensalada verde**	en-sa-*la*-dah *ver*-dey
salad with tuna	**ensalada mixta**	u-na en-sa-*la*-dah *mix-tah*

Meat

English	Spanish	Pronunciation
meat	**carne**	*car*-ney
poultry	**aves**	*ah*-veys
ham	**jamón**	ham-*on*
pale sliced ham	**jamón Cork**	ham-*on* york
Serrano ham	**jamón serrano**	ham-*on* sir-*ran*-o
chicken	**pollo**	*po*-yo
duck	**pato**	*pa*-toe
partridge	**perdiz**	per-*dith*
turkey	**pavo**	*pa*-voh
lamb	**cordero**	cor-*der*-oh
rabbit	**conejo**	con-ey-ho
sirloin	**solomillo**	sol-o-*mi*-yo
steak	**bistec**	bi-*steck*
hamburger	**hamburguesa**	ham-bur-*geh*-sa

Fish

English	Spanish	Pronunciation
fish	**pescado**	pes-*car*-doh
shellfish	**marisco**	ma-*ris*-co
catch of the day	**pescado del día**	pes-*car*-doh del *di*-ah
breaded / cooked in breadcrumbs	**empanado**	em-pa-*na*-doh
anchovies	**anchoas**	an-*show*-az
clams	**almejas**	al-*mey*-has
cockles	**berberechos**	ber-be-retch-oz
cod	**bacalao**	ba-ca-*lau*
crab	**cangrejo**	can-*grey*-ho

English	Spanish	Pronunciation
lobster	**langosta**	lan-*gost*-ah
mackerel	**caballa**	ca-*bai*-ya
monkfish	**rape**	*ra*-pey
mussels	**mejillones**	meh-i-*yon*-ez
prawns	**gambas**	*gam*-baz
red mullet	**salmonte**	sal-mo-*net*-tey
sardines	**sardinas**	sar-*di*-naz
scampi / large prawns	**langostinos**	lan-gost-*ti*-nose
salmon	**salmón**	sal-*mon*
swordfish	**pez de espada**	peth duh es-*pa*-dah
tuna	**atún**	a-*toon*

Vegetables

English	Spanish	Pronunciation
vegetables	**las veduras**	lass ve-*du*-raz
artichoke	**alcachofa**	al-ka-*chof*-a
asparagus	**espárragos**	a-*spah*-ra-goose
aubergine	**berejena**	be-re-*hen*-a
beetroot	**remolacha**	re-moh-*latch*-a
broccoli	**brócoli**	*bro*-co-lee
cabbage	**col**	kol
carrots	**zanahorias**	than-a-*or*-ri-az
cauliflower	**coliflor**	co-li-*floor*
celery	**apio**	*a*-pi-oh
courgettes	**calabacín**	ca-la-ba-*thin*
endive	**endibia**	en-*di*-bi-ah
fennel	**hinojo**	in-*o*-hoe
garlic	**ajo**	*a*-hoe
green beans	**judias verdes**	ju-*di*-az *ver*-dez
leeks	**puerros**	*poer*-roz
mushrooms	**champiñones**	cham-pin-*yon*-ez
onion	**cebolla**	th-*boy*-ya
peas	**guisantes**	gi-*sa*-tez
peppers (green, red, yellow)	**pimientos (verdes, rojos, amarillos)**	pi-mi-*en*-toe (*ver*-dez, *ro*-joz, a-ma-*ri*-yoz)
potatoes	**patatas**	pa-*ta*-taz

English	Spanish	Pronunciation
baked potatoes	**patatas asadas**	pa-*ta*-taz ah-*sa*-daz
mashed potatoes	**puré de patatas**	pur-*rey* duh pa-*ta*-taz
spinach	**espinacas**	es-pi-*nac*-az
sweetcorn	**maiz**	my-*eez*
turnips	**nabos**	*nah*-boz

Spices & Condiments

English	Spanish	Pronunciation
salt	**sal**	sal
salted	**salado**	sa-*la*-do
pepper	**pimienta**	pi-mi-*en*-ta
rock salt	**sal gruesa**	sal gru-*e*-sa
vinegar	**vinagre**	vi-*na*-grey
capers	**alcaparras**	al-ka-*pa*-rras
mayonnaise	**mayonesa**	mai-on-*ei*-sa
ketchup	**salsa de tomate**	*sal*-sah duh to-*ma*-tey
mustard	**mostaza**	moh-*sta*-tha
curry	**curry**	*kur*-ree
cinnamon	**canela**	can-*eh*-lah
coriander	**cilantro**	si-*lan*-troh
cumin	**comino**	ko-*min*-oh
ginger	**jengibre**	gen-*gee*-bra
nutmeg	**nuex moscada**	noez mos-*ka*-da
saffron	**azafrán**	a-tha-*fran*

Cooking Methods

English	Spanish	Pronunciation
baked	**al horno**	al *orr*-no
boiled	**hervido**	er-*vi*-doe
cooked over a coal fire	**a la brasa**	a lah *bra*-sa
cooked on a skewer	**un pincho**	*oohn pin-show*
deep fried	**frito**	*fri*-toe
grilled	**a la parilla**	a lah pa-*rri*-ya
medium (cooked, i.e. steak)	**al punto**	al *pun*-toe
rare (cooked, i.e. steak)	**poco hecho**	*pock*-o *etch*-o

English	Spanish	Pronunciation
roast	**asado**	a-*sar*-do
simmered	**cocer a fuego lento**	ko-*cer* a *fey*-go *len*-to
steamed	**al vapor**	al vap-*hor*
sautéed	**salteado**	sal-te-*ar*-do
stuffed	**relleno**	re-*yen*-o
well done (cooked, i.e. steak)	**muy hecho**	mui *etch*-o

Drink

English	Spanish	Pronunciation
water	**agua**	*ag*-wa
drinking water	**agua portable**	*ag*-wa por-*ta*-blah
spring water	**agua mineral**	*ag*-wa min-er-*ral*
still mineral water	**agua mineral sin gas**	*ag*-wa min-er-*ral* sin gas
sparkling mineral water	**agua mineral con gas**	*ag*-wa min-er-*ral* con gas
milk	**leche**	*lech*-ey
apple juice	**zumo de manzana**	*thu*-mo duh man-*tha*-na
orange juice	**zumo de naranja**	*thu*-mo duh na-*rang*-ha
pear juice	**zumo de pera**	*thu*-mo duh *pair*-ah
fizzy drink	**un refresco**	oonh rey-*fres*-ko
beer	**una cerveza**	u-na sir-*vey*-sa
red wine	**vino tinto**	*vee*-no *tin*-toe
white wine	**vino blanco**	*vee*-no *blan*-ko
coffee (black)	**un café americano**	oohn caf-*ey* a-mayor-ri-*ka*-no
coffee (with milk)	**un café con leche**	oohn caf-*ey* con *lech*-ey
coffee (decaf)	**un café descafeinado**	oohn caf-*ey* des-caf-ey-*nah*-do
coffee (espresso)	**un café solo**	oohn caf-*ey*
tea	**un té**	oohn tey
herbal tea	**una infusión**	u-na in-fu-sea-*on*
hot chocolate	**un chocolate caliente**	oohn choc-oh-*la*-te cal-ee-*en*-tey

Desserts

English	Spanish	Pronunciation
dessert	**el postre**	ell *poss*-trey
fruit salad	**una macedonia**	u-na mass-a-*doh*-ni-a

English	Spanish	Pronunciation
ice cream	**un helado**	oohn eh-*lah*-doe
	vanilla	vai-*knee*-ya
	fresa	*frey*-za
	chocolate	choc-oh-*la*-te
ice-cream cone	**un cucurucho**	oohn ku-ku-*rutch*-o
scoop	**una bola**	u-na *bol*-lah
yoghurt	**yogur**	*yo*-gur
whipped cream	**nata montada**	na-ta mon-*ta*-dah
waffles	**gofres**	*goph*-rez
pastries	**pasta**	*pas*-ta
cake	**pastel**	*pas*-tell
sponge cake	**bizchocho**	bis-*scotch*-o
baked apple	**manzana al horno**	man-*tha*-na al *orr*-no
chocolate mousse	**mouse de chocolate**	moose duh choc-oh-*la*-te
thick custard dessert with caramelised topping	**crema catalana**	*cre*-ma cat-a-*la*-nah *krem* bruh-*lay*
egg custard	**flan**	flan
tart	**una tarta**	u-na *tar*-ta
doughnuts	**donuts**	*dough*-noot
cream puffs with chocolate sauce	**profiteroles**	pro-fit-a-*ro*-lez

Family Travel

Travelling as a family can be fun, exciting and create memories to savour, but a bit of preparation will go a long way in forging a smooth journey and holiday. There are plenty of sites providing parents with essential holiday information and even sites popping up for youngsters, too. From what to pack and coping with flights to childcare and accessories, the sites below will help give you a headstart.

www.babygoes2.com: An innovative guide for parents travelling with babies and children with independent recommendations.

www.all4kidsuk.com: Links to tour companies offering family-friendly holidays.

www.youngtravellersclub.co.uk: Currently in its early days, this is a site for children themselves, which deserves to succeed.

www.deabirkett.com: The website of *Guardian* journalist Dea Birkett, who specialises in travelling with children. It includes a very useful Travelling with Kids Forum.

www.babycentre.co.uk: The travel section throws up some interesting articles on family holidays.

www.mumsnet.com: Set up by a journalist, TV producer and radio producer. Product reviews, interviews and planning help.

www.travellingwithchildren.co.uk: Comprehensive site with lots of handy tips for travelling parents.

www.travelforkids.com: An American site that has some good information on different countries with 'what not to leave at home'-type tips.

www.familytravelforum.com: Lots of useful stuff on family travel in general.

www.travelwithyourkids.com: Easy to navigate with advice you feel comes from real experience of things having gone wrong!

www.thefamilytravelfiles.com: Heavily American, but with a section on Europe.

www.family-travel.co.uk: Independent advice on travelling with children. Lots of sound general advice.

Responsible Tourism

Although one could argue any holiday including a flight can't be truly 'green', tourism can contribute positively to the environment and communities UK visitors travel to if investment is used wisely. Firstly, by offsetting carbon emissions from your flight, you can lessen the negative environmental impact of your journey. Secondly, by embracing responsible tourism practises you can choose forward-looking companies who care about the resorts and countries we visit, preserving them for the future by working alongside local people. Below are a number of sustainable tourism initiatives and associations to help you plan a family trip and leave as small a 'footprint' as possible on the places you visit.

www.responsibletravel.com: A great source of sustainable travel ideas run by a spokesperson for responsible tourism in the travel industry.

www.tourismconcern.org.uk: Working to reduce social and environmental problems connected to tourism and find ways of improving tourism so that local benefits are increased.

www.climatecare.org.uk: Helping UK holidaymakers offset their carbon emissions through flying by funding sustainable energy projects

www.thetravelfoundation.org.uk: Produces excellent material on how to care for the places we visit on holiday. There is also a special guide for children aged 7–10 and parents incorporating 'Hatch the Hatchling Hawksbill' with a play and puzzle book. Highly recommended.

www.abta.com: The Association of British Travel Agents (ABTA) acts as a focal point for the UK travel industry and is one of the leading groups spearheading responsible tourism.

www.aito.co.uk: The Association of Independent Tour Operators (AITO) is a group of interesting specialist operators leading the field in making holidays sustainable.

Index

Accommodations

Restaurants

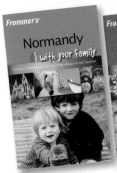

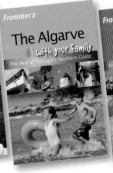

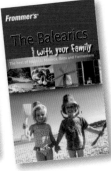